From the Modernist Annex

From the Modernist Annex

American Women Writers in Museums and Libraries

KARIN ROFFMAN

THE UNIVERSITY OF ALABAMA PRESS
Tuscaloosa

Manufactured in the United States of America

Typeface: Minion

∞

The paper on which this book is printed meets the minimum requirements of American National Standard for Information Sciences-Permanence of Paper for Printed Library Materials, ANSI Z39.48-1984.

Library of Congress Cataloging-in-Publication Data

Roffman, Karin.
From the modernist annex : American women writers in museums and libraries / Karin Roffman.
p. cm.
Includes bibliographical references and index.
ISBN 978-0-8173-1698-3 (cloth : alk. paper) — ISBN 978-0-8173-8396-1 (electronic)
1. Women authors, American. 2. American literature—20th century—History and criticism. 3. Libraries and women—United States—History. 4. Museums and women—United States—History. 5. Wharton, Edith, 1862–1937. 6. Larsen, Nella. 7. Moore, Marianne, 1887–1972. 8. Benedict, Ruth, 1887–1948. 9. Libraries in literature. 10. Museums in literature. 11. Libraries—Social aspects—United States—History—20th century. 12. Museums—Social aspects—United States—History—20th century. I. Title.
PS151.R64 2010
810.9'39—dc22

2009036280

Cover art: Frank Waller (American 1842–1923), *Entrance Hall of the Metropolitan Museum of Art when in Fourteenth Street,* ca. 1881, Oil on wood, 12 × 16 in. The Metropolitan Museum of Art, Purhcase, 1920 (20.77). Image © The Metropolitan Museum of Art.

For Aranka and Paul Kaplan and Cynthia and Alfred Roffman

Contents

Illustrations

Acknowledgments

This is a project about women writers in museums and libraries that was built very much out of the discoveries those archives make possible. I am very grateful for a grant from the Lilly Library at Indiana University, which allowed me to work with the library's Edith Wharton papers. Two grants from the Beinecke Rare Book and Manuscript Library and the essential guidance of Patricia Willis and Nancy Kuhl were crucial in developing the Wharton, Larsen, and Moore chapters. I want to thank Evelyn Feldman, Michael Barsanti, and Elizabeth E. Fuller at the Rosenbach Museum and Library, Philadelphia, and Marianne C. Moore, literary executor for the estate of Marianne C. Moore, for their kindness in answering my questions and their enthusiasm for Moore's work. For the 1972 photograph of Moore's Greenwich Village apartment, a special thanks goes to Nancy Crampton. More than a year spent reading Ruth Benedict's papers at the Vassar College Libraries Archives and Special Collections was made much easier by Dean Rogers's professionalism.

This book has gathered a great many debts along the way. My thinking emerged first with the encouragement of Langdon Hammer and Ruth Yeazell, for whose thoughtful guidance, intellectual rigor, and patience with the various stages of the writing process I am very grateful. I also want to thank other readers and friends in the Yale English Department from whom I have learned so much: Wai Chee Dimock, Jill Campbell, Robert Stepto, Alan Trachtenberg, Linda Peterson, William Deresiewicz, Lena Hill, Vanessa Ryan, Becca Boggs, and Gabriel Alkon. During the last three years my wonderful colleagues at West Point have provided new friendships and ideas. I would like particularly to thank Elizabeth Samet, James R. Kerin Jr., Tony Zupancic, Scott Krawczyk, Michael Stoneham, and Peter Molin.

The staff at The University of Alabama Press has been wonderfully supportive as I actively revised this book over several drafts. Both of my readers provided useful feedback, but "Anonymous Reader B" went above and beyond, reading the entire manuscript carefully twice and providing some of the most helpful and detailed criticism that I have ever received. I am enormously indebted to her for the hard work, for it really helped me to see how I could best incorporate my new thinking and research into crafting a stronger book.

My parents, Dorothy and Eric Roffman, have always been fond of books, and I am grateful for their general belief that it is worth the time and effort to bring one into being. To that end they have provided me with an immense amount of help—from encouraging words to many hours of babysitting—and, though it is small compensation, I would like to thank them for all of it. Many thanks go also to Kim, Franz, Audrey, and Margot Field; Ian, Jennie, Sam, Eli, and Zachary Roffman; Bob and Roz Rosenblatt; and Sharon Roffman, Elizabeth Basset, Dan Libenson, and Irwin Chen. Jennie Roffman and Beth Niestat carefully read and edited multiple drafts of this project, performing a time-consuming and thankless task so graciously. I am enormously grateful to Fu-Ming and Katherine Chen for being so supportive and such wonderful grandparents. Melvin has contributed a tremendous amount to this book, not only by being a generous reader and honest critic but also by providing wit, perspective, and a fabulous sound track. Milo is the newest member of our family and already a delighted reader. My apologies to him that neither trains nor helicopters nor even a single power shovel appear in the following pages.

For granting permission to quote from unpublished material in their archives, I thank the Rare Book and Manuscript Library, Columbia University; 135th Street Branch Collection in the Schomburg Center for Research in Black Culture Records of the New York Public Library; Vassar College Libraries Archives and Special Collections; the Rosenbach Museum and Library, Philadelphia; Marianne C. Moore, literary executor for the estate of Marianne C. Moore; the National Gallery Archive, London; the Metropolitan Museum of Art Archives; the Lilly Library, Indiana University, Bloomington; and the Beinecke Rare Book and Manuscript Library, Yale University. An earlier version of chapter 2 appeared in *Edith Wharton and Material Culture*, ed. Gary Totten (Tuscaloosa: University of Alabama Press, 2007); an earlier version of chapter 3 appeared in *Modern Fiction Studies* 53, no. 4 (Dec. 2007): 752–87; parts of chapters 3 and 4 appeared in *Institutions of Reading: The Social Life of Libraries in the United States*, ed. Thomas Augst and Kenneth Carpenter (Amherst: University of Massachusetts Press, 2007).

Abbreviations

AAW	*An Anthropologist at Work,* by Margaret Mead
AI	*The Age of Innocence,* by Edith Wharton
DH	*The Decoration of Houses,* by Edith Wharton
HM	*The House of Mirth,* by Edith Wharton
MMC	Marianne Moore Collection, Rosenbach Museum and Library
PC	*Patterns of Culture,* by Ruth Benedict
RP	*The Rise of Professionalism,* by Magali Larson
S	*Sanctuary,* by Edith Wharton
SF	*Social Freedom,* by Elsie Clews Parsons
SR	*Social Rule,* by Elsie Clews Parsons
VCASC	Vassar College Libraries Archives and Special Collections

From the Modernist Annex

Introduction

No literary episode better reveals the distinct attitude of the women writers chronicled in this book than the following negative example. In the opening scene of Henry James's *The American* (1876) Christopher Newman lounges at the Louvre:

> On a brilliant day in May, of the year 1868, a gentleman was reclining at his ease on the great circular divan which at that period occupied the centre of the Salon Carré, in the Museum of the Louvre. This commodious ottoman has since been removed, to the extreme regret of all weak-kneed lovers of the fine arts; but our visitor had taken serene possession of its softest spot, and, with his head thrown back and his legs outstretched, was staring at Murillo's beautiful moon-borne Madonna in deep enjoyment of his posture.[1]

Given Newman's confident and relaxed pose, it may be a surprise to learn that he actually does not understand most of what he sees and experiences in the museum and that he strains to make some sense out of his afternoon. Yet his approach to this new and confusing aesthetic experience of the museum is to establish an attitude of serenity and comfort.

None of the women writers on whom this book directly and indirectly focuses ever include a scene such as the one James writes above. For these women writers museums and libraries are new places that require alertness and a serious commitment of intellectual and emotional attention. In their view no museum visitor would behave with Newman's ease, confidence, or serenity. Although James suggests in the novel's preface that Newman's "ease" at the start of the novel had much more to do with the author's own feelings while writing the scene than with his attitude about the museum, women writers did not feel—or write—about moments of contemplation inside museums, or any other cultural institution for that matter, with anything like that sense of well-being (even a false or temporary feeling, as James suggests he experienced). Instead, the women writers on whom this book focuses, especially those who set their works in museums and libraries, always have their characters standing at a kind of attention in front of a collection or inside a cultural institution. A sense of anxiety prevails in the works of these women as their characters try to understand themselves in relation to collections and cultural institutions toward which they find themselves increasingly drawn.

From Dorothea's intensity for Casaubon's library and her complex museum trips in *Middlemarch* (1872) to Virginia Woolf's raging concern that women do not have as much access to institutional collections as men do in *A Room of One's Own* (1929), no woman ever has the time or inclination to relax on a sofa. Indeed, the opening scene in Virginia Woolf's *A Room of One's Own* is probably the most famous literary depiction of the opposite experience to Newman's. After Woolf is denied access to a famous university library, she becomes so angry that she can no longer write. She spends a half-day fuming and then explains exactly what happened:

> Here I was actually at the door which leads to the library itself. I must have opened it, for instantly there issued, like a guardian angel barring the way with a flutter of black gown instead of white wings, a deprecating, silvery, kindly gentleman, who regretted in a low voice as he waved me back that ladies are only admitted to the library if accompanied by a Fellow of the College or furnished with a letter of introduction.
>
> That a famous library has been cursed by a woman is a matter of complete indifference to a famous library. Venerable and calm, with all its treasures safe locked within its breast, it sleeps complacently and will, so far as I am concerned, so sleep for ever. Never will I wake these echoes, never will I ask for that hospitality again, I vowed as I descended the steps in anger.[2]

Although Woolf initially assumes that the library bars women to protect them from the danger of knowledge, she wonders what this danger could possibly be. She decides that it must have something to do with disturbing the "treasures safe locked within." The rest of the text is testimony to her desire to disturb those "treasures" simply by having women write books. Woolf argues that the only way to ensure that a cultural institution can never again shut out (nor shut up) a person is to introduce new works to undo its sense of the inviolability of its "treasures." By adding new books written by women, the existing "inviolable" system will be disrupted and subsequently require rearranging; through this shift women will literally belong to spaces that currently bar them. The recognition of this exclusion, however, does provide Woolf with something important: exactly the material she needs to write.

Woolf's 1929 essay is a culminating statement on ways women can become part of the very institutions that try to keep them out. Yet her voice, understood more completely now, was by no means the only one at the time thinking about the relationship between women and cultural institutions, nor was her sharp and angry response the primary reaction to these new observations. Even earlier in the decade a group of American women writers were thinking intently about how women use museums and libraries and how knowledge of the ways these spaces operate shapes their thinking and writing. For these American women writers, museums and libraries provide a similar kind of emotional and intellectual drama as Woolf's library-university and a similarly charged relationship to writing. Yet their specific stories, crucial not only to the development of individual modern American women writers but also necessary to our recognition that there even was such a thing as modernist American women's writing, still remain largely unknown.

The primary reason for this absence is that the story of the development of American modernist literature has been told alongside the story of the rise of the university at the expense of the very institutions that early twentieth-century women used much more. In the last fifteen years there has been a proliferation of texts on the history of American universities and on the roles of particular schools in the creation of American male artists who emerged from the university system in the first half of the twentieth century.[3] Critics explore how modernism developed out of the culture of the university, particularly at places such as Harvard University and the University of Pennsylvania, where writers, artists, and theorists gathered to exchange ideas. Although T. S. Eliot, William Carlos Williams, and Ezra Pound attacked academia in letters and speeches, they also used their access to these institutions to develop friendships, make connections, and publish. The important group of writers, collectors, and artists who began to meet after New York City's iconic 1913 Armory Show at Walter Arensberg's Central Park West apartment, for example—including Wallace Stevens, William Carlos Williams, Marcel Duchamp, and Alfred Kreymborg—was initially introduced through collegiate connections since Arensberg and Stevens had known each other at Harvard. American modernist writers are linked through their connections to the universities that helped to shape their ideas and aesthetic goals.

This narrative, however, largely excludes women writers, who tended to have fewer connections to these institutions or were only peripherally part of men's experiences there. Gertrude Stein, for example, began attending the Harvard Annex—which became Radcliffe College—in the 1890s. The composer Virgil Thomson, who attended Harvard in the late teens, liked to explain his affinity for Stein's writing and personality by claiming that "Gertrude and I got on like Harvard men." This charming point about their shared affinities is also revealing of their shared ability as fellow artists to connect as unlikely friends by cutting through the closed-door, boys'-club quality of the university experience that they both recognized (and enjoyed mocking).[4] Hilda Doolittle and Marianne Moore, who both attended Bryn Mawr College, at the time had a less profound sense of the kind of shared experiences and loyalties that the phrase "Harvard men" conjures. Bryn Mawr students were only beginning to develop that tremendous sense of ingrained traditions and likely destinies that early twentieth-century Harvard students already openly claimed. Although "Bryn Mawr girls" was the comparable epithet to "Harvard men," and in use when H.D. and Moore arrived there, the diminutive "girls" versus the established "men" already demonstrates the difference between the cultural weights of the terms.[5] Not only do the phrases describe a different degree of traditions, but they also signal somewhat divergent professional expectations for the future.

For women learning during this period, whether they had the opportunity to attend college or not, the museum and the library played a central if distinctly different role from the university in the development of their thinking and writing. For a writer such as Edith Wharton (whose most direct connection to a university occurred in 1923, when Yale University awarded her an honorary degree), examining private art and book collections provided for the bulk of her early education and a genuine source of wonder and creativity. She also had the access, interest, and cultural acumen to recognize in the transformation of museums and libraries from private to public spaces a compelling subject for fiction. She observed these spaces shift from small, modest spaces to massive buildings and collections and made comparisons between these new American spaces and established museums she knew well in Europe. Nella Larsen, younger and less affluent than Wharton, had direct contact with a number of schools through her long and erratic process of self-educating: as a student and later as a professor's wife at Fisk University, as a nurse at Tuskegee, as a nursing student at Lincoln Hospital, and as a library student at the New York Public Library School. Larsen's brief period of intensive writing coincided with her work as a library student and as a librarian. She worked in libraries and studied artwork in museums, developing insights about the relationships among individuals, race, and culture that were as biting as they were authentic to her own intellectual experience in those places. Because libraries seemed more welcoming to women than universities, and particularly welcoming to black women beginning in the early 1920s, Larsen's subsequent realizations of the serious limitations of a library career helped her to focus her criticisms about the interchange of race and culture around these particular spaces.

Marianne Moore, who graduated from Bryn Mawr in 1909 and eventually found her way to a job in a library at the same time as Nella Larsen, also spent a great deal of time visiting New York City museums and exhibitions as she prepared her first official volume of poetry. For Moore, too, the experience of working in a library and of educating herself in museums inspired her at first to keep track of every visit in diaries and later to question her own devotion to the idea of collecting and organizing information. Ruth Benedict, who was a full-time anthropology professor at Columbia University when she died, would seem to be the writer most shaped by the experience of the university rather than by the museum or the library. Yet Benedict gauged the development of her career in relation to the work of the previous generation of women, particularly her mother's career as a librarian. Benedict carefully observed her own career at Columbia through the lens of her mother's sharp criticism of the library as negatively contributing to the long history of professionalization of women. Benedict struggled to advance professionally at Columbia and certainly never saw herself as one of the "Columbia men," despite her twenty-five years at the school.

By looking at each woman's writerly relationship to museums and libraries, I tell a different story of literary modernism's development than the one offered through accounts of relationships and intellectual interests formed by connections at American universities. One of the interesting things about the museum and the library in the early twentieth century is that women writers had to discover and often imagine a sense of tradition and devotion within these places for themselves—there certainly was not an equivalent of "Harvard men," for example, in the New York Public Library branch system in which Nella Larsen and Marianne Moore participated at exactly the same time. Yet these writers' interests in museums and libraries created a similarity of experience that shaped seemingly unrelated writers in remarkably related ways. Because the museum and the library created a kind of isolating experience for those who worked within them, it becomes that much more important to show the unexpected connections that dependence on these spaces produced. Unlike the university, which from an early point in its development recognized that an effort to produce a feeling of connection (through identification with such things as a common song, an insignia, and school colors) would create the sense of an obviously shared experience, the museum and the library did not try to forge those sorts of emotional links among their users. This disparate group of women writers did not recognize that they shared work experiences and a set of concerns and questions. Instead, the connections among them must be reproduced through research that uncovers the related questions their work raised and how each writer imaginatively transformed her experiences into her own writing voice.

Though contemporaries with overlapping careers and interests, the four authors on whom I focus—Edith Wharton, Nella Larsen, Marianne Moore, and Ruth Benedict—never officially met. This book initially grew out of a recognition of their mutual concerns, despite also serving as their first formal introduction through their writing.[6] While the obvious connections between them consist primarily of an absorbing general interest in museums and libraries and the women who use them, a closer inspection of their works reveals how this fascination helped complicate their individual relationships to writing in overlapping ways.

A brief account of the role that museums and libraries have played in American institutional history in the first chapter will serve as a short introduction to the issues that these writers bring up in their own writing. While there have been great histories of the rise of the museum and excellent accounts of the transformation of the American library system, both of which I discuss in chapter 1, there have been almost no texts that consider the ways these institutions interacted during their development.[7] I argue that the histories of the museum and the library are more intertwined and mutually reinforcing than the accounts of their individual stories reveal. I discuss the ways in which these institutions transformed over approximately one hundred years, in part shifting their focus and a sense of their mission by observing and learning from one another. This combined history of the museum and library is one with which the writers were familiar; not only did all four authors think about museums and libraries through multiple friendships with those who officially occupied (and wrote about their experiences in) these places—including private collectors, librarians, curators, and museum directors—but they also moved back and forth between these spaces in their visits, reading, and writing.

In chapter 2 I consider how Edith Wharton's insider knowledge of a transforming American museum culture during the period from 1870 through 1920 shaped what I call her "museum-novels": from *Sanctuary* (1903) through *The Age of Innocence* (1920). I frame my reading of these novels through a discussion of how ideas about the educational purpose of American museums shifted in those years, resulting in both private and public debates about the purpose of aesthetic ideas, of connoisseurship, of methods for display, and of creating a population of Americans genuinely interested in culture. The extent of Wharton's knowledge of these debates is a story that has not been told. Wharton's uncle (and her mother's only brother), Frederick W. Rhinelander, was one of the founding trustees of the Metropolitan Museum of Art and served in a variety of administrative roles for more than thirty years until he was made its third president in 1902. His role in shaping the early development of the Metropolitan was much more than a source of passing family interest to Wharton; it helped to focus her analysis of American museums around the Metropolitan's specific and complex story of its early struggles and choices.

At the center of this chapter is a focus on Newland Archer's two trips to the Metropolitan Museum of Art in *The Age of Innocence.* In these two scenes, which take place in the original Cesnola antiquities exhibit twenty-six years apart, Wharton makes her clearest case for how she views the modernizing American museum. The Cesnola objects that Archer and Madame Olenska observe in the late 1870s, and that seem to stand for a lost era, were later proven to be inauthentic amalgams of many different eras. In the initial museum scene Wharton acknowledges that the controversy over the Metropolitan's first important purchase was not merely a historical footnote but is personally significant to her characters and to American culture. She is able to illustrate how the museum's early choices resonate in the larger culture and over time through the novel's double framing of this scene: Archer eventually looks back at this moment from the vantage of about 1900 (when he returns to visit the Metropolitan), and Wharton looks back fifty years through the long lens she uses to write the novel in 1919. Although Wharton has often been accused of losing touch with America in her later novels, her study of the professionalization of the Metropolitan Museum of Art links her museum novels closely to her New York novels of the 1920s. In these later novels Wharton chronicles modern society as suffering from an absence of memory and particularity, the very maladies that she identifies in these earlier novels as by-products of a combination of poor choices and social pressures within a developing American museum culture.

Wharton never went to college or held any official position in a cultural institution, facts representative of the period and class in which she lived.[8] Yet Wharton's deep curiosity about learning not only led to her interest in books and paintings but drove her to study the technical choices that museums and libraries make in exhibiting these objects. Through her close friendships with collectors, curators, and museum directors, Wharton visited an astonishing number of exhibitions in Europe and America and helped to build up her own private collections of books and art as well. Since she was not allowed to attend a university (a fact that she noted but never lamented), her curiosity and intellectual passions had to be satisfied through the cultural materials made available to her. Wharton provides a particularly useful introduction into the idea that museums and libraries shaped a generation of modernist women writers since her own creative development can be viewed almost entirely in relation to the detailed story she tells about the simultaneous maturing of American museums and libraries—a transformation that she understood both actually and imaginatively.

Wharton's theoretical ideas about ideal museums and libraries provide a stepping stone to Nella Larsen's practical ones. In my third chapter I discuss the ways in which Nella Larsen's novels recall her training as a librarian. The library plays a role in *Quicksand* (1928) as it also played a role in Larsen's life during the 1920s when she enrolled in library school, studied the Dewey decimal system, and worked as a librarian at the New York Public Library's 135th Street branch. The library facilitates discussion of Larsen's ideas about the institutionalization of knowledge—ideas that preoccupy her characters Helga Crane, Clare Kendry, and Irene Redfield in her two novels *Quicksand* and *Passing* (1929). Larsen's female characters understand that the production of knowledge is always also the production of new methods or theories of exclusion. One of the reasons these characters can recognize this idea of knowledge as exclusion is that they work in the places that employ the very same systems—such as the Dewey classification system—used to exclude them.

Nella Larsen makes clear from the opening paragraph of *Quicksand* that Helga Crane is on an intellectual quest. As Helga rejects each new job and responsibility she receives for offering anti-intellectual and unimaginative solutions to critical social problems, she despairs increasingly that she will ever find a space from which to create a new, productive form of knowledge. She looks for this space in art and culture and in institutions such as the museum and the library and the people who support them. She seeks new knowledge that will free her, both intellectually and imaginatively, from old and familiar ways of thinking about race, class, and gender. On the very first page of *Quicksand* Helga sits in her room, framed by light, as though she has been painted in a portrait. Although she does not yet have a vocabulary to express whether this framing device is tasteful or problematic, Helga will later become so effective a cultural analyst that she insightfully reads a portrait of herself destined for a prominent spot in a museum, in time to save herself temporarily from making a terrible mistake. *Passing,* Larsen's next, last, and angrier work is a reply to *Quicksand,* and it takes place in a far more suffocating environment. While Clare Kendry's nonchalance, her willingness to move between classes, races, and cities, and her surprising social life suggest that she embodies many of the traits Helga Crane most admired, it is Irene Redfield, anxious and imitative, who survives the battle between them. The door Larsen leaves slightly open in *Quicksand* is closed by the end of *Passing*. Helga Crane and Clare Kendry have very few of the characteristics of the typical heroine, but they are unwavering in their commitment to independent thinking and to discovering new ways to learn. While they are still trying to navigate their way through the maze of social institutions to which they belong and in which they want to believe, a new form of commitment emerges as the characters attempt to subvert these institutions from the inside, creating not only new knowledge but new systems through which knowledge might be produced.

Nella Larsen's library world is unexpectedly and intimately shared by Marianne Moore. The two writers worked at the same time as librarians in branches of the New York Public Library. Larsen worked at the 135th Street branch, uptown; Moore worked at the Hudson Park branch, downtown. Both authors managed the children's sections of their libraries, reported to the same central administrator (the well-known Miss Annie Moore), and passed the examination offered by the central library as a tool for promotion. The geographical distance between the two library branches (about one hundred blocks), however, signals the different literary worlds the two authors inhabited. The center of the Harlem Renaissance was 135th Street, and Arna Bontemps, Langston Hughes, and others published accounts of the library as the necessary first stop for artists arriving in Harlem; Greenwich Village was the center of the burgeoning modern art movement. As authors, Larsen and Moore are never discussed together; as librarians, however, both are mentioned in the same volume of New York Public Library minutes.[9] Larsen and Moore never met, and although their creative works differ significantly, their intellectual development as writers follows a remarkably similar trajectory.

Moore's ideas, like Larsen's, were shaped in large part by experiences at her early jobs. After attending college, she worked as a secretary for Melvil Dewey, a figure whose classification system was central to Nella Larsen's library training in the 1920s as well. Moore also worked for several years as a teacher in a vocational school and then as an assistant librarian at the New York City Hudson Park branch, where she readied her first official book of poems—*Observations*—for publication in 1924. To read Moore's early prose and poetry is to see her develop as an intellectual. She was clearly inspired and curious about almost everything, yet when Moore begins to put the book into its final form, her serious engagement with the ideas and ideals of museums and libraries becomes central to its final production. In this period, when she creates notes and an index and discovers an ideal order in which to present her poems, Moore elevates qualities of "enjoyment" and "accident"—terms and ideas that she identifies as crucial in her museum and library work—to poetic necessities in the volume.

In Moore's final written work—her will—she creates a museum and library for her papers and objects; in this gesture she underlines her serious commitment to the ideals of museums, libraries, and poetry that she had initially explored in *Observations.* Although T. S. Eliot's *Selected Poems* (1935) had eclipsed *Observations* critically by vetting, reorganizing, and renaming much of that initial volume, Moore returned to her thinking about museum and library ideals at several points in her later career. As she published her final editions of her works—*Collected Poems* (1951) and *Complete Poems* (1967)—and worked toward her final decision to sell her archive to the Rosenbach Museum and Library in Philadelphia, Moore continued to think about the relationship between museums, libraries, and poetry. She not only sold her papers to the Rosenbach, but in an addendum to her will she established the "Marianne C. Moore Room," a museum devoted to showcasing her personal possessions within the Rosenbach townhouse. This gesture toward creating a metaphorical and a physical space (the Rosenbach houses her poems—metaphorical spaces—and it is a museum and library—a physical space) is already identifiable in Moore's first volume of work, which begins to imagine how an interchange between museums, libraries, and poetry might benefit all three.

My final chapter focuses on Ruth Benedict's reflection on whether the university can exist as a place for women to achieve more professionally and intellectually than is possible within the museum and the library. This question leads Benedict to consider the relationship between cultural institutions and the development of imaginative thinking processes. She eventually decides that the practice of poetry is more important to cultural improvement in America than anything else, but her path to this revelation involves rejecting jobs in museums and libraries and achieving a PhD and a job at Columbia in anthropology. In poems that she writes and rewrites during a career spanning more than twenty-five years, Benedict theorizes about ways to resist the powerful shifts in thinking and beliefs that cultural systems can produce in individuals. As she explains in the first chapter of *Patterns of Culture* (1934), "knowledge of cultural forms is necessary in social thinking," and she increasingly argues in her anthropological as well as her literary works that a keen sense of these "cultural forms" could be obtained through close attention to the smallest details of an individual's life.[10] Arguing that "there has never been a time when civilization stood more in need of individuals who are genuinely culture-conscious, who can see objectively the socially conditioned behavior of other people without fear and recrimination" (*PC*, 10), Benedict explains that individuals often do not even know the ways in which their behavior and ideas are socially conditioned. She argues that writing can potentially undo some of these entrenched beliefs simply by awakening the reader to see firsthand the ways culture affects thinking.

The ideas behind Benedict's two most important contributions to anthropology—her explanation for how cultural conditioning occurs and her creation of new methods for ethnographic research—began in the library. Benedict's critique of the library as a place that employs women often unfairly under the guise of a professionalization program later develops into arguments about the ways seemingly benevolent systems often impose negative expectations on individuals (sometimes without their realizing these pressures). Benedict also promotes a new, more analytical and skeptical, approach to research after completing a dissertation as a young anthropology student undertaking a typical project using library sources. Benedict's frustration with this method of research helps her to push for more research out in the fields and greater efforts to question and correct older studies she sees as moldering in the library. Despite her eventual success as a professor at Columbia University, Benedict felt similarly frustrated as she saw universities working to instantiate some of the very same cultural ideas that she had worked hard to eliminate. Benedict eventually critiqued the university using terms similar to those she used to challenge the library (and, to a lesser extent, the museum).

Just as Wharton, Larsen, and Moore had hoped to transform the cultural lessons museums and libraries taught by transforming the way those spaces made their intellectual arguments in physical ways (for example, by shifting methods of display or the order of books on a shelf), Benedict demonstrated, quite powerfully, her belief that cultural institutions need to hear the voices and works of poets and writers who recognize the unending, probing nature of intellectual inquiry. She believed that writing, and poetry particularly, provides a mode of self-reflection and a means to resist system-making sorely missing from social science and cultural investigations. She came to believe that to become fully aware of the way culture affects people is the only way to begin to intervene positively and directly in a social system and change the way people think culturally. She found that even institutions ostensibly dedicated to this open spirit of inquiry—particularly museums, libraries, and universities—fell short under practical pressures to professionalize.

Benedict held to these beliefs even as her poems remained largely unpublished and her anthropological texts became enormously popular, even as she was increasingly discouraged as a poet and encouraged as an anthropologist. Despite her lack of success, Benedict knew the poetry scene that Marianne Moore was part of almost as well as Moore did. Many of her friends were Moore's friends, and the two writers published in some of the same journals and literary magazines. If Benedict hung back from that scene because of its frequent rejections of her work, she was still probably a greater champion of the possibilities for poetry and art to create lasting cultural changes than any of the other three authors. Perhaps because Benedict was fully aware of the annoyances and hypocrisies of professional life in a university, she never could hold professional work up as an ideal, as Wharton, Larsen, and Moore sometimes had. Benedict's bitterness about her own lack of artistic success did not extend to bitterness about possibilities for poetry and art broadly to affect the ways one perceived experience. Shortly before she died in 1948, Benedict sat in the audience at one of Moore's poetry readings, and she did so as a celebrated New York intellectual—a famous anthropologist—instead of as a poet and artistic personality, yet Benedict's presence at that event underlines her hope that poetry and aesthetic ideas might enable greater possibilities for thinking imaginatively than her own academic position could ever achieve.

I conclude this study with a brief meditation on this group of radical thinkers—critical of museums and libraries and yet still willing to work in them and use them in order to get needed jobs, continue their education in whatever form they could discover it, and mine those spaces for writerly material. These women not only used museums and libraries as points of inspiration or a way to reflect generally on American culture and morality—certainly male writers such as Henry James and Sinclair Lewis used the settings of museums and libraries to critique American cultural development—but they studied the mechanics of how these places were created and operated quite consciously as a means to understand the basis of their own intellectual and social ideas. They hoped their creative achievements would help to ironize the very institutions that they sometimes needed to foster a connection with in order to gain credibility and prestige in a world increasingly reliant on those places to give women professional approval. Their works have generally not been read this way; instead, women writers' interests in museums and libraries have been taken literally as reflective of their gender and class. This view of their writing arises from the ways museums and libraries continue to be read—often unconsciously—as middle-class, feminine spaces. Women writers sometimes struggled against succumbing to the same biases in their own thinking, considering their work in these places to be less revolutionary and intellectual than it really was because early twentieth-century American cultural critics—particularly Van Wyck Brooks, George Santayana, and Malcolm Cowley—viewed the spaces in these ways.

In exploring how museums and libraries shape powerful cultural notions about gender, race, and class through a seemingly benign process of democratizing the acquisition of knowledge, these writers' works illustrate the need to observe the formation and stabilization of these spaces when and where they continue to occur. Their commentary about this complex process, and their effort to explain it as both a practical issue and a cultural one, is becoming increasingly relevant in the twenty-first century. Recent debates about Google's plans to become the world's most comprehensive library have raised remarkably similar concerns—anxieties about power, authority, and who will gain control over vast amounts of information—to those that Wharton, Larsen, Moore, and Benedict brought up almost a century ago. These women recognized, as we are only beginning to, that the methods through which we receive information have already transformed that information, often in crucial ways. They argued that how we receive information ought to be studied because it always affects how we use it. The secrecy with which Google regards its search algorithm, and the speed at which this set of organizational concerns is constantly updated to reflect new expectations for what material can be found and how we ask for it, is increasingly a subject of contemporary interest. Wharton, Larsen, Moore, and Benedict took intelligent steps to understand details of the equivalent early twentieth-century process, to identify where women fit into it, and to expand those possibilities, discovering through their intense reactions and critical reflections a new way to write.

1

Women and the Mutual Development of Museums and Libraries

Museums and libraries share a history as places whose related processes of institutionalization and professionalization profoundly shaped the early twentieth-century intellectual woman.[1] Although today libraries and museums conduct different kinds of cultural work, they developed as public institutions in part by observing each other and recognizing that they shared many of the same goals. Libraries were younger but developed institutional character first. Museums observed the early history of the library and modeled their institutionalization on the library's progress. Debates in the mid-nineteenth century considered what kind of political influence a library or museum ought to have and whether such places had the potential to exercise less obviously the same kinds of social controls as the church or the court. Because cultural institutions were relatively new social institutions overtly concerned with the development of a national culture, and were not obviously involved in any regulatory or authoritarian action (as, for example, the court or the church had been), politicians debated how to make these cultural spaces, particularly libraries and museums, do certain kinds of "persuasive" institutional work, influencing beliefs and attitudes of patrons without overtly doing so.

The fear that American scholars would have to continue to travel to England to find the material that they needed for their work, along with the desire to create an independent American culture, spurred the earliest library movement forward.[2] Discussions about the role of the library in national politics became clearly articulated through the extensive debates surrounding the creation of the Boston Public Library. When the Boston Public Library Board of Trustees asked George Ticknor and Edward Everett to draft a report about the plans for the creation of the library, board members expected that the librarian-scholars would provide them with the rhetoric that they wished to use to describe the library project. The report, which was drafted on July 6, 1852, set out the reasons for establishing the library: "In this way the Trustees would endeavor to make the Public Library of the City, as far as possible, the crowning glory of our system of City schools; or, in other words, *they would make it an institution,* fitted to continue and increase the best effects of that system, by opening to all the means of self-culture through books, for which these schools have been specially qualifying them."[3] In the document the two men clearly state that the collective aim is to make the library into "an institution." This was not merely a general desire to make the library an important cultural center in Boston. They carefully chose the word *institution* to represent the plan for a library that would exercise a certain amount of intellectual and political control over the masses:

> It has rightly been judged that—under political, social, and religious institutions like ours—it is of paramount importance that the means of general information should be so diffused that the largest possible number of persons should be induced to read and understand questions going down to the very foundations of social order . . . for no population of one hundred and fifty thousand souls, lying so compactly together as to be able, with tolerable convenience, to resort to one library, was ever before so fitted to become a reading, self-cultivating population. By a little judicious help in the selections for a Free City Library, rather than by any direct control, restraint or solicitation, [the taste for books may] be carried much higher than has commonly [been] deemed possible; preventing at the same time, a great deal of mischievous, poor reading now indulged in.[4]

The idea that the institution will fit seamlessly into the project of the "political, social, and religious institutions" that already exist was an old argument for the close relationship between the creation of the library and the continuation of the national political project. The document also made an argument, however, for what institutions do. Namely, they control without obviously controlling, they prevent mischief, and they teach self-culture, which will eventually lead to self-control and self-restraint. The plan for the Boston Public Library was to offer "judicious help" to "one hundred and fifty thousand" Boston souls by offering free books that would help create a restrained, controlled, and patriotic population.

Whether the motivation behind the creation of these early cultural institutions was the promotion of an ideal nation of educated people or the desire to create institutions of control was a source of debate that historians continue to probe. As Michael Harris and Gerard Spiegler argue in their revisionist study of the public library, the early plans for public libraries, and particularly the national plans for libraries, brought about aggressive discussions between competing intellectuals who had very different reasons for supporting such plans. These debates intensified in the years leading up to the opening of the Boston Public Library in 1854: "Great enmity developed between the transcendentalists, who were anti-institutionalists, and other high-placed Bostonians. The transcendentalists insisted that each individual was capable of seeking, and finding, truth through a communion with nature, and they rejected the need for institutions designed to 'educate' or 'control' society . . . while the more authoritarian Bostonians sought to bolster the controlling influence of existing social institutions while creating new ones that were designed to control the common man, not to liberate him."[5] Playing on the term *librarian-scholars,* a phrase that has often been used to describe the men who helped create the earliest libraries, Harris and Spiegler describe the men who helped found the Boston Public Library as "authoritarian-elitists." They argue that these men wanted to create libraries in order to stamp out any form of social instability that might undermine the government and that they understood that social meaning could be made more powerfully in seemingly benign institutions than directly through the government.

While Harris and Spiegler may overstate their argument, lumping Ticknor and Everett (two very different thinkers) together through their joint authorship of the report, there is no question that a few intellectuals feared that the library was being created as an institution of social control and ought to be resisted.[6] Although Ralph Waldo Emerson was known to support libraries, beginning with the part his father played in founding the Boston Athenaeum and through the speech that Emerson gave in 1873 at the dedication of the new library building in Concord, he also worried about the effect that reading books in libraries had on students. In several essays, including "The American Scholar," Emerson commented on the possible dangers of reading books in libraries: "Meek young men grow up in libraries, believing it their duty to accept the views which Cicero, which Locke, which Bacon, have given; forgetful that Cicero, Locke, and Bacon were only young men in libraries when they wrote those books."[7] If readers approach the library with too much passive veneration, they might be tempted to accept books that have made it onto the library's shelves as containing a greater truth than the perceptions they bring to their reading. Behind Emerson's seemingly straightforward advice are statements about what libraries are. Simply put, they are archives, and as such, they institutionalize certain kinds of works by displaying them. Furthermore, by virtue of how they choose to display books and where they might place a particular work in relation to other books, libraries instantiate ideas to such an extent that the library, Emerson feared, could endanger original thought.

At the same time, of course, Emerson's essays are replete with evidence that he used libraries. In "Quotation and Originality," published first in *The North American Review* (1868) and later in *Letters and Social Aims* (1875), Emerson offers an interesting analogy to describe libraries:

> Whoever looks at the insect world, at flies, aphides, gnats, and innumerable parasites, and even at the infant mammals, must have remarked the extreme content they take in suction, which constitutes the main business of their life. If we go into a library or news-room, we see the same function on a higher plane, performed with like ardor, with equal impatience of interruption, indicating the sweetness of the act. In the highest civilization the book is still the highest delight. He who has once known its satisfactions is provided with a resource against calamity. . . . In every man's memory, with the hours when life culminated are usually associated certain books which met his views. Of a large and powerful class we might ask with confidence: What is the event they most desire? What gift? What but the book that shall come, which they have sought through all libraries, through all languages, that shall be to their mature eyes what many a tinsel-covered toy pamphlet was to their childhood, and shall speak to the imagination?[8]

Because Emerson recognizes that the library has the potential to be a source of control, he fights against the idea that a man could sit in a library in "the extreme content" that a fly would "take in suction." Although books are "the highest delight," Emerson continues to argue against the idea that a person searching after genuine knowledge ought to sit passively in a library.

While in the early national period there was a search for the means to keep political stability in a postrevolutionary world, by the beginning of the twentieth century many of the questions that had been raised and seriously debated during these earlier periods were considered resolved or were simply dropped. A new attitude finds expression in Ainsworth Spofford's famous 1897 essay "The Function of the National Library," in which the librarian of Congress argues that "a fact pregnant with meaning [is] that the nations which possess the most extensive libraries maintain the foremost rank in civilization."[9] Rather than consider the library a tool of the government to keep peace within the nation just as it had been in the past, librarians and politicians were beginning to view the library as an emblem of the government's power outside of the nation. This new perception is also evident in the 1896 congressional reports on the Library of Congress, which include long interviews between members of Congress and the librarians Spofford, Melvil Dewey, and Herbert Putnam (who would become the librarian of Congress in 1899 and would serve in that capacity for forty years). While the congressional meeting was held ostensibly to discuss the construction of the new wing of the building, the conversation was much more about the general interest in transforming the library further into an emblem of the new, industrial nation. Earlier concerns about the library's status as an institution had been replaced by newer ones considering the library's power as a symbol. Discussions centered on questions of perception—issues such as women as librarians,[10] the hanging of artwork inside the library, and the desires of some speakers, such as Dewey and Putnam, to rename the Library of Congress "the National Library." The library as a site for debate between politicians about the role of the government and the power of institutions had been generally replaced by a notion of the library (even the Library of Congress) as standing outside of politics and requiring experts and professionals in the library field to explain its goals to politicians.

It was at this point in the library's history that the museum caught up to it. Although the American museum was officially older than the library, its status by 1876 was much less secure. John Eaton, the commissioner of education, had completed a centennial survey of libraries in 1876, but the centennial of museums in 1873 went unremarked. Museum historians have noted this absence:

> If the condition of museums in 1876 could have been viewed with understanding, not to say prescience, a classic document might have been produced. The heyday of public museums had begun. The principal elements of the modern museum scene (except for some recent developments) had appeared. . . . There was evidence, in 1876, of a change in form of museum organization. *The old societies, academies, and lyceums had begun to give place to institutions*—conspicuous examples in Washington, Boston, and New York—suggesting that in the future the typical museum would be a corporation piloted by trustees. And to these harbingers had come city support—tax funds being given to the American and Metropolitan museums in New York. Nothing like this had happened before. . . . Here worldly responsibility was laid

> upon the new kind of museum to be "as important and beneficial an agent in the instruction of the people as any of the schools or colleges of the city." It was at this time also, well in view of centennial reporters, that the aim of public service—as contrasted to club activity—began to be realized through educational exhibits and the earliest cooperation with schools.[11]

Laurence Vail Coleman describes the evolution of the history of museums and libraries. The period of the American museum renaissance began slowly in 1870 with the founding of both the Metropolitan Museum of Art and the Boston Museum of Fine Arts. Newspaper and magazine articles about both spaces suggested that "very few persons in the land even [knew] what is meant by a Museum of Art" at the time.[12] Magazines and newspapers publicly debated what a museum *is* and what effect it would have on people. Partly as a reply to these kinds of questions, there was an increasing emphasis on discussions about the social responsibility of these new spaces. The museum's perception of itself as an institution corresponded with its efforts to become more central to education. Coleman describes the museum's transformation to the status of institution as effectively providing a set of recognizable goals and ideals to achieve.

For Coleman the progression from buildings that house art to the big-city art museum was a fantastic change carried through during the Industrial Revolution. The growth of museums coincided with a period of massive political expansion in the United States, aptly described as "the incorporation of America."[13] This much-analyzed fifty-year period in American history, extending from 1870 to 1920, encompassed the massive industrial and commercial revolution that transformed the American material and intellectual landscape. Museums and libraries were swept up in this period of change, and they not only expanded in size and scope but were reorganized on the model of the businesses that their new trustees successfully managed. Individuals such as Andrew Carnegie and J. P. Morgan helped to turn these institutions into loci of power and privilege through their contributions of money, book and art collections, and management expertise. As the centralization and organization of administrative functions in museums and libraries was transformed, so the status of the institutions *as* institutions was transformed as well. To receive state and federal money, they had to play up their educational goals and their training and employment systems. The change was rapid and powerful. By the early twentieth century, museum curators and administrators such as Benjamin Ives Gilman at the Boston Museum of Fine Arts and

Roger Fry at the Metropolitan Museum of Art were publishing texts about how museum education had transformed the exhibition and display of museum objects and had changed the experience of going to a museum.[14]

By this point the status of museums and libraries as institutions no longer produced the same kind of controversy. Instead, the maturation of these spaces was completed through the process of their professionalization. As specific types of educational training and expertise became increasingly required to work in and write about these spaces, museums and libraries sought to embrace their new status as professional organizations. Formerly politically charged institutions, they became anxious to shift the public perception of their relationships with the political and the economic worlds. Publicly they were increasingly perceived as symbolic and stable cultural (as opposed to political) spaces.[15] Their symbolic value as institutions was in large part a result of their founding as political institutions. Ideals that had been abstracted from their specific histories, including the arguments surrounding the importance of their early development, still clung to them but in a new and vague form. The original meanings of the terms of the postrevolutionary political debates about social control and national spirit in the library had over time become obscured and were replaced only by a sense that libraries and museums were both central symbols of democracy.

Professionalizing Late Nineteenth-Century Culture

The professionalization of the museum and the library helped to cement ideas about them in the mind of the public.[16] In his essay "The Profession," published in the first issue of the *American Library Journal,* Melvil Dewey, who had spearheaded the founding of both the journal and the American Library Association (ALA) that year, and whose ideas would later play a direct role in educating Nella Larsen and Marianne Moore, announced that the new era of librarianship had arrived:

> The time has at last come when a librarian may, without assumption, speak of his occupation as a profession. . . . It is in the interest of the modern library, and of those desiring to make its influence wider and greater, that this journal has been established. Its founders have an intense faith in the future of our libraries, and believe that if the best methods can be applied by the best librarians, the public may soon be brought to recognize our claim that the free library ranks with the free school. . . . The time *was* when a library was very like a museum, and a librarian was a mouser in musty books, and visitors looked with

> curious eyes at ancient tomes and manuscripts. The time *is* when a library is a school, and the librarian is in the highest sense a teacher, and the visitor is a reader among the books as a workman among his tools. Will any man deny to the high calling of such a librarianship the title of profession?[17]

Dewey's call to professionalize the library made the library new, and it seemed to do this at the expense of the museum. Yet this remaking of the library also demonstrated that the process of professionalization involved an effacing of history. By making the library new, Dewey was altering—or even purposefully erasing—the library's previous history. He established a clear line of demarcation between what he wanted remembered about the library's dusty pre-1876 past and its modern, gleaming post-1876 future. His notion was a powerful one. Generally, historians have agreed with Dewey's assessment. "The Profession," an often-quoted essay, has been used as a sound bite to illustrate the clear distinction between two eras in library development.[18]

Certain aspects of Dewey's pronouncement, however, were misleading. By claiming that the pre-1876 library was premodern, he was focusing necessary attention on his singular vision for the future of the field, but he was also ignoring the past. He made no mention of the important place the library had occupied in the early nineteenth-century debates about the making of the nation and the relationship between free and continuing education and democracy; nor did he discuss the arguments made by mid-nineteenth-century intellectuals both for and against the establishment of the public library as an American institution. This critique is not meant to challenge Dewey's importance to the library profession—his roles in founding the American Library Association, the *Library Journal,* and the first library science program at Columbia; in creating a classification system; and in recruiting women to the field are all well documented.

Dewey's pronouncement ought to be considered a watershed moment not only because it permanently and profoundly marked a change in the direction in which the library had been moving up to that point but also because part of what was altered was the library's relationship to time and history. While the professionalization of the library assumed the already existing institutional status of the space, it also created a mild case of amnesia about its past. Dewey's essay ushered in a specific definition for what it meant to be professional. Rather than continue to promote the library as intimately linked to national politics, as had been done in the past, Dewey asked that librarians consider the library's position in relation to other professions (such as law or medicine, whose professional societies were more advanced by that time) or other institutions (such as schools or museums) that were at different points along the path he sought to follow.

Part of the success of Dewey's pronouncement occurred because the call to professionalize and the new emphasis on the organization of ideas occurred simultaneously. As the creator of a classification system, library schools, and journals, Dewey helped to make organizational systems essential components of professional life. In the post–Civil War period massive growth in the field of American technology produced equally massive changes in the "structure and strategy" of the businesses that were formed as a result.[19] An increase in technology brought with it an increase in production and the desire to create a body of workers whose job it was to organize these new, large enterprises and to create an effective and efficient way to run them. Often referred to as the "organizational revolution," this period that followed the first wave of the Industrial Revolution began at the end of the nineteenth century and sought to make management into a science in order to run businesses efficiently and consistently through new methods of organizing and evaluating work. This emphasis on effective organization transformed the educational missions of museums and libraries. To achieve their educational goals, these spaces adopted new systems of classifying and exhibiting the boundless knowledge that they were dedicated to disseminating. Dewey argued that educational spaces could improve their administration in order to serve the public more efficiently: "[The Library of Congress] has become a great administrative machine, and the library that we hope will be the first in the world requires an administrative organization of the highest order . . . a national head for the vast educational work of American libraries."[20] To serve the public at this level, librarians needed proper training at accredited schools and programs. Dewey argued that librarians ought to learn to run the library as a business and to participate in the standardization of the goals of American educational institutions.

Philanthropic grants to schools, libraries, and museums helped to make this ideal of standardization through efficient education a possibility. Growth in industries and an increase in effective management skills had created enough surplus capital to enable wealthy businessmen to donate money and art objects for the creation of institutions of culture and education.[21] The institutions then turned back to these businessmen to set up organized internal systems of management, often run on the model of the effective and efficient businesses that had helped to fund their creation. By 1904 Andrew Carnegie, who became wealthy as an "organizer of industry," had donated money to create more than fourteen hundred public libraries throughout the country. He stated by this action his desire to become an "organizer of opportunity."

As accredited programs became an increasingly established route to jobs, as libraries standardized the use of the Dewey decimal classification system, and as museums made certain choices in lighting, labels, and design through annual association meetings, Dewey's model for the standardization, centralization, and organization of cultural institutions became closer to a reality. Carnegie's gifts and other influential endowments like it helped to further remove museums and libraries from the sphere and influence of the government into that of the businessman and philanthropist and to further preserve their place as "enduring . . . symbols."[22]

By the early 1920s, with the war over, the economy beginning to improve again, Dewey's systems firmly in place, and the number of new museums and libraries built having slowed, these institutions had a personality. They were genteel, apolitical spaces that employed women and promoted self-culture and were standardized throughout the country.[23] Museums and libraries had completed most of their growth, organization, and transformation. At this point directors of museums and libraries turned their attention to using their institutions' status to attend to the influx of immigrant populations and their new role as "the people's university." This moniker crystallized their acceptance as benign social spaces. One of the results of this process of institutionalization was that these spaces were considered (by the public, through the language that described them) to be in the hands of the people.

Feminization, Cultural Institutions, and the 1920s

Part of the excitement of professionalization was that it seemed to offer a meritocratic system of advancement. Professional movements promoted the idea that careers were open to anyone who was willing to work hard, regardless of class or race. Indeed, this attitude helped inspire Edith Wharton, Nella Larsen, Marianne Moore, and Ruth Benedict to consider (in their lives and in their writing) careers in librarianship. As the development of the university as a school for training expanded, it "appeared to offer to a rapidly growing number of teachers, a refuge and an alternative to the business world" (*RP*, 153). Debates raged, however, over whether these educational spaces were truly "refuges" or whether they simply reproduced some of the class issues more overtly apparent in other institutions. Were these museums, libraries, and universities really "organizations of centers for the production of knowledge" (*RP*, 44)? The idea that knowledge was classless helped to create a seeming paradox: if knowledge and expertise could be obtained through hard work, ensuring thereby that everyone had equal access to the same opportunities, then some could argue that those who were able to achieve success were entitled to positions of greater power. Some argued that democratic institutions actually were "central reproducers of the class structures" (*RP,* 145) because they helped to satisfy through the idea of expertise the desire for a class society.

As each of these four authors would recognize at some point in their writing, invoking the idea of expertise became the means by which authority could be established in a seemingly legitimate way. Critics argued that "these apparently classless organizations" invoked "the legitimacy of expertise" in order to "transmute power into authority" (*RP,* 145). The problem with legitimizing expertise was that doing so also legitimized the kinds of classification systems that made it possible to identify who the expert was. In *The Rise of Professionalism* Larson explains how professionalism—a standardizing and regulating system that women helped to promote since it gave them greater access to schools and jobs—perversely made it more possible for institutions to offer a seemingly legitimate excuse to exclude women from positions of power. Some women resisted the "ideology of expertise" because they recognized that expertise is "implicitly proposed as a legitimation for the hierarchal structure of authority of the modern organization" and that "professionalism, in turn, functions as an internalized mechanism for the control of the subordinate expert" (*RP,* 199). Some women questioned the "legitimacy of expertise" or, at least, wanted to resist the kinds of classification and totalizing systems they believed institutionalized ideas about them that kept them from being viewed *as* experts. Although they had increasing access to schools and training, women were not being put in positions of power in their jobs, an exclusion that kept them from being considered experts and from gaining new levels of authority.

As the museum and the library professionalized, a cult of gentility grew up around them. Museums became associated with leisure-time activities, and libraries—in part because their workforce over a short period of time became predominantly women—became associated with women's work.[24] Library historians have repeatedly noted that these factors were mutually (and negatively) reinforcing: "During this period, paid employment in general was open to women only under conditions appropriate to the prevailing perception of women's role. As it developed in the late nineteenth century, librarianship, and particularly public librarianship, met these conditions because it came to be seen by society as involving service, focus on the individual, attention to detail, transmittal of societal values, and culture. . . . It was a genteel calling seen as a logical extension of a woman's traditional role in the home and family."[25] The publications that supported the library movement remarked on these changes. For example, in the journal *The Library Assis-*

tant: The Official Organ of the Library Assistants' Association, there was an increasingly vocal call for female librarians. In an 1899 essay the author offers an explanation for the growth in the employment of women in libraries and why he supports the change:

> The reason that women are so largely employed in our libraries is that they stay better than men, and although paid as high a salary as a man would be under the circumstances, are more loyal, more trustworthy, and more faithful. It is much better to pay a woman 900 dollars as first assistant than to pay a man that sum. The woman does not think of marrying, while the man would, and then begin fussing about his salary being inadequate for the support of a family. This may be true, but what business has he to marry on such a salary? With no reflection on the men, I say that women make better assistants than men. . . . The American woman has done much to endear the library to the populace, and a great deal of the popularity of the American libraries is due to her faithfulness, conscientiousness, genius, and patience.[26]

The author argues that the reason women ought to be employed is that the job of the librarian and the natural traits of a woman are well suited to one another—that is, a woman need not develop any additional intellectual or technical skills to become a librarian because of innate characteristics such as "patience," "faithfulness," and an uncomplaining acceptance of lower salaries. These attitudes became quite destructive to the work of women librarians (resulting in lower salaries and fewer possibilities for advancement). In *The Feminization of American Culture* Ann Douglas critiques this period of industrialization for leading to what she considers a disappointing cultural transformation. As the power of the church eroded, it was replaced by a feminine culture that, Douglas argues, did not improve the religious culture it had displaced. Douglas feels betrayed by "the drive of nineteenth-century American women to gain power through the exploitation of their feminine identity as society defined it."[27] Although the feminization of culture was meant to replace the masculinist culture that women wished to resist, Douglas argues that this attempt unfortunately resulted in the creation of an even more pervasive set of cultural ideas that did not ultimately help women or culture.

From the Modernist Annex argues that the process by which these spaces came to be seen as always having been feminine, however, actually occurred much later than generally believed—in fact, primarily during the periods when the museum and the library completed their institutionalization and professionalization processes—ending around 1920. The 1920s, sometimes called the period of "normalcy," were the seemingly stable moment following a fifty-year period of remarkable growth and change. The year 1920 is located as an end-date to this period in part because it marks the end of World War I, in part because it marks the beginning of a period of sustained economic prosperity, and in part because the "centralization and consolidation" in business, industry, and education through which the nation had come to identify itself was relatively standardized by this point and did not change very much during the next decade.[28]

Early twentieth-century women writers embraced the opportunities that museums and libraries offered for continued education, but they also recognized through their close association with these spaces that their institutionalization and professionalization processes ironically had created an environment of ideas that often worked against them. Edith Wharton critiqued the way the organization of museums effaced time and history; Nella Larsen argued that the Dewey decimal system inscribed exclusionary ideas about gender and race under the guise of genuine knowledge; and Marianne Moore and Ruth Benedict suggested that museums and libraries missed opportunities to promote innovative ways to think.

Work in museums and libraries helped modern American women writers shape their thinking and their writing. By the early twentieth century, women perceived their relationship with these spaces as necessary for their intellectual advancement, especially as prevailing cultural views of higher education for women were only beginning to change.[29] By the 1920s, as women (and American culture in general) increasingly viewed higher education as a viable option for continued study, professional women's reliance on libraries and museums for intellectual and career advancement began to shift.[30] As a result, this period was particularly fraught for professional women, and an intense creative response to conflicting ideas about how primary these spaces should be in shaping an intellectual woman's work and life developed around museums and libraries. These concerns find their way into novels and poems as American women writers examine their thinking about the relationship between transforming professional opportunities and their creative lives.

2
Museums and Memory in Edith Wharton's Modern Novels

Edith Wharton's analysis of her experience reading James Joyce's *Ulysses* (1922), which she details in a letter—like Virginia Woolf's similarly negative journal entry about the book—has been used by critics to illustrate how out of touch she had become with modern writing after 1920.[1] Although Wharton later published *The Writing of Fiction* (1924), which traces the evolution of modern fiction through Marcel Proust, and several novels that deal explicitly with the development of the modern writer—particularly *Hudson River Bracketed* (1929) and *The Gods Arrive* (1932)—the general consensus is that Wharton's writing suffered after *The Age of Innocence* (1920) because she failed to understand the direction in which modernist literature, and the modern world, had moved. She was getting older and had lived away from America (the inspiration for much of her creative work) despite continuing to set her novels there, and critics contend that these factors conspired to make her unresponsive to modernist literature.

I want to propose a new view of the development of Edith Wharton's writing after 1920 by exploring her thinking about the history of American museum culture, particularly her knowledge about the creation and early days of the Metropolitan Museum of Art. By 1920 she had completed *The Age of Innocence,* a novel that not only used the Metropolitan as the backdrop to its central love story but also began to explore in a new way the relationship between the modernizing museum and the transforming culture of writing. By this point in her life she had explored American and European museums both as a tourist and in a much more personal way: as a close friend and intellectual partner to some of the most important art critics, museum curators, and presidents and directors of art and educational institutions. More than that, however, the subject was one she had prepared for all of her life; her earliest direct contact with the American museum movement had begun

1. F. W. Rhinelander, president of the Metropolitan Museum of Art from 1902 to 1904, was Edith Wharton's uncle and a founding trustee of the museum. Photo courtesy of the Metropolitan Museum of Art.

in 1870, when she was eight years old, as her uncle Frederick W. Rhinelander (fig. 1), her mother's only brother, became one of the founding trustees for the Metropolitan Museum of Art and eventually its third president.[2]

Wharton continued to have other important and consistent connections both to the American museum movement and to the European response to these developments: through her correspondence with the art historian Charles Eliot Norton, a relationship that began after he admired her first novel; the art historian Royall Tyler; the art critic and connoisseur Bernard Berenson; Geoffrey Scott, the author of *The Architecture of Humanism;* Edward Robinson, who, after beginning his career at the Boston Museum of Fine Arts, moved to become the first assistant director of the Metropolitan Museum of Art in 1905 and then its director from 1910 to 1931; the art critic Royal Cortissoz; and Eric MacLagan, the keeper of architecture and sculpture at the Victoria and Albert Museum until he became its director in 1924; and, finally, her close relationship during the years before her death with a young Kenneth Clark, initially Berenson's student and later the keeper of the Ashmolean Museum in 1930 before becoming director of London's National Gallery in 1933. She visited exhibitions and galleries with these curators and critics, corresponded with them, read their works, and sent them hers.[3] These close friends stayed with her at her homes, and she visited them at their homes and offices, often taking personal tours of museums and collections with them. Wharton's correspondence with these artists and curators, chronicled in letters and journal entries, provides a sense of her commitment to the study of art, the language that she used to talk about culture, and her enthusiasm and respect for museums.[4]

Wharton sent the letter criticizing *Ulysses* to Bernard Berenson. In this letter Wharton's assumption that a currency already exists between the two worlds of museums and writing is apparent through the abbreviated style she uses to shift between the two subjects. She begins the letter by imploring Berenson to visit and mentioning a dinner she recently had with a mutual friend just after she read *Ulysses*. After discussing the book at dinner, she writes that "Mack carried it off with him that very evening." Mack is Eric MacLagan, a close friend who was about to be promoted from a curatorial position to that of director of the Victoria and Albert Museum. *Ulysses* moves from a writer's hands to a museum director's hands and eventually back again (as Wharton writes about the exchange). The letter ends with an invitation to Berenson to please "come here and be cured!" This injunction contains within it the notion that moving between worlds—the museum-like world of Berenson's Villa I Tatti estate (a place that would later become an official museum and library for Harvard University) and the writerly world of Wharton's home—is curative. More generally, the letter suggests that, for Wharton, provoking a conversation between those engaged in thinking about the future of museums and those concerned with the novel's future feels necessary and natural.

Wharton suggests that her thinking about the modern novel develops in relation to the evolution of her ideas about the modern museum. She begins this conversation on the relationship between museum culture and writing with her first book, a nonfiction work on interior design, *The Decoration of Houses* (1897), which she published with Ogden Codman during perhaps the most transitional moment in American museum history, and continues it through her last, "A Little Girl's New York" (1938), her follow-up essay to *A Backward Glance* (1934). As the turn of the century approached, Wharton—reflecting much of what museum trustees and contemporary newspapers seemed to suggest about the American museum—also expressed optimism about the positive influence museums could have on the public.[5] She believed that if America was going to develop its own aesthetic culture, it was going to do so by changing the way people thought and talked about art and by creating beautiful places for artistic self-immersion. *The Decoration of Houses* was her first public attempt to direct this cultural conversation from within it.[6] She recognized that for the first time in its history the museum was beginning to see itself in broader terms. While American museums had been officially in existence since the mid-eighteenth century, it was not until the founding of both the Metropolitan Museum of Art and the Boston Museum of Fine Arts in 1870 that an idea about the museum began to form in the minds of the American public.[7] Although the founding of both those museums went relatively unheralded and was treated with skepticism in newspapers and magazines, it was clear within the first twenty-five years of their existence that museums were acquiring a central cultural role in America; what this role was going to be, however, was still a source of debate.[8]

After *The Decoration of Houses* Wharton explores even more directly what the cultural role of American museums ought to be and how to accomplish those goals, primarily through her novels from *Sanctuary* (1903) to *The Age of Innocence*. In her fictional works she repeatedly shows how these cultural institutions can be powerful catalysts for social change. In *Sanctuary* Wharton's museum is an ideal place. The notion of a museum as a sanctuary, a space that exists within the social world but can also provide solace from that world, is comforting to the characters who hope for its continued existence and improvement. Wharton's idealized vision of the quest for a new public institution that, because it functions as a potential sanctuary, affords individuals access to heightened consciousness and memory is also a fleeting one in this novel. In her next few museum-novels Wharton offers accounts of what she views as a rather problematic exchange between the social world and modernizing American museums. In works such as *The House of Mirth* (1905) and *The Custom of the Country* (1913) museums function less as educational institutions that inspire reflections on beauty and refinement in the public (as characters in *Sanctuary* hope museums will become) than as authoritative sources of cultural expertise enabling new acquisitive behavior.

As she had earlier suggested in *The Decoration of Houses*, Wharton was aware of a developing obsession among American consumers for the acquisition of art objects. She felt that acquisition alone was not necessarily a cause for concern; Wharton never thought that art objects were sullied by a too-close connection with money or that conspicuous display of luxury was necessarily bad. In fact, *The Decoration of Houses* is one of the first books to celebrate and make a positive case for the value of artistic reproductions in American culture, a subject that museum administrators were avidly debating during the early days of the museum (when sometimes the only access to certain great works of art within the new American museums was through expert reproductions). The work embraced the idea that there was something profound and moving about certain kinds of ideas and objects and that even copies of them would retain that uniqueness. Wharton did, however, have a growing anxiety about what she saw as the connection between the public's attitude toward acquisition and museum administrations' seeming encouragement of this obsession by translating acquisitive urges into educational terms through new definitions of usefulness. In *The Decoration of Houses* Wharton states that "one of the first obligations of art is to make all useful things beautiful."[9] For Wharton the utility of an object was a quality of its aesthetic concerns. The political need, however, to adopt a vocabulary of usefulness—an attitude felt powerfully by politicians and museum administrators particularly during the years preceding World War I—became increasingly untenable to Wharton because it meant that the American museum relied on a social and political vocabulary to attract and to educate visitors rather than an aesthetic one.[10] She despaired over the possibility of ever creating an important new cultural language through the museum that would both reflect on society and have the power positively to influence it.

By 1919 Wharton's growing distrust of the idea of "usefulness"—a term that had always been part of the early museum administrations' educational goals but was increasingly being defined in a new way—developed alongside her observation of the expanded cultural authority of the museum. She held a front-row seat for this phenomenal transformation as it unfolded during the fifty years from 1870 to 1920. Not only did she view her uncle Frederick's frustration (openly voiced in the annual reports by the Metropolitan Board of Trustees) at the complete lack of engagement of her own society in the initial plans of the Metropolitan Museum of Art during the 1870s, but her novels and memoirs make clear that she also watched closely and critically museum administrators' efforts to eradicate this complacency.[11] Wharton understood exactly when her fellow Americans embraced the museum, and she clearly thought she knew what this embrace looked and felt like and why it happened when it did. That she tells this story of the development and overt success of the Metropolitan Museum of Art in *The Age of Innocence* as the backdrop to—but also through the emotional lens of—a failed romance is crucial because the story was one that she knew intimately and felt personally.

By the time Wharton published *The Age of Innocence*, she knew that her hope for a particular future of the museum had not been realized. The novel, which takes place between the 1870s and 1900s and ends a few years after she published *The Decoration of Houses,* revisits some of the hopeful aesthetic ideas of that earlier book from the perspective of knowing how the museum would continue to develop over the next twenty years. Whereas in *The Decoration of Houses* she imagined the possibilities for using culture optimistically in American social life, in *The Age of Innocence* she writes with a mixture of nostalgia and dismay of what she believes—while composing the novel in 1919—has happened instead. Her hope that the ideal museum will develop a language and a set of ideas and concerns that can help to reflect critically on society has been replaced by a belief that the museum has—despite its good intentions, high purpose, and ideals—been a victim of its own success: it has developed a cultural authority so seemingly authentic that the public has come to rely on it not only to *preserve* a historical record but to actually *do* the remembering. Despite museums' overt focus on preserving history, Wharton accuses them of some responsibility for what she sees as a particularly American malady: a lack of visual memory (and an accompanying sense of disorientation). What the museum focuses on as its educational achievements by 1919 when she writes the novel, Wharton views much more cynically. The novel looks both backward through the historical development of museum culture and forward to the way Wharton will continue to analyze the results of this modernization process in the late 1920s and early 1930s. After *The Age of Innocence* she writes novels that explore the world she believes the museum both willingly and unwittingly helped to create, even at the expense of some of its own goals.

From *The Age of Innocence:* Looking Backward to the Early Museums

> Italians I have met here [are] completely insensitive to their surroundings and ignorant of the treasures of art and history among which they have grown up. I begin to think it is better to be an American, and bring to it all a mind and eye unblunted by custom.
>
> —Edith Wharton to Sara Norton, March 8, 1903[12]

In one of the last chapters of *The Age of Innocence* still set in the 1870s, Newland Archer jokes about museums. Married to May Welland, but in love with Madame Ellen Olenska, Archer asks Ellen to meet him somewhere private. "In New York?" she asks, underlining the lack of privacy she feels there compared to Europe. Archer replies: "There's the Art Museum—in the Park . . . at half-past two. I shall be at the door."[13] His response illustrates the desolate cultural landscape of New York in the 1870s. The city lacks an accessible public location for the exhibition of art and a reflection on culture. Central Park, where the Metropolitan Museum of Art is situated, is still a "wilderness," in the vocabulary of the novel. The inhabitants of the city view this space as truly uninhabitable. The art museum is set in a rural space in the midst of what is clearly—as several leisure-class characters in the novel bemoan—a transforming and modernizing city. The art museum is also, as Archer's awareness of its emptiness makes clear, not yet central to this process of modernization. Archer hopes that the connection between the places where people live downtown and a place of culture uptown will be bridged (by both traffic and interest).

To make the joke about the still uninhabited art museum really work, however, Wharton exaggerates its history. Critics who have written about *The Age of Innocence* have noted the novel's many anachronisms: Archer, for example, reads books that were not yet published in the 1870s, when the novel takes place.[14] Wharton, who was careful about checking period details, admitted that at certain moments in a novel she knowingly moved details around to highlight a certain feeling or idea. In the first scene in the museum Wharton transfers the location of the museum to Central Park despite the fact that the novel takes place in the early 1870s and the museum did not actually move to that site until 1879 (and opened there in 1880). She also includes the Wolfe exhibition of impressionist paintings (despite the fact that these paintings were not exhibited until 1887).[15] The precise details merge with the anachronisms in the description to create a scene in which several key moments in the museum's early history are brought together—in part to emphasize that old New Yorkers initially avoided the museum.

Wharton's biting depiction in *The Age of Innocence* of the empty museum of the 1870s as representing American society's lack of interest in culture seems at first quite different from the generosity she exhibited toward American tourists' cultural innocence in her writing earlier in the century. In her letter to Sara Norton of March 8, 1903, Wharton interprets Americans' lack of aesthetic knowledge and vocabulary in a positive way. Americans, she suggests, unlike Europeans who seem inured to art because of their constant close contact with it, are charmingly "unblunted by custom" and can come to view art with both a fresh eye and a new language with which to describe their observations. She had recently made a similar argument in *The Decoration of Houses* as she called for the creation of a new American language to talk about art: "In short, our civilization has not yet developed any artistic creed so generally recognized that it may be invoked on both sides of an argument without risk of misunderstanding" (*DH,* 196). Wharton suggests that Americans need to develop an aesthetic language in order to be understood within and outside of America. Critics such as Charles Eliot Norton and John Ruskin were making similar suggestions (though their comments had a more resigned edge to them) at this same time.[16] They were asking how America could transform itself artistically and to what extent a nation was a civilization if it had not yet learned to use its language to share aesthetic ideas. Wharton admired Ruskin's writing, but his ideas were decidedly negative about the possibility of America ever creating an aesthetic vocabulary.[17] Wharton, however, hoped in 1903 that as American museums matured, so would the general level of American conversations about art and culture.

By 1919, however, when Wharton writes the first scene inside the museum in *The Age of Innocence*, she knows that her earlier positive interpretation of Americans as culturally innocent—the image of characters "unblunted by custom"—was not only too optimistic but a misreading of their character. The anthropological language in this novel, noted by several scholars, is the first clue that her definition of custom is much clearer to her at this later point in her career than it was when she first wrote the letter to Sara Norton. Before writing the novel, she read James Frazer's seminal *The Golden Bough* and also annotated her copies of several works by Edward Tylor on primitive customs and the evolution of culture. Tylor, who succinctly defined custom as "common habits" in several works, argued that "the growth of culture" was "developmental"; in other words, he subscribed to an evolutionary model of culture. The Archer and Welland "clans" seem culturally innocent—they are more often called "clans" than "families" in the novel, suggesting their connection to primitive societies—but Archer becomes increasingly aware throughout the novel that this cultural innocence is not real. He gradually recognizes that these groups have manufactured their cultural innocence through an attachment to custom.[18]

The more Archer recognizes that "custom" rules the lives of leisure-class New Yorkers, the more despairing he becomes about the possibilities for culture to intervene in this habitual and unexamined process. His transforming view of May Welland is perhaps the best example of this understanding. Although he first likes that May Welland is the "product of a system," and one who understands the "recognized custom" of her set of friends, as the novel progresses Archer gains an increasingly sophisticated vocabulary in which to give a context for her inscrutable personality (*AI*, 6). He considers the world that created her:

> In reality they all lived in a kind of hieroglyphic world, where the real thing was never said or done or even thought, but only represented by a set of arbitrary signs. . . . The result, of course, was that the young

> girl who was the centre of this elaborate system of mystification remained all the more inscrutable for her very frankness and assurance. She was frank, poor darling, because she had nothing to conceal, assured because she knew of nothing to be on her guard against. . . . He returned discouraged by the thought that all this frankness and innocence were only an artificial product. Untrained human nature was not frank and innocent; it was full of the twists and defenses of instinctive guile. (*AI*, 29)

The primary interests of the new anthropology that Wharton was studying at the time were in examining the behavior of "untrained human nature" and in studying the process by which a so-called primitive culture is civilized. Archer, who reads "the books on Primitive Man" (Tylor's most famous book is *Primitive Culture* [1871]), understands how to describe May Welland as the product of a kind of clannish education using an ethnographic analysis of her behavior (*AI*, 29). He observes her in her natural setting (with her family and in St. Augustine) in order to better understand who she is. He decides that her inscrutability is a product of how she was made, or actually "manufactured" (*AI*, 29), by her family. He begins to resent the idea that modern civilization uses its intelligence to manufacture innocence.

This paradoxical process of unenlightenment so frightens him that he searches for further evidence. He notices that May's modern manufacturing is betrayed by her eyes. Throughout the novel Archer remarks on May's "too-clear" (*AI*, 91) and "transparent" (*AI*, 194) eyes as a symbol of her lack of engagement with culture. He worries that this loss of the use of her eyes is not her problem alone but a symptom of the society that created her: "He shivered a little, remembering some of the new ideas in his scientific books, and the much-cited instance of the Kentucky cave-fish, which had ceased to develop eyes because they had no use for them. What if, when he had bidden May Welland to open hers, they could only look blankly at blankness?" (*AI*, 52–53). Archer concludes that May's eyes only reflect but seem to be unable to view critically the world that created her. Archer initially sees this as a positive by-product of following the custom of her "set," but later he considers that it reflects her lack of engagement with ideas or thinking. The artist Roger Fry came to a similar conclusion about modern eyes and modern art: "Biologically speaking, art is a blasphemy. We were given our eyes to see things, not to look at them. Life takes care that we all learn the lesson thoroughly, so that at a very early age we have acquired a very considerable ignorance of visual appearances. . . . The subtlest differences of appearance that have a utility value still continue to be appreciated, while large and important visual characters, provided they are useless for life, will pass unnoticed."[19] Fry's argument that the kind of observation necessary to look at art is biologically unnecessary, and will cease to exist unless forced into practice, is Archer's recognition, too. Archer despairs that modern life deems the ideal work of a museum, or the development of culture in general, unnecessary, and he fears that evolution is already producing human beings that will turn this misconception into a permanent fact. May Welland, as a representative product of the clan that raised her, cannot conceive of any reason to discover a visual world outside of her immediate surroundings (she has no interest in the museums Archer wants to take her to on their European trips, for example). She has no idea that she might be losing her sight, and Archer cannot adequately explain to her the distinction he makes between seeing and looking since, as her expertise at archery indicates, she knows that she can see just fine.

Archer's realization develops Wharton's discussion of the relationship between custom and culture. The process of identifying the "custom[s] of the country" and their relationship to culture, which is the central plot of *The Age of Innocence,* is also the title of Wharton's satiric 1913 novel. These customs, *The Custom of the Country* makes clear, have quickly adapted to new material—responding directly to the ascendency of the museum as a cultural institution. In *The Custom of the Country* the connection between the museum and social custom (for example, the fact that Undine Spragg goes to the museum to learn what to buy) is purposefully overplayed and comical, but in *The Age of Innocence,* set in an earlier period, Archer can only silently despair about the development of a society ruled by custom rather than culture. Archer realizes repeatedly, however, that society's initial lack of interest in art and its eventual passion for the museum—by the end of the novel the museum has become a highly public and popular place—arise from the same misunderstanding of the terms. By redefining *culture* and *custom* in *The Age of Innocence* as concepts in direct relation to (and in conflict with) one another, Wharton revises her original hopeful analysis of American tourists looking at art. Archer recognizes that he, too, at first misinterpreted May Welland positively as "unblunted by custom" and therefore capable of education and cultural training. He misunderstood May Welland's innocence as genuine rather than as something "manufactured" by the custom of the country. By the end of the novel Archer recognizes that the museum also may not be able to provide the kind of education and cultural training that it seemed destined to be able to accomplish, and—despite (or perhaps because of) its phenomenal growth and some good intentions—it may only be capable of servicing and supporting some of society's most entrenched customs.

The Possibilities for the Ideal Museum: The Observation of the Art Object

Wharton recreates the beginning of the modern American museum in *The Age of Innocence* by staging a scene in the original Cesnola rooms of the Metropolitan Museum of Art. In this scene Newland Archer watches Madame Olenska walk around the Cesnola room with the kind of concentration with which Wharton felt one needed to look at objects in order to know them, a practice that she had described in *The Decoration of Houses* through her emphasis on simplifying and decluttering the space in which a work of art resides. Much of Wharton's early work is dedicated to the issue of how Americans can learn to look at objects more closely as a means of becoming more culturally literate. One of the arguments her interior design book emphasizes is that it is essential in cultivating one's sense of taste to learn to recognize the intrinsic merits of certain objects and the lack of those merits in others.

This question of the best way to observe and know an object as an object of art was one that her close friend Bernard Berenson was also contemplating.[20] Early in his career he explained his process to Roger Fry: "You will do well to rest assured that I am not in the first place 'scholarly' and 'learned.' I hate to read about art, and love to use my eyes."[21] During the years prior to Wharton's first meeting with Berenson in 1903, his career as a connoisseur developed rapidly. By 1892 Berenson's study of Lorenzo Lotto illuminated how his "method [of connoisseurship] worked by attempting to reconstruct the artistic personality of this painter through close scrutiny of correctly attributed works. . . . Ever mindful of the unreliability of such evidence [as signatures and documents], the Morellian connoisseur placed more faith in visual evidence."[22] Berenson argued that the connoisseur could discover a more correct attribution for a work of art than any other method available: "a problem cannot be treated dialectically and forensically alone. It has to be experienced and lived, it has to be tasted and felt. . . . The most authentic evidence, nevertheless is there, beyond the realm of discourse."[23] Mary Ann Calo describes Berenson's *The Drawings of Florentine Painters* (1903) as the "monumental study" in which Berenson finally successfully merged "his formidable skills as a critic, psychologist, and historian, a synthesis that has come to define the modern connoisseur."[24] Berenson described the experience of connoisseurship simply in a diary entry late in his life, writing that "what amazes me is how alive and alert I get before unknown or long unseen pictures. I see through them to the characteristic which is most decisive as never before."[25]

Wharton's consideration of the issues involved in being able to look effectively at a work of art draws on Berenson's ideas and anticipates later works on the subject. In "The Work of Art in the Age of Mechanical Reproduction" Walter Benjamin explores how modern life complicates the process of seeing, because of both the excitement that mass-reproduced objects create and the contradictory desire for an object still to be able to reveal "the essence of all that is transmissible from its beginning, ranging from its substantive duration to its testimony to the history which it has experienced."[26] Wharton's *The Decoration of Houses* shares a similar combination of excitement and anxiety over the proliferation of objects that modern technologies have made possible: "It is an open question how much the mere possibility of unlimited reproduction detracts from the intrinsic value of an object of art. To the art-lover, as distinguished from the collector, uniqueness per se can give no value to an inartistic object; but the distinction, the personal quality, of a beautiful object is certainly enhanced when it is known to be alone of its kind" (*DH*, 192). Underlying this discussion is Wharton's attachment to the skills of the connoisseur—the individual who is able to distinguish between an object with an "intrinsic value" and a fake.[27]

Returning to the first scene inside the Metropolitan Museum of Art, Wharton offers evidence that she is thinking about how an art museum might participate in the development of a class of connoisseurs—those capable of determining the authenticity of an object of art—and what circumstances might limit those possibilities. She describes Archer and Olenska's visit:

> Avoiding the popular "Wolfe" collection, whose anecdotic canvases filled one of the main galleries of the queer wilderness of cast-iron and encaustic tiles known as the Metropolitan Museum, they had wandered down a passage to the room where the "Cesnola antiquities" moldered in unvisited loneliness.
>
> . . . "It's odd," Madame Olenska said, "I never came here before."
>
> "Ah, well—. Some day, I suppose, it will be a great Museum."
>
> "Yes," she assented absently.
>
> She stood up and wandered across the room. Archer, . . . as always when they first met, was wholly absorbed in the delicious details that made her herself and no other. Presently he rose and approached the case before which she stood. Its glass shelves were crowded with small

> broken objects—hardly recognizable domestic utensils, ornaments and personal trifles—made of glass, of clay, of discolored bronze and other time-blurred substances.
>
> "It seems cruel," she said, "that after a while nothing matters . . . any more than these little things, that used to be necessary and important to forgotten people, and now have to be guessed at under a magnifying glass and labeled: 'Use unknown.'"
>
> . . . Suddenly he heard a step echoing far off down the empty rooms, and felt the pressure of the minutes. . . . The step drew nearer, and a guardian in a braided cap walked listlessly through the room like a ghost stalking through a necropolis. They fixed their eyes simultaneously on the case opposite them, and when the official figure had vanished down a vista of mummies and sarcophagi Archer spoke again. (*AI*, 185–91)

Wharton describes in detail a part of one of the original exhibits of the museum: the Cesnola antiquities collection.[28] The meticulousness with which she describes both the exhibit and the encounter that occurs in front of it suggests that Madame Olenska and Archer do not only meet at the museum simply because they believe it is the one secret place to meet in New York City. This is the last time in the novel that they will ever meet alone. For Wharton, who considered so carefully in all of her works the details of place, the fact that this scene between the lovers takes place in this room of the museum is essential to what happens in it. The details included in the scene suggest a further explanation for her inclusion of anachronisms here; she merges several different eras of the early museum (from 1870 to 1887) into this scene to heighten her focus on the antiquities and argue that any accurate narrative of the modern American museum movement, in fact, has to begin in the Cesnola room.

As Archer walks into the "Cesnola antiquities" room, Madame Olenska announces that she "never came here before." The timing of her statement suggests that "here" refers not to the museum in general but specifically to the Cesnola room. Archer's reply is apologetic: one day the museum will be great, he says, suggesting that what he means is that he hopes one day the museum will be worthy of the inclusion of something like Madame Olenska. He knows that she does not belong "here." Archer cannot completely articulate this idea, but he instinctively recognizes the difference between the authenticity of Madame Olenska and the lack of quality of the objects that surround her.

Wharton's description of how he looks at her highlights this distinction.

Archer looks at Madame Olenska as "she stood and wandered around the room. . . . [He was] absorbed in the delicious details that made her herself and no other" (*AI*, 186); the emptiness of the rooms and the lack of competing objects of interest help to illuminate Madame Olenska's beauty for him. He knows that she belongs in the museum; she is an ideal and authentic museum piece. Archer studies her closely, absorbing all the details of her beauty that make her unique. She briefly glances at the unimpressive objects on display in the room, her look suggesting that they are not worth studying. She notes the cruelty of looking at something so forgotten and so unattached to any knowledge of culture that even the original use of the objects can no longer be identified. The objects are labeled "use unknown," which Madame Olenska interprets automatically as a statement about a lack of present understanding. Archer's love for Madame Olenska and his desire for culture are linked inside the museum space at this moment as Wharton choreographs a scene that showcases Archer's intuitive recognition of the disparity between Madame Olenska (a real museum object) and the Cesnola objects on display.

The potential for what an American museum might be able to accomplish through promoting an ideal kind of looking is the central issue of Wharton's first museum-novel, *Sanctuary.* Written the same year as the letter suggesting that a person "unblunted by custom" can look at art in an ideal way, this novel earnestly contends that a well-designed museum can save a disintegrating society by creating a model for observation and a space in which to practice it.[29] This short work questions what a new American museum ought to look like and how this building choice might affect what happens inside it. Wharton plays with the idea that one type of building or another might better promote the kind of contemplation that she believes is necessary for the creation of an aesthetic culture.

The novel is concerned with the design of cultural spaces. This literal definition of design is also treated metaphorically in the plot as competing ideas about how a new museum's architectural look reflects the social, political, and moral designs on the use of that space.[30] Kate Peyton sees an article in the local newspaper advertising a public architecture competition established to discover who will design the new Museum of Sculpture:

> The evening paper was brought in, and in glancing over it her eye fell on a paragraph which seemed printed in more vivid type than the rest. It was headed, *The New Museum of Sculpture,* and underneath she read: "The artists and architects selected to pass on the competitive designs for the new Museum will begin their sittings on Monday, and

> to-morrow is the last day on which designs may be sent in to the committee. Great interest is felt in the competition, as the conspicuous site chosen for the new building, and the exceptionally large sum voted by the city for its erection, offer an unusual field for the display of architectural ability."[31]

Her excitement over the competition is, in part, due to the very new civic interest in museums and the willingness to support the creation of one with public money. Kate believes that her son, Dick, a recent graduate of the Beaux Arts, will create the best plans for the museum. In her mind his design could demonstrate the combination of moral and aesthetic values she instilled in him as a child; he could showcase her efforts to raise him to contemplate beauty as itself and not be moved by displays of wealth or material goods. She feels confident that "as long as the inner eye had food for contemplation, he cared very little for the deficiencies in his surroundings; or, it might rather be said, he felt in the sum-total of beauty about him, an ownership of appreciation that left him free from the fret of personal desire" (*S*, 79). It does not matter whether Kate's idea of an "ownership of appreciation" as a kind of freedom seems impractical or that it seems about to be crowded out; she believes that if individuals learn how to contemplate art, they will be able to withstand the "deficiencies" of the system. It is the close examination and slow consideration of objects, she has always believed, that is the best defense against the pressures of one's "surroundings."

While the competition is advertised as a wonderful example of the democratic spirit of the country and the growing importance of culture in the cities—the newspaper refers to it as an "unmatched opportunity" (*S*, 89)—the promotional materials also illustrate how well the political and economic offices of the city function and how much money the city allocates for culture. Kate wonders, however, whether the competition will negatively affect the future museum because it will link that space too closely to the political, economic, and professional issues that are a central aspect of winning. Dick's desire to design a grandiose building for his competition entry, a style one associates more with Renaissance churches than with modern city buildings, suggests the symbolic value that he assigns to the museum as a result of absorbing Kate's ideas. He struggles over the problem of how to resolve the conflicting symbols of the museum through a design—he wonders if the museum he designs needs to function as a symbol of democracy, a symbol of economic power, or as something else entirely?

As a result of the museum competition, Kate understands that the museum is a product of the particular system that creates it—the same political system that removes sewage and material waste from public view is responsible for establishing the museum as a cultural and educational center—but she still believes that the museum needs to provide people with a space to reflect on those systems. Her recognition of this irony, however, is at the center of her struggle to understand all the forces that are battling within her son as he prepares for the competition. The announcement of the museum competition triggers the final battle she will wage over her son's soul. The novel itself puts the issue into such apocalyptic terms. Despite Dick's upbringing, Kate is never certain that he can understand the complexities of the museum completely enough to design a good one. Instead of working on his designs for the ideal museum, Dick falls in love with a young woman, Clemence Verney, who believes the world ought to run on the model of a business. For Clemence, the museum is important simply because it represents modern success: it costs a great deal of money to build; it is politically sanctioned; and whoever designs it will be powerful by association. Dick recognizes that her view of the museum as an economic center "simplifie[s] life so tremendously" (*S*, 163–64), and he finds it compelling.

In *Sanctuary* Kate pits the social and political system, which she sees as corrupt, against the museum, which she insists on believing can still be separate and good. Not surprisingly, given the melodramatic extent of the conflict here, Wharton's later novels will suggest that no such separation is possible, however disappointing that might seem to some of her characters. At the end of the novel Kate walks through her house as though it were a museum, still trying to hang on to her ideal vision:

> In her round of the rooms she came at last to Dick's study upstairs. It was full of his boyhood: she could trace the history of his past in its quaint relics and survivals, in the school-books lingering on his crowded shelves, the school photographs and college trophies hung among his later treasures. All his successes and failures, his exaltations and inconsistencies, were recorded in the warm huddled heterogeneous room. Everywhere she saw the touch of her own hand, the vestiges of her own steps. It was she alone who held the clue to the labyrinth, who could thread a way through the confusions and contradictions of his past. (*S*, 167–68)

Kate studies the objects in Dick's room as though they were antiquities in a museum; this scene is both nostalgic and critical. She looks at "relics" and "vestiges" that contain "clues" to other meanings and resonances. By observing and concentrating on the objects, she begins to remember the past more clearly and understand her relationship to it. She reacts to Clemence Verney's interpretation of museum culture as economically and politically expedient by reasserting her own relationship to objects and to the importance of understanding their histories and meanings to establish intimacy not only between objects of beauty but between people as well. She "alone" can navigate the maze of this room and make sense of it because she alone studies each object closely.

The novel's depiction of Clemence Verney and Kate Peyton in a Faust-like struggle over Dick's soul and his architectural designs for the museum anticipates the public conflict over the museum itself that will develop over the next few years, a conflict that the Metropolitan Museum of Art and many other American art museums will try to sort out during their early years. In 1906 the American Association of Museums reported in its minutes the interest of some of its members in merging with the National Education Association, a much older and more established group. An important issue was at stake: the question of whether the museum ought to consider itself an institution of education or whether education was merely one aspect of the broader aims of the museum project.[32]

Since there never was any question within the American Association of Museums that education was an important part of the museum project, it might seem surprising that the subject produced any argument at all. The possible scope, however, of the educational goals of the museum was closely debated, and the argument became increasingly centered on the issue of aesthetics and on competing definitions of usefulness. Benjamin Ives Gilman, museum historian and secretary at the Boston Museum of Fine Arts, sought to resolve this debate by arguing that the aesthetic quality of a museum should be the guiding principle behind any discussion of the future of museums.[33] In his paper "The Triple Aim of Museums of Fine Art," which he presented to the association, he clearly stated his antipathy for the idea of the usefulness of museums, precisely because he saw that term as counteracting the real usefulness that an aesthetic perspective enabled: "Aristotle was the first western thinker to differentiate clearly between fine art, as that whose product is valuable in itself, and useful art as that whose product is valuable through some result external to itself. Laotze in China two centuries before, had spoken of beauty as 'the usefulness of the useless.' The conception reappears in Kant's definition of beauty as 'Zweckmässigkeit ohne Zweck' (purposiveness without purpose). Emerson repeats it in his 'Beauty is its own excuse for being.' "[34] This point of view was seductive to many members of the organization who believed that the museum should take aesthetic issues seriously. Despite some support for Gilman's attachment to the idea that visitor comprehension could be accomplished through greater attention to aesthetic matters, many museum administrators did not know how to reconcile those ideals with what they perceived to be the educational mission of the museum. In the presentation of his paper "Labeling in Museums," Henry Ward, director of the Milwaukee Museum, argued that the museum ought to accept "as a cardinal principle that one should avoid pedantry, or the appearance of trying to teach . . . [but] nevertheless that sufficient teaching should be accomplished to enable the visitor to take an intelligent interest in the exhibits."[35] Gilman's open reply to the paper stated definitively that "labels as ordinarily used do more to interfere with the artistic effect of exhibitions than anything else."[36] This desire for a museum to teach without ever seeming to do so was one that many members believed an impossible compromise. Other museum educators wished to work out how they could better use the techniques available to them: lighting, labels, and didactic panels all became issues in these debates. Some curators believed that a resolution ought to be passed that would require all museums to use the same labeling system. Though this resolution was never formally made, the debates about whether labels ought to be aesthetically pleasing or informative and clearly useful to the visitor continued, and the arguments on both sides became increasingly heated.

The controversy surrounding the exhibition of the Cesnola antiquities in the late 1870s and early 1880s publicly raised questions on the educational goals of the early American museum and pointedly directed those at the Metropolitan Museum of Art. The narrative of Cesnola's discoveries—which was reported in newspapers and several of the new art journals published in the 1880s—also draws together ideas about art and museums from several of Wharton's museum-novels. The controversial history of the Cesnola antiquities, although forgotten today, is a narrative that was not only generally known and discussed at the time but one that had specific meaning in Edith Wharton's intellectual and personal world. Wharton's uncle Frederick W. Rhinelander was a member of the executive committee, one of two internal committees at the Metropolitan that investigated the collection when charges against the authenticity of the objects began to appear in art magazines and New York newspapers.[37] Wharton also knew about the Cesnola antiquities from Henry James's description of the Metropolitan Museum of Art in *The American Scene* (1907), a work she heavily annotated.[38] In this description James mentions the Cesnola antiquities as an aside: "I know not if all past purchase in these annals (putting the Cesnola Collection aside), has been without reproach, but it struck me as safe to gather that . . . the Museum, in short, was going to be great, and in the geniality of the life to come such sacrifices, though resembling those of the funeral-pile of Sardanapalus, dwindled to nothing."[39] These words anticipate those in the scene inside the Cesnola room in *The Age of Innocence* when Archer and Madame Olenska first walk inside:

> They had wandered down a passage to the room where the "Cesnola antiquities" moldered in unvisited loneliness. . . .
> "It's odd," Madame Olenska said, "I never came here before."
> "Ah, well—. Some day, I suppose, it will be a great Museum."
> "Yes," she assented absently. (*AI*, 185)

Both passages describe the museum vaguely and uncertainly as "great" yet apply the term to two different eras in the Metropolitan's history: the 1900s and the 1870s. James's use of the term to describe what he sees in 1904 offers both the sense of his excitement about and his wariness of the conspicuous displays of American wealth and power that he observes on his first trip back to America; Wharton's "great" signifies Archer's uncertain hopefulness about the museum's future. In James's passage the word *great*—invoked in relation to the story of Sardanapalus, who builds his funeral-pile out of the vast treasures he collects through his life—underlines the link he sees between massive accumulation and death; he pursues the metaphor of museum as gaudy mausoleum. Wharton's concern is less about death, however, than about process. James is interested in explaining what the museum is; Wharton is interested in explaining why the museum developed the way it did. This distinction helps explain the difference between the ways the two passages treat a discussion of the Cesnola collection. James "put[s] the Cesnola Collection aside," but Wharton makes the collection the central space of her discussion, suggesting that to fully understand the future of the museum (both the turn-of-the-century version that James sees and the post–World War I version that Wharton considers) is to go back and understand the first and crucial purchase by the museum trustees of the Cesnola antiquities.

Cesnola's Antiquities

The narrative of how the Cesnola antiquities were bought by the Metropolitan Museum of Art, the history of how they were exhibited, and the controversy over their authenticity within and outside of the museum are central to an understanding of that exhibit as the principal location for museum scenes in *The Age of Innocence*.[40] Louis Palma di Cesnola (fig. 2) was an Italian who immigrated to the United States in the mid 1800s, fought in the

2. Louis Palma di Cesnola, director of the Metropolitan Museum of Art from 1879 to 1904. Photo courtesy of the Metropolitan Museum of Art.

Civil War, and spent several months in a Confederate prison. Abraham Lincoln learned of his story, in part through Cesnola's skills at self-promotion, and appointed him consul to Cyprus in 1865. In Cyprus, without much to do politically (Lincoln was assassinated shortly after Cesnola left for Cyprus), Cesnola hired locals to excavate sites reputed to be full of treasures. In most accounts of Cesnola's history, including his own, his ascension to the political rank of consul and his career as an adventurer-archaeologist through his appointment to the board of trustees in 1877 and then to the first directorship of the Metropolitan Museum of Art in 1879 are treated as a testimony to his enormous energy, intelligence, and dedication to America's emerging cultural life.

Cesnola's unquestioned confidence that it was his right to excavate the Cypriote antiquities and sell them to a foreign museum infuses his description of his experiences in Cyprus in the 1860s and early 1870s. As it became increasingly clear that there were valuable antiquities to be found in Cyprus, international arguments escalated over who had the right to claim those treasures. At various points over a twenty-year period the British Museum, the Berlin Museum, and the Turkish and Greek governments and national museums competed over the right to the land and the treasures.[41] Cesnola wrote of his success in outmaneuvering the difficult local authorities in Cyprus with a great deal of pride in his 1878 account of his diggings, *Cyprus: Its Ancient Cities, Tombs, and Temples:*

> Two important steps had now to be taken at once. One was the purchasing of the ground in which the diggings had been commenced, thus acquiring a right to all objects found therein. The other was the prohibition of all further excavations by unauthorised persons. [The peasants] knew that I had the power of taking those [treasures] from them by force if I chose to use it, and they were therefore very glad when they found that instead, I offered them a liberal sum for the acquisition of each object, though . . . it required a good deal of tact and maneuvering to find out where all the pieces that had been abstracted were.[42]

In this example Cesnola's certainty that his money, his access to superior archaeological tools, and his competitiveness ensure a right to the treasures illustrates the spirit of the age and the opportunistic, expansionist, post–Civil War moment that enabled the creation of the great American museums.[43] To Cesnola the objects are not the "spoils" others (like Wharton) would later call them but rather the prize awarded for what he deemed a fair and fruitful competition. Embedded in such a view was also the notion that any kind of moral or national obligation could be eliminated with money. Cesnola praised his own "liberality" (in both political and economic senses) and suggested that although he did not even have to offer money, the fact that he chose to pay the peasants well for excavating the antiquities obviated any claims they might have had against him for taking the objects out of the country.

Cesnola's wholehearted embrace of antiquities as commodities and his desire to sell his discoveries to the nascent American museum were crucial to some of the earliest plans and decisions of the board of trustees of the Metropolitan Museum of Art. The annual reports of the museum suggest that Cesnola's energy, his promotion not only of himself but of the importance of the Cypriote pieces in telling a complete history of art, and his excitement about the role his treasures would play in catapulting a new American museum into functioning as a major international player convinced the trustees of the necessity of buying the objects, finding new temporary quarters in which to house them, and installing them immediately for visitors to see. In fact, buying and installing the Cesnola collection was the driving force behind many of the new innovations the museum trustees planned—including guidebooks, new lighting, and the reorganization of exhibits—to increase attendance, interest, and donations (fig. 3).[44]

Although the board of trustees believed that the purchase of the Cesnola antiquities would simultaneously fill a gap in the known history of art and excite interest in the new American museum, Wharton's museum-novels suggest a less noble motivation. She suggests that in their rush to buy and exhibit the Cesnola collection, museum trustees abandoned some of their early ideals about the kind of educational space that they wanted to create in favor of a quicker return on their investment. In short, they saw in the antiquities and in Cesnola himself the opportunity to put on a good show and bring in an audience.

From the beginning the promotional efforts used to arouse interest in this new exhibition provoked confusion about whether a distinction even existed between the aesthetic and the commodity, an issue Wharton's characters struggle with in *The House of Mirth* and *The Custom of the Country.* In *The House of Mirth* the public art museum becomes the main inspiration for home decoration and social communication. Carol Duncan explains in "Art Museums and the Ritual of Citizenship" how the public art museum developed out of the private gallery, which displayed a royal family's unparalleled access to culture and in doing so helped make a silent but strong claim to the legitimacy of their rule: "Historically the modern institution of the museum grew out of sixteenth- and seventeenth-century princely collections. . . . Public art museums would appropriate, develop, and transform the central function of the princely gallery . . . to impress both foreign visitors and local dignitaries with their splendor and, often, through special iconographies, the rightness or legitimacy of their rule. The function of the princely gallery as a ceremonial reception hall wherein the state presented and idealized itself would remain central to the public art museum."[45] Whereas the royal home may have been the basis for the grand museum historically, in Wharton's modern analysis the grand museum becomes the model for the parvenu's princely home: "[The Brys'] recently built house, whatever it might lack as a frame for domesticity, was almost as well-designed for the display of a festal assemblage as one of those airy pleasure-halls which the Italian architects improvised to set off the hospitality of princes."[46] In the well-known tableau scene in *The House of Mirth,* Mrs. Wellington Bry, desperate to be accepted

3. Archival photograph of terra-cotta sculptures from the Cesnola collection on display at the Metropolitan Museum of Art, 1907. Photo courtesy of the Metropolitan Museum of Art.

by high society, hires Carrie Fisher to orchestrate a public event that will provide her an entrance into society. Fisher's plan is to turn the Brys' museum-like house into a live museum for one evening; her sense that society will respect a house (if not the owners of it) that looks and acts like a museum is accurate. The leisure-class New Yorkers ignore the upstart Wellington Brys by focusing on the correctness of a home built on the model of a museum. This museum-like home gives the family the cultural authority that they lack on their own.[47]

While Carrie Fisher recognizes that Mrs. Wellington Bry's house can be transformed symbolically into a museum in *The House of Mirth*, by 1913 Undine Spragg in *The Custom of the Country* can only recognize the museum as an acquisitive space. Undine, a woman who belongs so completely to the acquisitive world that she is named after the commercial hair product that made her father wealthy, walks into a museum because she wants to be seen in a place that she recognizes for containing everything she hopes to have: wealth, respectability, and status. She has no feelings for art or culture and cannot conceive of visiting a museum to contemplate an art object, but she has a great respect for the unrestrained acquisition that museums seem to sanctify. Undine considers her first foray into the museum successful because she leaves it knowing the next two things she will possess—jeweled eyeglasses and Peter Van Degen—making no apparent distinction between their different qualities. Wharton suggests that Cesnola's simultaneous commodification and aestheticization of the antiquities contributes to the creation of a society unable to distinguish between the two ideas. In this account she implicates the early choices of the Metropolitan Museum of Art's board of trustees who encouraged Cesnola to put on a show (and appreciated that he very much wanted to do so), since the immediate result was a huge spike in attendance, attention, and interest in the museum.[48]

The ensuing controversy over the authenticity of Cesnola's discoveries and the museum's responsibility to the public was related to the political maneuverings that made it possible for Cesnola to dig in Cyprus. No one had superintended his excavations there or the later unpacking of crates at the Metropolitan; as a result, questions arose later over the origin of the objects and unbilled restorations that might have been undertaken to make the collection seem more complete and important. The Metropolitan paid close to $140,000 for the collection.[49] The collection consisted of objects that he claimed had been found in the Temple of Golgoi, said to be the worship site for Aphrodite, and gems that he claimed were from the site of the royal city of Curium. The Golgoi find was eventually partially discredited, and the Curium find was completely discredited by the 1920s, when Wharton wrote *The Age of Innocence*.[50] In March 1880, when the Central Park site opened, however, both collections were exhibited in the main hall as the museum's primary attraction.

Despite the important position that the museum gave to the objects, reports had already started to appear in the late 1870s attacking the credibility of the finds. Cesnola at first answered his critics by writing the book *Cyprus: Its Ancient Cities, Tombs, and Temples*, which detailed his excavations. His statements in the book, however, that his excavations "were carried out systematically . . . [though] perhaps not conducted in all their details according to the usual manner advocated by most archaeologists," did not satisfy some of the skeptics.[51] Reports surfaced from other archaeologists who were attempting—and failing—to find any of the excavation sites he described in the book.

In fact, a few months after the Metropolitan Museum opened in March 1880, an article appeared in a new magazine called the *Art Amateur* calling for a public investigation into the authenticity of the objects and, by extension, the museum.[52] Gaston Feuardent, an antiquities dealer in London who had temporarily housed the objects, accused Cesnola of altering the Golgoi statues so as to make a better sale. He also argued that either the Metropolitan Museum knew about Cesnola's activities and covered them up to protect its purchase or that its ignorance suggested that the museum needed a more expert staff. Feuardent's explicit public comparison of American and European museums was a particularly bitter one to the Americans since one of the reasons the Metropolitan Museum had purchased the Cesnola collection was to compete with and outbid the British Museum. The Metropolitan Museum trustees had heard, not necessarily reliably, that the British Museum was about to purchase the objects.[53] Feuardent's argument ends with the admonition that museums "must be absolutely trustworthy in the information they give" and a plea to "those who take an interest in the Museum of Art" to be aware that these objects are only valuable to the museum as a part of the "history of the art" if they are "reliable."[54] Implicit in this article and many that came after it were suggestions about what makes a good museum. The issue of the credibility of Cesnola's finds became one about the reliability of the American museum. This question of reliability connects the discussion about the Cesnola antiquities to the debates about the museum's role in education, discussions that would become increasingly central to the museums' future in the early twentieth century. Particularly during World War I, museums scrambled to comply with government suggestions concerning operating hours and relevant exhibition subjects in order to continue to receive state and federal grants.[55] The ideological value of reliability became very closely connected to the practical issue of obtaining limited supplies of public funding.

Feuardent's charges against Cesnola grew increasingly specific over the next few years. Feuardent accused Cesnola of "a barbarous anachronism"—altering one of the statues by replacing a lotus flower (held in a hand) with a mirror: "The antiquity of this mirror of recent revelation must be decided by an examination of the object itself, by either antiquarians or persons accustomed to stone-carving. The shape it bears, the undercut work round its edge, its state of preservation when compared with the rest of the statuette . . . all these points will, I feel certain, prove that its antiquity dates from the time of its said discovery, A.D. 1879."[56] This alteration was important to Cesnola, Feuardent stated, because the revelation of the mirror would more directly support his contention that the statue was "Venus" and that its origin was the site of her temple at Golgoi; the proof of both facts would make the excavation finds seem that much more significant. Cesnola replied that the mirror was revealed after cleaning the statues and that no serious alterations were ever made to any part of his collection.

The public response to these charges was strong enough to convince the Metropolitan's administration to investigate. Rather than appoint an outside council of experts, however, or send some of the seriously contested works to other museums for verification, it appointed its own investigating committee to respond to the accusations. This committee submitted a report on January 28, 1881, stating that Feuardent's charges had no merit.[57] The *New York Times*, however, which had not commented on the story before, published some rather scathing articles denouncing the museum's investigating committee: "It is, then, a matter of deep regret to think that henceforward the confidence placed in the authenticity of the Cypriote objects will be sensibly diminished. . . . If the [members of the] committee are willing to put the statuette to the test, let them send it either to the British Museum or to the Louvre, and the determination of it there by competent European experts would settle the matter."[58] Newspapers and magazines quoted leaders in the field of art and archaeology as saying that "the . . . value of the museum depends on a determination of the authenticity of the works."[59] The museum responded to these charges by placing several statues uncovered by glass in the main hallway and inviting the public to bring hammers and chisels to examine the statues more closely.[60] Although the museum was pushed to respond to these charges, significantly, the annual reports of the trustees for this period contain no mention of the controversy at all. Not until December 31, 1883, in the Fourteenth Annual Report of the Trustees, is the controversy alluded to, and this discussion occurs entirely in brackets.[61]

In part because the museum trustees reacted in a particularly silent and exclusive way, seemingly going to extremes to protect one of their own, newspapers and magazines capitalized on this controversy to lobby for what the museum should become for the public. The *Art Amateur* opined that one of the purposes of the museum ought to be for visitors to learn to distinguish "what is good from what is meretricious" in order to be able to "[cultivate] the art perception" and know what is "a true work of art" and something "genuine."[62] According to the articles the ability to tell the difference between a real and a fake was the job of the museum expert. Amateur visitors could then trust that at a museum they were seeing genuine objects approved by experts. The desire for the creation of a class of experts to run the museum was the beginning of the process by which the museum was professionalized.[63] The call for the professionalization of the museum did not come, at first, from within the administration (though there was some internal discussion about hiring curators); rather the call for the creation of museum professionals came from a magazine devoted to the idea of creating an amateur class of museum-goers.

In an effort to increase the number of visitors to the museum, the trustees were also already appealing to the art amateur, but they were sending mixed messages. In its guides to the collection, the museum described the Cesnola rings as having "the same shape as our American wedding rings" and the Cesnola vases as "afford[ing] the visitor ample material for study[ing]" the perpetuation "of these shapes . . . in our own houses at the present day."[64] A year later, in 1878, in celebration of the installation of Cesnola's second excavation in Cyprus, Tiffany and Company created and sold a special jewelry line inspired by the Curium finds, an event that the trustees noted with pride in its annual report.[65] One can already see the museum trying to appeal to the readers of the *Art Amateur,* the people going to the museum to learn what to wear or how to decorate their homes. This is the new usefulness of the museum that the Wellington Brys capitalize on in designing their new home in *The House of Mirth* and that Undine Spragg assumes in attending museum exhibits in order to discover what to buy in *The Custom of the Country.* For the reader of the museum guide or the *Art Amateur* a visit to the museum served to establish and perpetuate a modern standard for taste.

If there were similarities between what *Art Amateur* magazine thought the museum ought to be like and the way the museum was beginning to present its collections in relation to the public, *Art Amateur* wanted more. In a series of editorials called "Our Mismanaged Museum" the magazine argued that the administration of the museum had not embraced its proper mission as an educational institution. The magazine suggested that the only way for the museum to undo the scandal was to become useful to contemporary society. "What might be a valuable institution [is] a useless, water-logged hulk, lying across the very current of our progress," the magazine wrote, explaining that its intention in uncovering the scandal was not to hurt the museum but rather to "[purify] its management and [secure] for it a career of usefulness."[66] Even in the phrase "career of usefulness," the rise of the professional classes—the possibility that a museum can have a "career"—is connected to the new attitude that the museum must be useful.

The Cesnola controversy enabled newspapers to call for what they saw as the museum's need for "reliability" and "usefulness," and it gave a voice to those who wanted the trustees of the museum more clearly to stand by their claims that the function of the museum was an educational one. These articles maintained that the example of Cesnola showed that those in charge of the museum were protecting him as one of their own, despite a blatant example of fraud, and that this deception was an illustration of the larger fact that the trustees did not really wish to share the museum with the public. They pointed to the museum's limited hours and the unwillingness of the trustees to open the museum on Sunday, when working-class visitors could attend exhibits, and they concluded that the antidote to this obvious elitism was this idea of usefulness applied to the entire idea of the museum and the objects in it.

In *The Age of Innocence* Wharton highlights the complexity of this controversy, and all the competing issues inherent in it, in the initial scene inside the Cesnola room. In a kind of sweeping call for reform, many aspects of the early museum project (even ideals that were shared by the trustees and the newspapers) came under attack under the banner of elitism.[67] The trustees were certainly trying to find an audience for the museum, but they were not entirely consistent about indicating whom this invitation was for. They had always promoted the museum as a tool for "education," but their officially stated desire to improve the "education of all classes of people" and to function as a "visible influence for good on the public" was tempered by their fears about whether a general population of visitors could be trusted among beautiful things.[68] Wharton had written about her support of the arts and thought likewise that any and all observation of art was a necessary part of education, but at the same time her ideas about how to develop this mode of observation and for whom were sometimes narrow.[69] Yet by 1919, when she went back inside the original Cesnola room in her novel, she saw a great deal more at stake in that space than simply a question of who should be there looking at museum pieces; in Wharton's representation of the Cesnola room she sees that as the museum tries to extend its reach and appeal, it compromises its goals of authenticity and its concerns with developing the public's contemplation and concentration of beautiful objects. She sees in the purchase and exhibition of Cesnola objects the beginning of the modern American museum project: not an educational or contemplative space but a spectacle and a show.

Wharton contrasts Archer's "wholly absorbed" way of looking at Olenska with the new way of seeing that this new museum, even in its awkward infancy, is beginning to demand (*AI*, 185). Archer and Olenska stand together in front of the Cesnola antiquities looking at "glass shelves . . . crowded with small broken objects—hardly recognizable domestic utensils, ornaments and personal trifles—made of glass, of clay, of discolored bronze and other time-blurred substances" (*AI*, 186). The description of the Cesnola objects as "time-blurred" underscores the novel's argument that the insistent and prominent display of the Cesnola purchases signals the new attitudes driving forward the modern American museum. In Wharton's papers at the

Beinecke Rare Book and Manuscript Library, *time-blurred* is the one term that Wharton changed in the scene. The word that she originally chose—"undistinguishable"—would connect this passage simply to the fact that she knew the Cesnola antiquities were amalgams of many different eras and substances purposely hidden by him. But *time-blurred* connects what Cesnola did to the statues more closely to the larger issue of what the Cesnola statues illuminated about the American modern museum project.

As Madame Olenska stares uncertainly at the Cesnola fragments, she also considers the beginning of the American museum, a space reserved for objects that she assumes at one time had specific social and historical contexts but are now promoted in a new context that highlights their existence in the museum as perhaps their most crucial quality for the public. Through the museum's efforts to entice visitors, objects are displayed to excite the interest of the modern museum-goer (as the Cesnola guidebook and the museum's tacit partnership with Tiffany and Company are already doing).[70] Archer and Olenska sense the "pressure of the minutes" (*AI*, 186); they feel hurried and watched. In the Cesnola room, evidence of "time-blurred" objects—suggesting a willingness to condone (or ignore) evidence of inauthentic experience—is merged with an insistence on the primacy and authority of the contemporary moment (as a guard walks by and their conversation ceases). This museum room, even as it suggests to Archer the beginning of the American cultural life that he craves and that he hopes might eventually serve to enlighten his fellow New Yorkers, also indicates within itself the very limits of that project.

That Wharton takes very seriously the social ramifications of early museum administrators' choices by the time she writes this scene is clear from a comparison with her 1900 story "The Rembrandt." This clever story about authenticity, the lack of knowledge of museum trustees, and the behind-the-scenes maneuvering at an American museum (never named but clearly intended to depict the Metropolitan) illuminates both how sharply aware she was of the issues confronting the early American museums and her biting sense of humor about them. The story follows the ethical and intellectual dilemma of a curator who buys a "Rembrandt" from an old and destitute woman on behalf of his museum because he cannot bear to tell her that her prize possession is a fake. The story hinges on the curator's belief that no one will notice the purchase; he knows that with the single exception of Crozier (who is in Europe), none of the other trustees can distinguish an authentic Rembrandt from a fake. No example of early museum trustee escapes Wharton's satirical gaze: neither the gullible, unknowledgeable, gentlemen trustees nor figures such as Crozier—the energetic businessman who does not like to be interrupted and who thinks of the curator's job as "capturing" art—nor even the well-intentioned curator, who knows his job exists at the whim of powerful men like Crozier. The story serves as a list of the real problems inherent in the museum's creation that Wharton understood threatened its future despite her sympathy for the genuine kindness of many involved in these early and crucial decisions: its amateurism; its insiderism; its pettiness; its willingness to cede its future direction (in large part because of a lack of knowledge) to whoever showed sufficient energy, panache, and authority. Wharton's analysis is certainly biting, and the ending of the story is ironic—instead of firing the curator, Crozier thanks him for his act of philanthropy on behalf of the other trustees by giving him the "present" of the awful painting—but because the story always remains behind the scenes at the museum, she does not yet consider the wider effects of the weaknesses she identifies.[71]

In the museum scene in *The Age of Innocence,* however, the label—"use unknown"—which adorns the Cesnola objects, not only underscores the kinds of mistakes, evasions, and complications that she already has identified as inherent in the early museum project, but also suggests their larger reverberations. Madame Olenska reads the label—which evades the facts of the objects' journey to the museum, including their questionable origins, under an official banner—and she interprets it as a statement of the museum's authority over how history is told, an idea that immediately depresses her.[72]

In this scene the crude label on the object relates to the way society views her as well. To Olenska's relatives the fact that her estranged husband is willing to return her money if she will sit at the head of his table once in a while is a reasonable exchange. They believe that his offer renders her moral claims against him immaterial. She recognizes that because they want to efface her painful marital history, they present the idea of Count Olenska's offer as altruistic rather than what it is—a chance to buy a kind of social forgetting. This idea is similar to Cesnola's belief that his offer of money to the native Cypriotes obviates any need to attend to the moral or national claims made for keeping the antiquities in Cyprus and also to the trustees' efforts to pretend within the museum that there is no controversy surrounding the Cesnola collection. Wharton suggests in this scene that Cesnola's objects are already being exhibited in the museum in this new context—preserved, collected, labeled, and removed from the true facts of their excavation, removal, and reconstruction. The museum discourages the consideration of an object's relationship to its entire complex and problematic history. The novel suggests that this way of exhibiting objects helps to create a society that also wants to view Madame Olenska as a subject without a history. Inherent in the scene is the suggestion that a loss of history, a willing forgetfulness, is already resulting in personal losses, too—of intimacy and understanding. Archer and Madame Olenska, critical of the society in which they exist, have fantasized about escaping it in order to pursue a superior relationship outside of time. Faced, however, with the Cesnola collection, they perceive similar evasions and blurrings of history and experience at work in this new museum project, an example that makes them unable to continue to develop a relationship based on these same kinds of evasions despite its promise of something better.

By the time Wharton writes this scene at the end of World War I, she also knows how the idea of "use" will continue to shape the development of the museum. As a result of the outbreak of World War I, a new earnestness about the educational role of American museums began to appear in essays and discussions. The war gave the American Association of Museums the impetus to state publicly its belief in the necessity of usefulness. The association behaved as though the question of the intellectual and aesthetic issues of usefulness could no longer be debated now that it had become a political concern. The government stated that if culture was not made politically useful, then it should not exist. It became a matter of urgency for the museum to redefine itself and its plans for the future in the concrete terms of usefulness that would allow it to continue to function and grow. The title-page essay in most issues of the journal *Museum Work* between 1918 and 1919, a journal supported by the American Association of Museums, turned previously controversial topics into decided, unarguable statements. The essay "War-Time Service by Museums and by Museum Men" (1918) begins: "Museums are primarily educational institutions. On their staffs are many specially trained scientific and technical workers. . . . Museums are doing their part in the war service."[73] The idea that museums are educational and can offer valuable information is certainly not a new idea, but its connection to preparations for war is a new and strongly stated validation of a museum's political utility. The essay becomes a list, and it offers nine numbered points that show how museums have helped the war effort through such means as "designing posters for war work." Other articles in the journal illustrate shifts in the language with which the museum describes itself. The new museum is less about aesthetics than it is "patriotic" and provides a "service." The difference between a specific museum's focus (for example, art, ethnology, history, science) and that of another museum, an important concern of the early association meetings, becomes immaterial in the new environment, since every museum is encouraged to have the same service-oriented aim. This new version of the museum—the museum of lists and goals—is presented as a unified organization with a clear mission by the end of the war.

In the post–World War I museum world the issue of aesthetics did not disappear, but it was absorbed into the idea of utility that became a primary museum language. John Cotton Dana, the curator of the Newark Museum, published *A Plan for a New Museum: The Kind of Museum It Will Profit a City To Maintain* (1920), which capitalized on the changing attitudes toward museums that the war had helped set in motion. He wrote that he was pleased by "the recent annual reports of the American Association of Museums [which gave] museum revolutionists much encouragement for they show that the one ever-present desire of many museum workers is to discover and exploit new avenues of definite usefulness."[74] The seeming victors in the long-standing debates on the purpose and aim of the museum were those museum workers who wanted the museum to focus primarily on practical and educational goals.

The post–World War I issues of the journal *Museum Work* went even further in making the ideals of the new museum seem central to the goals of the nation. One essay on museums and democracy argued that the current evil is distance: "for the part it plays in dulling our sense of justice, and in delaying the action of legislative bodies until grim necessity knocks at their council chambers, we loath it." The antidote to distance, the essay stated, is education, specifically, the kind of education that museums can provide: "To eliminate distance, to bring the truth home through science, art and history is the part Museums have to take in this new era of democratization of the world."[75] This new idea of the museum's political role in the "democratization of the world" through the organization of objects meant eliding the differences between objects or collections to illustrate closeness, a further act of time-blurring.

For Wharton this development was an empty victory for the museum. While the journal's view is ostensibly more democratic (to bring unlike objects together, to eliminate separations and differences) than the aesthetes' views of art it criticized, Wharton suggests through her analysis of Cesnola's objects in *The Age of Innocence* that these same pressures to be a democratic space and to make exhibitions educational were felt from the very beginning of the museum project. The museum administrator's early efforts to make the museum more accessible to a general audience, Wharton suggests, helped to inspire some of its earliest missteps just as much as its exclusiveness also slowed its progress. Both elitism and an attitude about democracy inspired the kind of American expansionist policies that led to Cesnola's initial trip to

Cyprus, as well as the excavation and removal of the Cypriote objects so that they could be viewed by the American public.[76] The Cesnola guide, which makes clear the connections between the objects and modern American life, also serves an educational purpose. For Wharton, however, these sorts of choices, which result in the erasure of the history of the objects themselves—even through positive efforts to increase the number of museum visitors and make their experience inside museums more accessible and enjoyable—robbed a viewer of the different quality of usefulness inspired by simply reflecting on beautiful objects. She had hoped for a long time that museums would help to create an American aesthetic language through a concentration on ways of seeing inside museums. Instead, museum education was increasingly being shaped toward "this new era of democratization of the world" by becoming politically useful.[77] As she imagined in her novels up to *The Age of Innocence,* museum administrators' efforts to convey the utility of their objects to contemporary society, through the design of exhibits and the limited didactic information selected for display within them, would ultimately serve to extend the authority of museums, simultaneously enhancing and debilitating the society they served.

After *The Age of Innocence:* Memory and the Modern Novel

The last chapter of *The Age of Innocence* begins with a reflection on the museum twenty-six years after the events of the novel take place. Newland Archer sits at his writing desk in the library and tries to remember his first visit to the museum with Madame Olenska:

> He had just got back from a big official reception for the inauguration of the new galleries at the Metropolitan Museum, and the spectacle of those great spaces crowded with the spoils of the ages, where the throng of fashion circulated through a series of scientifically catalogued treasures, had suddenly pressed on a rusted spring of memory.
>
> "Why, this used to be one of the old Cesnola rooms," he heard someone say; and instantly everything about him vanished, and he was sitting alone on a hard leather divan against a radiator, while a slight figure in a long sealskin coat moved away down the meagerly-fitted vistas of the old Museum.
>
> The vision had roused a host of other associations. (*AI,* 206)

Archer's first experience of the museum with Madame Olenska, which he seems to have forgotten, eventually returns to him. Hearing the word *Cesnola* helps him return to that earlier visit with her and the feeling that "everything about him vanished" except for the one figure he observed.

In the new museum, by comparison, there is no room for even a brief version of this kind of contemplation because it has been crowded out. The place is now officially and obviously a "spectacle," instead of a potential "retreat"; there are "spoils of the ages," instead of "personal trifles." There are crowds of people and crowds of objects, and all of these are "scientifically catalogued" so that their usefulness, relevance, and presence in modern life is now fully organized and made obvious and clear. In fact, the organization and display of the cases in the Cesnola room (and throughout the museum) had changed by the beginning of the twentieth century to reflect more current museum practices. Objects were crowded together in glass cases standing on the floor in order to show the wealth and mass of the collection.[78] In his essay "The Problem of Museums" (1923) Paul Valéry acknowledges this shift and despairs that modern museums have become places of "cold confusion"; they are too crowded to allow for any kind of concentrated observation.[79] Theodor Adorno, writing about Valéry's essay, argues that "an excess of riches impoverish man" in part because "the unique work of art kills the other ones around it."[80] Archer notices this reorganization; his experience inside of the museum is not conducive to a developing relationship between an art object and a viewer, but rather everything from the well-dressed crowds to the overabundance of objects contributes to illustrating the centrality and authority of the museum to culture: to highlight the degree to which it has fully succeeded in embracing its role as a "spectacle."[81]

This attitude toward the museum is one that the earliest museum trustees helped to instill in the public and one that had driven not only the purchases of Cesnola's collections but also the choice to hire him as director. Cesnola, as adventurer-archaeologist, showman, and museum administrator, instinctively understood this goal and was able to capitalize on it. In 1902, at approximately the moment this scene takes place, the Metropolitan celebrated the opening of the Main Entrance Hall, its newest wing. This event was the first major occasion at which Frederick W. Rhinelander spoke as president of the Metropolitan; the celebration was well attended, and all of the major newspapers published stories about it.[82] In Wharton's scene the museum's reflection of its position at the center of American culture is immediately clear to Archer as he absorbs the spectacle that the museum has become and feels overwhelmed by it.[83]

The museum's act of modernizing itself, Wharton suggests, is related to the way modern memory works as well. The reason Archer has a "rusted spring of memory" is connected to the destruction of the past. In "The Work of Art in the Age of Mechanical Reproduction" Walter Benjamin discusses the same moment in time that Wharton highlights in *The Decoration of Houses* (*DH,* 192): a moment "around 1900 [when] technical reproduction had reached a standard that not only permitted it to reproduce all transmitted works of art and thus to cause the most profound change in their impact upon the public, [but] it also had captured a place of its own among the artistic processes."[84] For the first two-thirds of his essay Benjamin explores how this new mechanical age extinguished or at least interrupted the relationship that an observer could have with an object and the ability of an object's "aura," its authentic core, to be recognized. He writes that "the authenticity of a thing is the essence of all that is transmissible from its beginning, ranging from its substantive duration to its testimony to the history which it has experienced" and specifically that what the reproduced object lacks is "its presence in time and space, its unique existence at the place where it happens to be" (220–21). Wharton increasingly worried about what this loss of authenticity, this blurring of a sense of time and place, could do to people.[85] In her reassessment of her work, "Introduction to *The House of Mirth*" (1936), which she prepared for a new Oxford edition of the novel, she imagined the dislocating experience of reading the novel in 1936 and reflecting on a world that had since vanished because of "modern devices for annihilating time and space."[86] At the end of *The Age of Innocence* these "annihilating" devices are at work within the museum and help to produce the kind of modern amnesia that affects Newland Archer.

This shift in time that occurs at the beginning of the last chapter in *The Age of Innocence* seems out of place. Archer does not appear to remember an event that was very important to him and has just happened in the novel. This lapse contributes to a feeling that Archer is suffering from something more serious than just a temporary loss of memory. Wharton not only characterizes the modernizing museum as contributing to his loss of memory, but her scene also offers an explanation for why she does not return to the subject of museums in her fiction again. In her novels after *The Age of Innocence,* although Wharton's characters continue to pass by museums on the street, they stop going inside. She explains why through her analysis of the development of the museum in *The Age of Innocence:* they do not need to. Her later novels contend that modern cities affect people in the same way modern museums do.

The relationship between the city and memory is central to the understanding of urban design, Kevin Lynch argued in his groundbreaking study of the relationship among the city, memory, and architecture in *The Image of the City* (1960). Lynch argued that the "legibility" of the city ought to be a key aim of architecture. He defined the phrase "the legible city" as the "means that we use today to locate ourselves in our own city world" and a place that encourages and enables memory to work:

> We need an environment which is not simply well organized, but poetic and symbolic as well. It should speak of the individuals and their complex society, of their aspirations and their historical tradition, of their natural setting, and of the complicated functions and movements of the city world. But clarity of structure and vividness of identity are first steps to the development of strong symbols. By appearing as a remarkable and well-knit *place*, the city could provide a ground for the clustering and organization of these meanings and associations. Such a sense of place in itself enhances every human activity that occurs there, and encourages the deposit of a memory trace.[87]

Lynch argues that when a city is well-designed, it can be remembered (an argument that Kate Peyton shares by the end of *Sanctuary*); a memorable city is a legible city. Reading *The Age of Innocence* in light of Lynch's ideas, I suggest that Wharton depicts Archer as suffering from a kind of amnesia caused by an inability to read his environment. With its inauthentic objects, the Cesnola room has always contained in it the seeds of this unreadability, even before it was so radically redesigned. Without Madame Olenska present—the only authentic piece from that original room—Archer cannot remember his previous experience in that place; it is only through conjuring up her image that he is able to reconstruct his related memories. In her later novels Wharton repeatedly returns to scenes of memory loss like this one, and she depicts characters who have completely lost their memories and their ability to read their environment. They live in New York City, but the city is as illegible to them as the modern museum is to Newland Archer.

This helps to explain why the novels that share with *The Age of Innocence* an ideological position (and in some ways a stylistic one) are not her earlier New York novels, *The House of Mirth* or *The Custom of the Country*, as most critics assume, but rather the later New York novels, which depict modern life as a dislocating experience marked by an absence of memory. Critics charge Wharton with losing touch after 1920, but her 1920s novels, and particularly the aspects of them most often criticized—such as their lack of attention to detail and their related antirealist attitudes—are the writerly applications of her conviction that the loss of places of contemplation and the ways that modern life makes things seem useful and relevant occurs at the expense of history and memory. These characters live in a kind of apocalyptic world; it is a place stripped of its authenticity and particularity to make room for spectacle and show. She represents this loss of memory and history as a fact of modernity; the modern world is a world with no real places to look at and no one trained to look.

Most critics of Wharton's work agree that something profound changed in the way she approached her fiction after 1920. The general feeling of modern critics on Wharton's late novels can be summed up in a statement by Eleanor Dwight in her 1994 biography, *Edith Wharton: An Extraordinary Life:* "As she separated herself more and more from the world in her precious retreat, she became increasingly out of touch with modern life as a subject for fiction. Her novels suffered."[88] Although there are some encouraging comments about Wharton's late novels from critics such as Millicent Bell, Mary Schriber, and Dale Bauer, Dwight's rather harsh assessment is echoed by most other critics.[89] In *Edith Wharton, 1862–1937* Olivia Coolidge writes that "the truth is, Edith's subtle powers of observation were being eclipsed by a hasty irritation which had nothing to do with art."[90] Cynthia Griffin Wolff makes a similar comment in *A Feast of Words.* Although Wolff takes the late novels seriously enough to analyze them in detail, she nonetheless prefaces a close reading with the statement that "one senses an attitude of resentment . . . has begun to infect her work—manifest in a tone of righteousness and a too-prompt condemnation of the modern world."[91] And if silence is the harshest criticism, then the fact that Ann Douglas's near-reference book of 1920s New York literature, *Terrible Honesty: Mongrel Manhattan in the 1920s,* fails to even mention Wharton at all shows the extent to which recent critics have undervalued Wharton's late novels.

Wharton's shift in writing style, however, does not come after *The Age of Innocence* as these critics contend. It occurs during it—at the beginning of the final chapter, when Archer sits at his writing desk twenty-six years after the action of the novel has occurred. This transformation in Wharton's writing style is directly related to her analysis of how the museum's both tacit and active participation in a blurring of time and space and of objects' histories results in Archer's—and society's—sense of confusion, memory loss, and disorientation. Even earlier in the novel Archer had recognized that society was already preparing itself for this new world: May has "transparent" eyes that he fears "could only look blankly at blankness" (*AI,* 53). If Archer's initial hope is that the new contemplative, authentic museum culture will slow or stop this loss of sight, he eventually recognizes that, instead, the spectacle of the Cesnola room hastens it.

Wharton's four post–World War I New York novels—*The Mother's Recompense* (1925), *Twilight Sleep* (1927), *Hudson River Bracketed,* and *The Gods Arrive*—share a task of representing this analysis of the modern condition. In choosing to set these works in present-day New York, and in a New York that she does not know intimately, Wharton is not creating pale imitations of her work in *The House of Mirth, The Custom of the Country,* or *The Age of Innocence* but is accomplishing something that she has already begun in *The Age of Innocence.* She uses a place not to help clarify and position a character in relation to something known but to displace and disarm by avoiding naming any fixed locations or objects. New York is simultaneously a central space in her post-1920 novels and a completely unspecific one. This seeming contradiction is not an example of poor or haphazard writing or a lack of knowledge about the changed city, faults of which she is accused. It is actually the point of these novels. Critical commentary claiming that Wharton no longer understood New York City ignores the fact that during the period in which she wrote the late novels, she also wrote the four novellas that make up the collection *Old New York,* which take place in a New York that she also did know. She did quite a bit of research on the New York of the 1840s to the 1870s and referenced in *Old New York* as many specific streets and locations from the past as she purposefully omitted from these late novels.[92]

New York becomes a modern character in that it has a past of great intensity from which it is as cut off as the characters that live in it. In *The Mother's Recompense* Kate Clephane returns to New York after almost twenty years of remembering it but cannot recover her own history there; in *Twilight Sleep* a family lives in a remarkably unparticularized New York—"a world bounded by Wall Street on the south and Long Island in most other directions"—and tries but cannot remember its own history.[93] In *Hudson River Bracketed* and *The Gods Arrive* Wharton mocks her own desire, as well as the desire of her contemporaries, to write a modern urban novel by telling the story of a young midwestern writer who comes to New York to learn enough about the streets to write "a big novel of modern New York," an epithet that repeats itself throughout both books.[94] In her final novel Wharton also suggests in a quiet way that a woman may be more capable of writing a good modern novel than a man. While Vance Weston is unable to write the impressive novel he has always planned, his lover, Halo Tarrant, realizes that *she* will be able to write a fine novel of New York that he cannot. Her novel will not be "big" the way Vance's was going to be, but it will more honestly represent her experience in the city. Wharton's idea serves to illuminate her critique of Joyce's *Ulysses* with which I began this chapter; in this final book she offers writing not as a cure for modern life but as one process—as Archer also employs it as he sits at his writing desk at the end of *The Age of Innocence*—by which to contend with the assault of modern life on an individual's ability to remember.

Wharton's concern with how people can continue to function in the modern world is one on which she ruminated, particularly during her last few years, as she considered her life and work. Writing about her second sea journey (this one on the *Osprey*, forty years after the first) in her memoir, *A Backward Glance*, Wharton notes that her trip occurred between two major earthquakes that shook the Mediterranean and resulted in the destruction of the objects in at least one museum. She concludes with the thought that "no treasure house of Atreus was ever as rich as a well-stored memory," shifting primary responsibility for remembering history back to individuals.[95] This argument—that individuals, not institutions, that perhaps books and not museums must try to be responsible for preserving cultural memories—also illustrates the degree to which her attitudes have shifted since writing works such as *Sanctuary* at the turn of the century.[96]

By the time Wharton writes *The Age of Innocence*, the museum she had hoped would exist to elevate the aesthetic language of American people had instead succeeded so completely in engaging the population that its original purpose seemed to her to have been forgotten. For Wharton the modern world's acceptance of the museum as a central repository for historical and cultural experience suggests an absence of oversight and an abdication of the individual's responsibility to remember and know. She blames the early museum administrators for allowing their ambitions, their exclusiveness, and their weaknesses to supersede their responsibilities, but she also blames the public for making the ideal museum an impossibility. In her works after *The Age of Innocence* Wharton explains the chaotic and empty society that results from this massive loss of cultural and historical memory. For the contemporary cultural critic Philip Fisher, the new post-museum museum world is the world of architecture. He argues that the kind of seeing Wharton once hoped to generate in a museum as a way of deepening cultural and historical knowledge cannot possibly exist any longer in the modern museum, but he suggests that this seeming loss is something to celebrate; the truly modern museum insists that people look at the building and not the art. He uses the creation of the Guggenheim Museum in New York as the prime example of this new kind of looking.[97] The museum building eclipses the art inside of it; visitors literally must follow a path past each artwork. According to Fisher this new idea of the museum will ultimately transform art for the better because it does not insist on having particular relationships to history or memory; it is aggressively contemporary and insistent about the necessity of the modern moment. Wharton already recognized by the time she wrote

Sanctuary in 1903 that the museum was the site of this contest; her novels explore how that contest played out over the next thirty years. They expose a writer deeply engaged in thinking through the ideal history and culture of a nation and a writer's efforts at articulating the museum's cultural responsibility and her own.

3
Nella Larsen, Librarian at 135th Street

Nella Larsen's work as a librarian was a catalyst in her rethinking of social issues, particularly her concerns about how systems of classification work to inhibit the creation of new categories of thinking. From 1921 until 1929, while pursuing a writing career, Larsen worked full- or part-time primarily at the 135th Street branch of the New York Public Library (fig. 4).[1] During 1922 and 1923 she attended the Library School of the New York Public Library. A survey of Larsen's library career—course records, library school required texts, employment records at the 135th Street Library, and the publications of the other librarians on the staff—suggests that in the 1920s Larsen was immersed in the education and practice of a librarian. This information stands in contrast to the view promoted in scholarly studies of Larsen that she was a genteel realist writer whose work as a librarian emerged from a powerful personal desire for gentility. Critics such as Thadious M. Davis and Cheryl A. Wall have suggested that Larsen's work in the library was an extension of her desire for social status, a desire that they claim is evident in her fiction and was ultimately crippling to her writing career.[2] Even these critics who respect what she achieved artistically in her brief career, which lasted ten years from 1920 to 1930 (and in only four of those was significant work done), have suggested that her work as a novelist may have been inspired more by a powerful desire to belong to a lauded community than by any intrinsic desire to write.

I suggest a different view of Larsen's intellectual development in the 1920s, based on readings of *Quicksand* (1928) and *Passing* (1929) and broadened by a more complete record of both the kinds of work she accomplished as a librarian and the kind of training she completed in library school. One of the difficulties with the arguments contending that Larsen lacked intellectual investment in her library training is that they promote what feminist library historians such as Dee Garrison call a "facilitating ideology," assuming that

4. The 135th Street branch of the New York Public Library. Photo courtesy of the New York Public Library Archives, New York Public Library, Astor, Lenox and Tilden Foundations.

Larsen must be a seeker of social status and gentility and that Larsen's writing must be genteel because her critics assume that the library was.[3] Rather than claim that Larsen's library work isolates her from the broader critique of middle-class values that she gives in *Quicksand*, I propose that Larsen's complicated reaction to the ideologies she was asked to absorb in library school helped her to sharpen her explorations of those critical attitudes in her fiction.[4] Claudia Tate has remarked that "the degree to which racism and sexism are culpable in her tragedy is an issue that reviewers and scholars have grappled with ever since the novel's first publication."[5] I contend that understanding Larsen's library work helps explain her novels as idiosyncratic efforts to invent a different system for conversing about gender and race than the one she saw popularized and instantiated through libraries and other cultural institutions—even those attempting to remake their own images, as the 135th Street Library was doing in the 1920s.

Those involved in the development of the 135th Street Library, where

Larsen worked, did not, however, consider themselves part of a genteel profession. Together they created a new attitude toward the library as a political tool in twentieth-century American culture. Whereas in the earliest days of the public library men such as Charles Coffin Jewett, George Ticknor, Edward Everett, and even Thomas Jefferson had been considered "librarian-scholars" as they pursued their aims of building a national library, improving academic libraries, creating the Boston Public Library, and serving on boards of trustees, increasingly, after 1876, the word *scholar* was dropped from the phrase when describing the newly trained, mostly female librarians. At the 135th Street Library a new type of what I will call the "librarian-artist" reconsidered what cultural institutions were meant to achieve in both their work and their writing. The librarians who worked there, in particular the branch supervisor, Ernestine Rose, who was hired in 1920, had a strong sense of how the library had developed since the early national period and how it should continue to evolve.[6] The team of librarians and volunteers at the library included, in addition to Larsen, such important thinkers and writers as Regina Andrews (librarian, playwright, founder of an experimental theater group with W. E. B. Du Bois, and author of a chronology of black history that was completed but never published), Gwendolyn Bennett (poet, artist, and author of the "Ebony Flute" column in *Opportunity*), Jessie Fauset (novelist and literary editor at *Crisis*), Catherine Latimer (full-time librarian who eventually helped create and publish catalogs of the Schomburg collection), and Ethel Ray Nance (Charles Johnson's assistant at *Opportunity*). These women shared an attitude about the library's potential to shape ideas and policies on a national scale; in their books and plays they would later write about how the 135th Street Library played a lasting role in shaping political and cultural ideas in the Harlem Renaissance.

Inspired in large part by the kind of intellectual questions Larsen had to consider in her library work, *Quicksand* and *Passing* are her aesthetic meditations on how social problems become institutionalized through the very structures that seem also to have the greatest potential to help solve them. Her novels trace real and imagined institutional spaces, examine how knowledge is created within and through them, and then consider what other kinds of knowledge or ways of thinking could be discovered outside them or what other kinds of institutions could conceivably be created that might do more. During the 1920s the women who worked and volunteered at the New York Public Library's 135th Street branch attempted to revolutionize both the library itself and a conception of cultural institutions and knowledge production that would give them a much more significant role in the shaping of both. Larsen continued to question and ironize the potential pitfalls of this undertaking in the novels she wrote at the end of the decade, after the 135th Street Library had completed the important restructuring and reimagining of its role and purpose.

Learning Systems of Classifying Knowledge

As the first black woman accepted into the New York Public Library School, Larsen recognized some of the problems inherent in the program.[7] Under the direction of superintendent Ernest Reece, the Library School used an educational model based largely on Melvil Dewey's ideas about library training. Reece contended in school documents and in his later publications on library education that the library is a form of technology and the librarian an "operator" of the library machine, and he aimed to improve the organization and the long-term efficiency of libraries through his administration.

As a librarian at the 135th Street branch Larsen was familiar with Dewey's system, but she may not have studied its ideology or the particular attitude behind it until she was required to do so in Reece's program. Although the New York Public Library's main library, where the library school was located, used (and still uses) the idiosyncratic system of classification designed by its first chief officer, John Shaw Billings (called the Billings classification system and employed in no other library), the branch libraries had always used the Dewey classification system. With Reece's articulation of Dewey's ideas through the choice of curriculum and of the five required texts—most of which were published by or related to the American Library Association (ALA) that Dewey helped to found—Larsen learned both Dewey's classification system and the ideas about knowledge that undergirded it.

The eleventh edition of Dewey's *Decimal Clasification* [*sic*] (1922) was a particularly noticeable required text: whereas the other required texts were rather thin and modest, *Decimal Clasification* was large (988 pages, 25 centimeters), with evident misspellings on the cover page. The entire book, in fact, as Dewey explained at several points in the text, used his phonetic spelling plan, which he believed fit the classification system particularly well because it was efficient, easy, and useful. Thus the title page of the book reads:

> Decimal Clasification
> and
> Relativ Index
> for libraries and personal use
> in arranjing for immediate reference

books, pamflets, clippings, pictures, manuscript notes
and other material
by
Melvil Dewey M A LL D
Edition 11, revized and enlarjd
Forest Pres
Lake Placid Club
Adirondaks N Y
1922

At the very top of this title page is a quotation: "To lern to clasify is in itself an education / *Alex. Bain*," a remark that any intelligent and critical reader of texts (as Larsen considered herself) might have paused over. What is the relation between classification and education? What does it mean to "lern to clasify"? Is that different from learning to operate knowledge? And what does it mean to be asked to "lern to clasify" (does the phrase mean something different if the spellings of the words carry their own agenda of efficiency and simplification)? Could one learn to do something without knowing what that thing was? The quotation's prominent location on the title page provokes obvious questions. The title page, with its glaring misspellings and seeming spelling inconsistencies—Why "placid" and not "plasid"? Why "edition" and not "edishun"? Why "lern" and not "lurn"? Why "relativ" without the silent "e" but "reference" with it?—provokes skepticism and perhaps misapprehension about the other system of classification described inside the book.

In "The Energy-Charged Life of Dorothy Porter Wesley," Harriet Scarupa recounts Wesley's life as a librarian and particularly the charge of embedded racism Wesley made against the Dewey decimal system. Wesley raised questions as the librarian for Howard's Moorland-Spingarn Research Center:

> In the fall of 1930, the board of trustees [at Howard] appointed her librarian in charge of the "Negro Collection." . . . Wesley's job was to organize the Moorland books as well as the library's other holdings related to black experience . . . [but] at the time [the Dewey decimal system] had no valid way to accommodate books dealing with the black experience. "Under the system, everything related to the Negro was classified under 'colonization,' or '326,' which was the number for 'slavery.' " . . . Having the richness and variety of black experience reduced to these two categories outraged Wesley. . . . "The woman in charge of the Dewey Decimal classification at the Library of Congress

couldn't see why I wanted to develop something else, why I didn't want to put a book of poetry by James Weldon Johnson under '325' or '326'—which was ridiculous!," she exclaims.[8]

Wesley's articulation of the problems inherent in Dewey's system in the 1930s came about a half-generation after Larsen's work at the 135th Street Library and during a period when several important libraries (including the 135th Street branch) began officially reclassifying their collections of black literature to expand the possible numbers that could be assigned to locate a text. Larsen's novels do not specifically attack the number "326" or the Dewey classification system, but they do repeatedly show how problematic systems of classification are and the ways in which these systems classify knowledge in an exclusionary way; her works challenge the ideology behind these systems and the institutions that promote them.

To an open-minded writer such as Larsen, Dewey's explanations for decisions on how to classify knowledge are problematic. Throughout his textbook Dewey explains that his program is meant to provide "practical usefulness" and to be flexible; his examples, however, clearly show the degree to which he believed his system of classification was totalizing and finished. For example, he explains in a section called "new subjects" that new topics will arise in the future. While this acknowledgment might suggest that he saw incompleteness as an inherent aspect of his project, or at least that he was open to including new information in the future, the paragraph is actually an argument for the completeness of his system. Dewey writes that "a new topic is always closely related to sum existing hed,"[9] and he offers evidence for the ways new information can be categorized using his already prepared model. This is a startling statement about the possibility of having created a system that can account not only for all present and past knowledge but also for all future knowledge.[10]

Dewey explains that part of the convenience of his system is that he has arranged the headings so that "each subject is preceded and followed by most nearly allyd subjects." Yet the decisions about what subjects are related to each other are his alone and have dramatic consequences for which books are shelved together. Consider, for example, the "326" headings about which Wesley complained. According to Dewey's precise system the books that are labeled in the "300s" are related to "sociology"; the books numbered "320" are related to "political science"; within political science are nine numbered categories, 321–329, including "form of state," "church and state," "internal or domestic relations," "suffrage-citizenship," "colonies and immigration," "slavery," "foren relations," "legislative bodies and annals," and "political parties." Dewey's system interprets "slavery" as most closely "allyd" to "foren relations" and "colonies and immigration," and his program suggests that these intellectual relationships are permanent. The indication that slavery is not a national concern and is more closely related to colonial issues or immigration than to domestic politics and economics, however, is potentially misleading. Within the nine classes, the one hundred divisions, and the one thousand general works categories that Dewey offers, these sorts of choices are made repeatedly throughout. Yet Dewey makes quite clear that attacking any part of the system is also an attack on a great effort to systematize, centralize, and organize; in other words, to attack Dewey's efficient, practical, useful system is to attack modernization itself. The very people who are excluded from his system, however, or whose identities are questionably defined by it, and who might want to challenge the kind of knowledge about themselves that might be generated by it, are the very people—primarily women and minorities—who are being accused (by self-proclaimed modernists such as Dewey) of not embracing the modern.

The library school superintendent Ernest Reece embraced Dewey's librarian training program to modernize the long-term efficiency of libraries. Reece argued that "the librarian need not discover knowledge nor create books . . . [rather] make the content of books more available and operative than otherwise it would be."[11] This idea, however, suggests that several assumptions about knowledge are underlined during Larsen's year in library school: first, that gaining knowledge and operating it are two different functions and that they can be separated; second, that librarians would want to learn to operate knowledge; third, that one can learn how to operate knowledge. To demonstrate his commitment to Dewey, Reece required the students to learn Dewey's ideas through the purchase of his five textbooks that would be used for the entire school year.[12] The result of this method is that "particularly since 1920" libraries have attempted to experiment in "simplifying and cheapening routines . . . to methodize an aggregate of tasks," in part through the graduating librarians' abilities to continue to organize and increase the management efficiency of libraries.[13]

In contrast to Reece's program, the 135th Street Library, under the leadership of Ernestine Rose (see fig. 5), established independent attitudes about its role in library history and in the production of knowledge. Though Rose was respectful of the 135th Street Library's status as a branch under the auspices of the central administration of the New York Public Library and understood libraries as modern institutions shaped by the ideas of Dewey and the American Library Association, she was also a revolutionary. Rose was the first white branch librarian to actively recruit black women for the staff. She made

5. The 135th Street branch adult reference area and Miss Ernestine Rose (lower left, foreground), Nella Larsen's supervisor. Photo courtesy of the New York Public Library Archives, New York Public Library, Astor, Lenox and Tilden Foundations.

an effort to court Arthur Schomburg and to have parts of his collection used at the library in the early 1920s, and she eventually played a significant role in encouraging the New York Public Library to use Andrew Carnegie's funds to purchase the collection on May 5, 1926. She fought to keep the collection at the 135th Street Library when the central administration considered housing it at the main branch. She helped develop, with Catherine Latimer and visiting librarian Edward Christopher Williams (a librarian at Howard University), a special classification system for the Schomburg collection. She had her own notion of public library history that was quite independent of the thinking of educators such as Ernest Reece. Rose was, however, as actively involved in the American Library Association as she was in the black community in Harlem, occasionally publishing the same article in both Charles Johnson's journal *Opportunity* and in the Melvil Dewey–originated, ALA-sponsored *Library Journal*.[14]

Through her work as a librarian at the 135th Street Library, the New York Public Library, and her involvement with the American Library Association, Rose developed an original conception of the public library that included a sense of its place in history and in the future. In *The Public Library in American Life* she demonstrated an understanding of library history that was quite different from Reece's and contributed to an analysis of the position of female librarian as scholar that was also quite different from Reece's image of the librarian as a manager or operator of the library machine. Unlike Reece, who saw the librarian's job as originating in Europe, Rose considered modern library history as beginning at the American Revolution:

> The stretch of one hundred years just following the American Revolution did see the emergence of the public library as a distinct institution; the beginnings of professional librarianship in terms of wide-awake association of librarians, a start in the development of more efficient techniques, and an effort to establish the library on a firmer administrative basis. From that time progress has been startlingly rapid in the process of transforming a reservoir of knowledge into a fountain of activity, and turning a cloistered, clerical operation, "keeping" the books, into a socially conscious profession, making books work for the public welfare.[15]

Rose's interpretation of library work as capable of "transforming a reservoir of knowledge into a fountain of activity" reimagined the job as an active and physical one. It was equally an understanding of knowledge as something meant to be transformed; to Rose, knowledge was not a static thing that the library simply housed. She reached this conclusion by outlining a history of the library movement that began during the active, transformative, post–Revolutionary War period. Unlike Reece, she did not think that Melvil Dewey's attitude toward knowledge as demonstrated by his modernization and professionalization of the library made it a more active or engaging place.

Rose saw the library's potential to play a more central political and cultural role by transforming its collections and goals. In an essay on the intellectual history of the Library of Congress, the historian Merrill D. Peterson argues that one connection between two such seemingly disparate thinkers as Jefferson and Emerson is through their shared interest in the "new nation's potentialities for intellectual achievement" and their consideration of how that might be worked out through the library and in public education in general.[16] This question of "the new nation's potentialities for intellectual achievement" is one that Rose also considered in terms of the library and its location at the center of the Harlem Renaissance. In her earliest essay on the 135th Street Library, "Serving New York's Black City," she discussed Harlem as a version of a new nation undergoing a cultural, economic, and political "awakening."[17] She considered the relationship between the development of a nation and the development of a library a close and necessary one, and she explained American library history in terms of national politics, arguing that the library reshaped itself according to political changes as much as it participated in shaping democracy: "All these important advances were undertaken by the public library during its formative years, which were also years of great national development. It is increasingly evident that in a democratic society the need for such an institution will be judged by the universality of its appeal and the accessibility of its resources."[18] Rose sounds positively Jeffersonian in her call for "universality" in librarianship. Her argument about the relationship between the contemporary public library and the early national period suggests that they were much closer than recent spokesmen for the library such as Ernest Reece or Melvil Dewey had wanted it to seem. Rose suggests that the library's productivity and development (its ability to turn "a reservoir" of knowledge into a "fountain") depends on the political and intellectual climate of its environment as much as it helps create that climate.

Rose's description of the library also sounds much closer to a description of what the library meant to librarians such as Larsen, Fauset, Bennett, Anderson, and Latimer, who were considering their work at the 135th Street Library in relation to larger questions about race, women, the nation, and culture. In *Black Feminist Criticism: Perspectives on Black Women Writers* Barbara Christian argues that in the 1920s and 1930s "black intellectuals in their struggles for independence glorified all things African and disdained all things European."[19] While the 135th Street Library did not disdain "all things European," there was an increasing focus on local cultures and exhibitions of black artists held at the library.[20] In this way the 135th Street Library's struggle for independence from the European model of librarianship and even from the administration of the central branch, and its effort to create a unique identity as a library, resemble post–Revolutionary War rhetoric more than Dewey's later statements on the professionalization of the library.

Jessie Fauset writes about this struggle for independence both metaphorically and literally in her first novel, *There Is Confusion* (1924), about a young black woman trying to find her identity as a dancer, an effort that results in a serious reexamination of her perspective on women, America, and culture. Regina Andrews, in addition to the plays she wrote for the experimental theater group founded by Du Bois that performed in the basement of the 135th Street Library, wrote an annotated black history textbook that she completed in the 1960s, a work that considers the close relationship among race, politics, and culture.[21] In addition to exhibitions and new collections, Anderson, Rose, and Latimer set up a small work area for Countee Cullen, Langston

Hughes, Eric Walrond, and Claude McKay. Arna Bontemps, and Langston Hughes often remarked on the independent spirit of the library.[22]

Much has been made of the importance of the 135th Street Library in the 1920s to writers and artists in the Harlem Renaissance. In his history of the era, *When Harlem Was in Vogue,* David Levering Lewis sums up the place briefly in the statement that "the intellectual pulse of Harlem throbbed at the 135th Street Library," and he discusses the frequent art exhibitions, theater events, and lectures that took place there and that made the library so important to writers and artists.[23] This library was a transformed and transforming space. It was a library, but it was also a museum, an experimental theater, a lecture hall, a community meeting hall, and a work space for writers. Another popular view of the library is given by Jervis Anderson in his book *This Was Harlem.* Anderson's library functioned as the antithesis to Harlem Renaissance nightlife. He writes that the library, "away from the surfeit of bars, clubs, cabarets, and other jazz joints," was "one of the most hospitable gathering places for aspiring black writers and literary intellectuals."[24] Here, the library is not Lewis's heart-racing center but rather something more genteel—it is a respite, safe, but also, in Anderson's word, "hospitable"; there is the lingering sense of something clean, a sanitized version of another, suggestively more real, Harlem. Though both views suggest that the library was a central space in the Harlem Renaissance, the experience inside it is described in divergent ways: in one the pulse races; in the other the pulse slows.

Ernestine Rose participated in creating these seemingly opposed ideas of the library. Despite her revolutionary restructuring of the library, Rose's views of race were relatively conservative. Although she was instrumental in encouraging Larsen to go to library school and helped her get accepted into the program, Rose also showed some ambivalence about changing racial views. Rose writes with obvious pride about the work that she has done to hire more black women in the library, but at the same time she seems nonplussed by the obvious racism that she still observes embedded in the library school system. In a July 1923 article, "A Librarian in Harlem," published in *Opportunity* after it was first delivered to the American Library Association, Rose calls for an end to racism and makes a statement about the library's continued value and importance in promoting certain ideas about the nation and national affairs. In the article Rose mentions Larsen, not by name but in a very identifiable way:

> So I have to offer you today a few examples of this racial drift. Perhaps that incident in New York which seems to me most significant is the

> acceptance by our Library School of a colored applicant on precisely the same terms as the white, and the following fact that all facilities offered by the school have been at her command. Before the practice trip to other libraries was taken, all hotels on the route were asked if they had any objection to admitting a colored woman, and without exception they answered that they had none.[25]

Though Larsen's library work may have meant something personal to her, in this article her attendance at library school is used merely to illustrate changes in racial policy, and Larsen herself plays the role of an anonymous example. As a voracious reader, and a known reader of *Opportunity* (in September 1926, at the request of Charles Johnson, she published a letter in *Opportunity* defending Walter White's novel *Flight*, which previously had been given a poor review), Larsen almost certainly read this article, and she certainly would have recognized herself in it. Though Rose encouraged black librarians, and in several different essays and official documents she mentions how well they perform their jobs, there is nonetheless a condescending, rather self-congratulatory, tone to much of what she wrote about this subject. One of the ways she argued for the continued hiring of black women as librarians was by saying "that educated and refined colored girls are of the same stuff as white."[26] Despite her support of black employees at the library, through her explicit comparisons between black and white employees, Rose still reinforced some of the same attitudes about race that she claimed her work at the library countered.

Rose was both revolutionary and conservative about classification and cataloging issues as well. She noticed the "books and journals about black history" that were overused and pulled them from the shelves. She set up a special collection for their use on the third floor and gave that room a new name and a curator (and this was before the Schomburg collection was purchased for the library), and she participated in the massive cataloging project for the new Schomburg materials after they arrived. At the same time, she also respected and used the Dewey classification system at the library.[27] Rose wrote in praise of the Dewey decimal classification system in her 1954 book. After discussing its use in most public libraries, she noted how "few library users realize that the orderly procession of books by which they are led to the titles they want is the result of painstaking labor and of the study of public use which started in the middle of the nineteenth century and is still continuing to meet new needs and new ways of seeking knowledge."[28] Rose praised the system and the methodology and ideology behind the system that made it, in her mind, necessary to use. Her effort to protect certain materials at the 135th

Street Library and to classify those materials separately was the very earliest example of steps the library would later undertake to recatalog almost its entire collection. Rose's writings show the degree to which she adhered to given systems while still interpreting them in such a way as to imagine them as inclusive rather than exclusionary.

Given Larsen's introduction to classification systems, it is not surprising that her novels suggest that she was increasingly skeptical of any institutions that produce comprehensive systems of knowledge. With library school completed and nearing the end of her career as a librarian by the time she wrote *Quicksand,* Larsen created a character who rejects all systems of knowledge as flawed and who seeks entirely other ways to learn—outside of libraries, museums, schools, and any other systematized forms of knowledge production. Helga Crane eventually acknowledges that there may be no position outside of institutions from which to learn, but as a result of Larsen's career within those places, Helga comes to her questions about institutions, systems, and knowledge production with the sophistication of someone who has been on the inside of spaces that claim only to exhibit or "operate" knowledge but are actually in the business of manufacturing it.

Knowledge, Uncertainty, and Education in *Quicksand*

Fittingly, *Quicksand* begins with a question.[29] As the epigraph to the novel, Larsen uses the last four lines of Langston Hughes's "Cross," a poem about a child thinking about his future:

> My old man died in a fine big house,
> My ma died in a shack.
> I wonder where I'm gonna die,
> Being neither white nor black?

Although critics have generally discussed this epigraph in terms of the interracial relationship that seems central to both the poem and the novel, these lines set up those interrelationships within a larger area of territory for the novel—race, class, gender, and knowledge.[30] Although in the complete poem it is clear that the father is a rich white man and the mother is a poor black woman, in the four lines that Larsen includes, the races of the rich man and the poor woman are left out. Instead, the emphasis is on the child and the fact that a child's natural sense of "wonder" at the world can be transformed into specific anxieties about race, class, and gender: Who will the child turn into? Will he or she be more like the mother or father? What race and what economic condition will the child inhabit in the future? At the same time, the poem ends with a question mark, a punctuation mark that leaves open the possibility of an answer or the possibility of more questions. The last four lines of the poem suggest that the child's desire to know something might be more important than any specific information he or she might be given. Larsen's novel is not so much an answer to the child's question as a meditation on the question itself and on the kinds of knowledge that are created, perhaps falsely, to answer such a question. In the world that the novel imagines, the ability to ask a question is a precondition of knowledge and an art that most adults have lost or forgotten in the effort to show that they have answers. By beginning a novel with a question about wondering, Larsen creates a space of open-ended possibilities for knowing that Helga Crane will spend the entire novel trying to find and inhabit.

Helga Crane begins the novel as a schoolteacher, an unquestionably intelligent and determined woman, who becomes aware of an increasing unwillingness in herself to participate in any program for which she does not have an intense and genuine intellectual commitment. Her main concern about her teaching at Naxos is that the school's ideology and policies seem hypocritical. Helga, present at the speech of "one of the renowned preachers of the state" during her lunch hour, is revolted by his patronizing sermon, which praises the school for teaching black people to have the "good sense" and "good taste" to "stay in their places" (37). She hates that white men such as the preacher endorse the education blacks receive at Naxos because they approve of teaching students that education has a ceiling and that there is a proper limit to ambition.[31] The white preacher says that "no other race in so short a time had made so much progress, but he urgently besought them to know where and when to stop" (37). This plea, particularly because it occurs at a school, a place that Helga believes ought to be an open and intellectually curious environment (an assumption that she will eventually dissect and question), not only makes her angry but sets in motion a counterresponse—to never stop moving and thinking. She tries to specify exactly what she is angry about—"The South . . . Naxos . . . Negro education"—but she cannot yet distinguish among these seemingly separate subjects and "suddenly she hated them all" (38). Helga's negative feelings toward the preacher's comments and the school's implicit endorsement of them shape her flight from that place and her subsequent revolutionary spirit.

At Naxos, on the evening that the novel begins, the constant, slightly irritated, sensation of personal insignificance that Helga has had for all of her two years of work there suddenly becomes so obvious to her that she can articulate it to herself and to others. She realizes that the school is not a human thing made up of individuals with ideas but rather an inhuman system—"a machine"—a piece of technology that rejects "ideas" in favor of methods or anything regulated, repeatable, and directed. Once Helga can articulate this recognition (as she does at length in Dr. Anderson's administrative office), she no longer wants to work at Naxos. Although it may seem as though Helga's tirade is against the school's hypocritical policies, her actual decision to leave only occurs after she has learned for herself how knowledge is produced there: "It was, rather, the fault of the method, the general idea behind the system. Like her own hurried shot at the basket, the aim was bad, the material drab and badly prepared for its purpose. This great community, she thought, was no longer a school. It had grown into a machine" (39). The school is a machine; knowledge is manufactured; methods and aims go in and systems come out; these systems produce more methods and aims; and no new knowledge is ever created. This realization that people behave inexplicably because they are trying to fit into an existing system gives her power to reject Naxos, a power that she claims she lacked before she realized that Naxos conspired to make her "powerless" (40). In leaving Naxos she upends her seemingly stable life of jobs, institutions, and connections and embraces the notion that there is a power to be found in a state of uncertainty, of not knowing. This state of not knowing will allow her an unexpected physical, emotional, and intellectual flexibility. It will enable her, if not yet to articulate her approach to undoing fixed distinctions, at least to upset certain individuals' expectations of their own positions.

Helga's interest in a state of not knowing is the beginning of a new relationship to knowledge and a more skeptical and questioning attitude toward the cultural institutions and educational programs that claim to help produce knowledge and ways of knowing. While at Naxos, before her moment of revelation, she is constantly irritated by the seeming hypocrisies in that place; after her release from it she can see more clearly that the seeming hypocrisies were not that at all; rather they were a necessary part of the system that maintained the status quo. Although it seems to her that the white preacher's comments oppose the philosophies of the school, and she cannot understand why others who hear the speech are not upset by it, she realizes that, in fact, he is simply repeating the school's own attitudes about the potential dangers of knowledge, the importance in setting limits, and the necessity for education to reinforce both of these principles. The preacher not only repeats the school's own beliefs, but he presents them rhetorically in the style that the school has trained students not to react against. Perhaps because the South still is new to her or because she has not been at Naxos long enough to become inured to its ideology, Helga finds the preacher's address racist and insulting. Her frustration is acute because she understands that for her colleagues and students to hear what the preacher has actually said to them will take an intellectual and educational revolution. She recognizes that the issue with which both the school and the preacher ought to be concerned is not race, with which they claim to be concerned, but how knowledge is created, a subject in which they have no interest but that she recognizes both bears on and is shaped by race.

After leaving Naxos, however, Helga discovers that although she has ostensibly freed herself from what she views as a poisonous and racist institutional ideology, these ideas are so pervasive that she has certainly not escaped them anywhere else. Once in Chicago, and in serious need of money, she plans to borrow from a kind uncle, the brother of her deceased mother, who has in the past paid for her schooling. When she goes to his house, however, his new wife, a woman Helga Crane has never heard about, answers the door, and although Mrs. Nilssen knows that her husband's sister had a child with a black man, seeing the actual evidence of this relationship makes her extremely angry. She refuses to give Helga any money, asks that she never come to the house again, and denies any tie of kinship: "Please remember that my husband is not your uncle. No indeed! Why, that would make me your Aunt!" (61). Helga's reaction to her aunt's denial of kinship is characteristic—she shrugs it off—and she quickly turns to seek the money she needs through an intellectual connection rather than the more personal one. She decides the moment after Mrs. Nilssen rejects her that there is nothing to worry about because she likes books and learning and will apply for a job at the library:

> She would find work of some kind. Perhaps the library. The idea clung. Yes, certainly the library. She knew books and she loved them. . . . After a slight breakfast she made her way to the library, that ugly gray building, where was housed much knowledge and a little wisdom, on interminable shelves. The friendly person at the desk in the hall bestowed on her a kindly smile when Helga stated her business and asked for directions. . . . Outside the indicated door, for half a second she hesitated, then braced herself and went in. In less than a quarter of an hour she came out, in surprised disappointment. "Library training"—"civil service"—"library school"—"classification"—"cataloguing"—"training class"—"examination"—"probation period"—flitted through her mind. "How erudite they must be!" she remarked sarcastically to herself, and ignored the smiling curiosity of the desk person as she went through the hall to the street. For a long moment she stood on the high

> stone steps above the avenue, then shrugged her shoulders and stepped down. (62–63)

Helga's brief but thorough analysis of her experience is made possible by Larsen's specific knowledge of and frustration with the library. This trip to the library also makes Helga reconsider her visit to her uncle's house, and she becomes angrier as she recognizes that the two events have a strong connection. It is not just that she is rejected at both places but that the particular form of the rejection at the library is related to Mrs. Nilssen's certainty that she is right to sever their relationship.

Larsen's training in library school is evident by the very specific list of terms that the library offers for why Helga cannot work there. Each term, "library training," "civil service," "classification," etc. is set off by quotation marks and dashes to emphasize both that someone spoke these words to Helga (and she heard them clearly) and that she registered them as representing a requirement for another form of schooling. Helga's sarcastic thought, "How erudite they must be!" is a protest against a place that "housed much knowledge and a little wisdom." Helga recognizes that when knowledge is treated as a passive thing (it can be simply "housed"), it becomes more silently destructive. The problem with the way knowledge is appropriated in the library is connected to the library school's attitudes about the training of librarians, specifically its ideas about how librarians ought to perceive and imagine what knowledge is. Helga has recognized that these attitudes are present. On her way out of the library, though, Helga sees perhaps another version of herself in "the smiling curiosity of the desk person." She pauses before leaving the building, perhaps wondering whether to view the smile as like-mindedness (perhaps she also is not allowed to work as a librarian) or see the woman's "curiosity" as additional evidence of how the library staff views Helga—as an oddity.

Helga's realization about herself after she left her uncle's house was that "she saw herself for an obscene sore in all their lives, at all costs to be hidden" (62). This issue of being "hidden" is connected to the kinds of systems that Larsen used to classify and catalog knowledge in the library. As a black woman, Helga would have recognized that Dewey's classification system was, like the kinship system devised by her uncle's new wife, manifested physically; it was created to show how certain ideas and people were not related to one another because they were not placed next to each other "on interminable shelves." For a librarian the physical relationship of books is related to an intellectual kinship of ideas between those objects according to the classification system employed. Dewey's ideas were to systemize these sorts of choices not only through the use of his classification and cataloging system but also through the promotion of library schools that required training and the mastery of a new vocabulary before the student was even allowed to participate in a discussion about the organization of knowledge. Helga, who has never been to library school, however, understands instinctively (in part because the events occur right after one another) that her rejection by her family is in some ways sanctioned by the library, by Naxos, and by all those "great institutions" that create intellectual systems that organize knowledge around an idea of "hidden-ness." The visit to the Chicago library reminds Helga of Naxos—how the preacher encourages the black students to remain an invisible part of the community by doing well but not too well and how the teachers take on this cultural role by dressing well but not standing out—and she begins to understand the pervasiveness and broader intellectual underpinnings of a racist ideology.

The 135th Street Library, nagged by questions about the organization of its books according to the Dewey decimal classification system since the early 1920s, eventually took active steps toward recataloging much of its collection in the late 1930s and early 1940s under the leadership of Dr. Lawrence Reddick. In the 1940 "Report of Cataloging for the Division of Negro Literature," the 135th Street Library tried to change and clarify its policies of cataloging. The result was an important decision: "To use the entire range of the Dewey classification . . . the use of the special numbers 326.93 and 326.94 has been abandoned and the 500 titles now in these numbers will be reclassified. . . . Further progress was made in the revision of the catalog at 135th Street."[32] In adopting the entire system of Dewey classification for the works that had previously only been allowed the prefix "326," the decision effectively and overtly reinterpreted the Dewey model to create a new system that fit the library's specific needs. Eventually called "the slavery reclassification project," it also sought to address "additional reclassification projects . . . books on suffrage, civil rights, housing."[33] The new process of classifying and cataloging material at the library is described in an undated "special report."[34] This report—which explains that for the person cataloging at the 135th Street Library to do her job successfully, she must not only know cataloging systems and employ them but also must have general knowledge, a liking for and an interest in books, and the intelligence, curiosity, and skills to do research and learn—is the antithesis of the kind of training in library school that Larsen received under Ernest Reece. In *Quicksand* Helga's trip to the library suggests that the Chicago library does not follow the Reddick or Rose ideal of librarianship but a model much closer to Dewey's or Reece's ideas; at the Chicago library one's knowledge of books will clearly not get one hired, only one's knowledge of a system concerning the placement of those books.

Helga's brief experience at the Chicago library serves to reinforce the negative notions about education, institutions, and knowledge that she had already developed by the time she left Naxos. She repeatedly discovers that the same term—*references*—is used to exclude (though with slightly different emphases) in each place she tries to work. It is the relation of one thing to another—people, books, ideas—and the ways those relationships get explained through references that determines how a book is read in a library or how a person is identified. Helga does not yet know how to go about reclassifying herself for the benefit of others, but she does begin to recognize the necessity of "cross-listing"—or the ability to move between and among different classification systems and definitions, thus upending rigid categories—in order to continue to survive. In Helga's case a lack of family and close friends and a subsequent lack of personal references make it extremely difficult for her to find a job after she arrives in Chicago. The word *references* is thrown at her so often as a barrier to her future work and life that she can only hear it "resentfully" (65). When she finally does land a job, as an editor of speeches for the "prominent 'race' woman" Mrs. Hayes-Rore, the sympathetic woman suggests to Helga that she keep her personal history, or lack of references, to herself in the future, as it would only hurt her to reveal it.

Although Helga likes Mrs. Hayes-Rore, and is grateful for the job, she finds the experience working for her as intellectually unsatisfactory as all of her previous jobs. The "race" speeches that she reads and corrects particularly irritate her:

> On the train that carried them to New York, Helga had made short work of correcting and condensing the speeches . . . patchworks of others' speeches and opinions. Helga had heard other lecturers say the same things in Devon and again in Naxos. Ideas, phrases and even whole sentences and paragraphs were lifted bodily from previous orations and published works of Wendell Phillips, Frederick Douglass, Booker T. Washington, and other doctors of the race's ills. For variety Mrs. Hayes-Rore had seasoned hers with a peppery dash of Du Bois and a few vinegary statements of her own. Aside from these it was, Helga reflected, the same old thing. (70)

Helga's attitude toward the speeches suggests that she is well-versed in debates about black education. She has not only thought about the education she was given and the one she was trained to impart to her students at Naxos, but she has considered other models for intellectual training. She seems surprised by Mrs. Hayes-Rore's lack of original interpretations. The speeches merely rehash "others' speeches and opinions" without any reflection on what those ideas mean or why they might be better rewritten than repeated. Helga's dissatisfaction with Mrs. Hayes-Rore's speeches is the beginning of her desire to move on to something else. Helga is not yet willing to settle into any existing system and transform it from within; rather, her restlessness simply enables her to identify more quickly what critical elements are missing.

Helga initially dismisses Mrs. Hayes-Rore's speeches as simply unoriginal, but later she sees many of the ideas in them as detrimental to the discussion of race despite their seemingly positive claims. The speeches reinforce problematic categories in which to think about race without reflecting on what those categories are or how to understand them. After moving to New York with the help of Mrs. Hayes-Rore's connections, Helga joins a crowd of well-educated race promoters in Harlem. At first she admires this group, particularly Anne Grey, the beautiful widow who invites her to stay in her house, but after spending almost a year in their company, Helga begins to see her companions as participating in an anti-intellectualism similar to the misguided attitudes she rejected at Naxos and criticized in Mrs. Hayes-Rore. In some ways, however, the Harlem group's ideas are more dangerous because the speakers are respected members of the black community, and their voices are heard widely: "Even the gentle Anne distressed her. . . . She talked, wept, and ground her teeth dramatically about the wrongs and shames of her race. . . . 'Social equality,' 'Equal opportunity for all.' . . . She hated white people . . . but she aped their clothes, their manners, and their gracious ways of living" (79). Despite Anne Grey's determination to improve the status of her race, her interest in "equality," and her seeming attachment to her cause, Helga recognizes within her a disdain of her own race. Helga understands once again that Anne is as much the product of her own education as she is an individual attempting to educate others. Anne is likable and kind, but Helga finds her values hypocritical. Anne's hatred for the sexual and mysterious Audrey Denny reveals to Helga that Anne views certain black women as better than others. At the cabaret one night, Anne insists that Audrey " 'ought to be ostracized' " by other black women (92). Helga, simultaneously attracted to and afraid of Audrey Denny's overt sexuality and beauty, understands Anne's desire to rein her in (she has some of the same feelings when she sees Audrey and Dr. Robert Anderson together), but Helga's reaction is never to limit and destroy others. As Anne's obvious sexism and covert racism become visible to Helga, their relationship weakens. For Helga, Anne becomes a symbol of covert classifiers—she helps to further entrench existing exclusionary systems under the guise of racially patriotic rhetoric.

Although Helga remains sympathetic to Anne, the bond between the two women continues to deteriorate. Helga observes that Anne, Mrs. Hayes-Rore, and even the white preacher are all products of the same education, the damaged products of "methods" and "aims" that have produced a "system" for thinking and talking about race. In his 1933 book on education, *The Mis-education of the Negro,* Carter Woodson would take aim at similar subjects and characters. He explains the project of his book as against no "particular person or class, but . . . as a corrective for methods which have not produced satisfactory results." These educational "methods" include "holding the Negro down" so that he learns quickly how to "find his 'proper place' . . . and stay in it." The victims of this educational system, however, are not only those trained in it but even those who learn to "feel that [their] race does not amount to much," including "the 'educated Negro' [who] is compelled to live among his own people whom he has been taught to despise . . . [so that he] prefers to buy his food from a white grocer."[35] Helga feels anger not only at Anne's professed beliefs but also at the "system" behind those beliefs. Anne's education has shaped her mind so that she does not question herself but rather accepts her unimaginative (and, Helga thinks, misinformed) ideas about race with the certainty that they are correct and ought to be promoted.

Helga's disillusionment with the ideas of the prominent race promoters in Harlem leads her, as it always has, to look elsewhere for more original or insightful possibilities. She leaves New York and takes an extended trip to visit relatives in Copenhagen, where she imagines that she has found something positive; she thinks that she is finally both happy and free. In America she has always felt torn between her material and intellectual desires, but in Denmark her upper-middle-class and generous relatives provide her with so much that she has no material anxieties whatsoever. She revels in this world of "Things . . . Things . . . Things" (97). But just as Polonius misunderstands Hamlet's reply that he reads "Words . . . Words . . . Words" as a sign that he is becoming happier, Helga's apparent satiation with "things" serves only as a temporary palliative.[36]

For a short time Helga's relief at the lack of conflict between the material and the intellectual makes her believe that Denmark and Europe in general are more advanced intellectually than America, but over the two years that she spends in Denmark she changes her opinion and decides that, in fact, the struggle between "things" and "words" is an intellectual and educational ne cessity. This realization extends back to her experience at Naxos and some of the arguments about vocational and industrial education that informed Larsen's discussion of that school. At the Hampton school, for example, and later mirrored by Booker T. Washington at Tuskegee, General Armstrong formulated ideas about the subject of "political economy" to students, including the notion that the interests of capitalists and laborers were not at odds and that sympathy ought to remain with the capitalists. Thus, according to one critic, "Hampton was deliberately teaching prospective black leaders and educators economic values that were detrimental to the objective economic interests of black workers."[37] The connection between Hampton's political and intellectual conservatism and its blatant support for capitalism and commercialism alarmed educators such as W. E. B. Du Bois, who attacked the school for not carefully examining the relationship between those ideas. In offering alternative educational plans, first in the critique of Booker T. Washington in the third chapter of *The Souls of Black Folk* (1903) and later in frequent articles on education, Du Bois consistently tried to show how commercialism weakened one's ability to think and that embracing intellectualism would ultimately lead to freedom for black people. In Denmark Helga does not go so far as to suggest that rampant materialism weakens thought, but after solely embracing the material world for a period of time, she slowly begins to yearn for the sense of conflict between the two desires that had always angered her in the past. She views this struggle between materialism and intellectuality as a sign of her attachment to America. If the intellectual quest that Helga initiates by leaving Naxos is, in part, a quest to find a balance between the possession of things and the possession of words, ideas, and knowledge—an anxiety that is present on the very first page of the novel, as Helga sits among her fine things in her room at Naxos seething over the ideas that are generated by the school—then her experience in Denmark helps cement her commitment to working through a genuine response for an acutely American conflict.

Helga's notion that the conflict between materialism and intellectualism might actually be a useful aspect of an American education goes against theories that were circulating at the time about America's intellectual weaknesses, often succinctly summed up by the charge of "gentility." George Santayana's 1911 address at the University of California at Berkeley, in which he officially vocalized a resentment toward what he had called "The Genteel Tradition" in literature, gave a name and a description not only to a type of writing but to an educational system that was producing peculiarly American personalities:

> America . . . is a country with two mentalities, one a survival of the beliefs and standards of the fathers, the other an expression of the instincts, practice, and discoveries of the younger generations. . . . America is a hundred years behind the times. The truth is that one-half of the American mind, that not occupied intensely in practical affairs, has remained, I will not say high-and-dry, but slightly becalmed; it has floated gently in the backwater, while, alongside, in invention and industry and social organization the other half of the mind was leaping down a sort of Niagara Rapids. This division may be found symbolized in American architecture: a neat reproduction of the colonial mansion—with some modern comforts introduced surreptitiously—stands beside the sky-scraper. The American Will inhabits the sky-scraper; the American Intellect inhabits the colonial mansion. The one is the sphere of the American man; the other, at least predominantly, of the American woman. The one is all aggressive enterprise; the other is all genteel tradition.[38]

Santayana's analysis of America leads him to criticize what he sees as a pro gressive and energetic country that is nonetheless intellectually backward. The address, which is as much a criticism of American higher education (Santayana left his professorship at Harvard in anger the same year and never returned) as an attack on American culture in general, is meant to point out an aspect of the culture that creates two disparate and contradictory personality traits that exist side by side but remain utterly separated from one another intellectually. The American will to build the skyscraper brings with it an equally strong desire to live life in the colonial mansion; the intensity with which Americans approach business only equals the lack of intensity with which they think about it; the aggressive man of enterprise is accompanied by the passive woman of tradition.

Van Wyck Brooks's *America's Coming-of-Age* (1915) developed Santayana's claims and considered these "crises in American culture" a crisis of "doubleness" when a mind is divided between high and low culture, "between university ethics" and "business ethics."[39] Malcolm Cowley would later describe Andrew Carnegie as the embodiment of this divided American spirit:

> The two sides of Puritanism might be united in a single man, Andrew Carnegie, who made a fortune by manufacturing armor plate and then spent it in promoting peace by impractical methods and in building libraries where the men in his rolling mills, who worked twelve hours a

> day and seven days a week, would never have time to acquire culture. . . . "Culture" was regarded as a foreign accomplishment to be learned and exhibited like golf or table manners, almost a commodity to be bought like a new Keats manuscript for Mr. Morgan's library.[40]

This image of a man who wants to have business concerns (during the week) and culture (on Sunday), but whose mind has so divided the two ideas that it cannot fully grasp an idea of "culture" as containing both, is the principal image, according to Cowley, Brooks, and Santayana, of America's lack of intellectual breadth and intensity and of the poor quality of its higher education. The fact that Cowley chose the man who had made a huge impact on the future of the library through expanding the number of public libraries in the country as the exemplar of this unfortunate tradition was pointed; not only Carnegie, but the libraries with which his name is unalterably linked, came under attack.

Helga's realization that the anxiety and self-questioning she feels in New York might actually be necessary to her future intellectual survival leads to her decision to leave Copenhagen. As with all her other decisions to leave one place for another, however, the inciting incident is a personal one: her refusal to marry the famous portrait painter Axel Olsen. Helga sees Olsen's marriage proposal as an attempt to institutionalize his racial views, ideas that are on display in the portrait he painted of her, which "had been hung on the line at an annual exhibition, where it had attracted much flattering attention and many tempting offers" from "collectors, artists, and critics" (119). While the portrait of her has a sensuality that she finds slightly disarming and which reflects a certain truth about her sexuality, it takes her a long time to realize that Olsen's view of her is not a reflection of his understanding of her feelings, intellect, or ideas but simply a representation of a visual category of blackness that he assumes is the truth and has never questioned. From the very first time he sees her "posed on a red satin sofa" (100) by her aunt's arrangement, he has seen her as nothing other than a particular type of painting. When he finally verbalizes this view to her—" 'you have the warm impulsive nature of the women of Africa, but, my lovely, you have, I fear, the soul of the prostitute' " (117)—she wants to laugh. While the novel begins with an image of an unselfconscious Helga, illuminated and outlined by a reading lamp in her room in Naxos, almost as she might exist in an ideal painting of her contemplative self, Olsen's rendering of her as symbolic of his view of race is not immediately recognized by her as worth challenging. Although Helga has always been quick to uncover evasions and exaggerations in language, and although she is instinctively drawn to art and to beauty, it takes her time and effort in Copenhagen to become a critical reader of categories of race in visual culture.

Although in Copenhagen she thinks "derisively" of the relentless "chattering about the race problem" (111) that had no doubt gone on during her absence from New York, in Harlem she recognizes that she has missed her irritation with it, an annoyance that may be more meaningful than she had given it credit for in the past. Helga claims that she will only be in Harlem temporarily, and this in-between status makes her recognize more than before how divided she feels: "This knowledge, this certainty of the division of her life into two parts in two lands, into physical freedom in Europe and spiritual freedom in America, was unfortunate, inconvenient, expensive. It was, too, as she was uncomfortably aware, even a trifle ridiculous, and mentally she caricatured herself moving shuttlelike from continent to continent. From the prejudiced restrictions of the New World to the easy formality of the Old, from the pale calm of Copenhagen to the colorful lure of Harlem" (125). But this new "knowledge" and "certainty" of a future of "division," of difficulty, and of "insecurity" (126) are exciting to her. She feels sorry for "those Negroes who were apparently so satisfied," and she feels contempt for "the blatantly patriotic black Americans" who march in parades in Harlem (126). In pronouncing, finally, her decision that she will stay in America, she understands that part of the attraction is the interest she feels in seeking new categories and new vocabularies to explain similar racial and sexual experiences that reappear. Helga's experience in Denmark, initially so distinct from her life in America, also allows her to begin to see patterns of her life emerge. Helga's restlessness, her constant searching, becomes a pattern, albeit an idiosyncratic one. Her experiences are unique to her and difficult for everyone else to comprehend in part because they stay put. Occasionally Mrs. Hayes-Rore or Dr. Anderson will move between two fixed points, but generally Helga is the only one in the novel who cannot stay still and whose response to the categories that are offered to her (black/white, American/European, teacher/house cleaner/speechwriter, wife/lover/loner) is not to pick one but to create more categories. Though Helga has discovered—through travel, multiple jobs, and unexpected responsibilities—the beginnings of her own system for thinking about issues of class, race, and sex, she does not have any platform yet from which to apply this understanding to anyone beyond herself.

Helga's recognition of the intellectual usefulness of internal conflict, however, has the potential to transform older notions of gentility. Whereas Santayana's description of the problem with the American mind is of "two mentalities" that remain separate and unexamined and Du Bois suggests in *The Souls of Black Folk* that the future of America rests on its ability to help mend the divided soul of the African American,[41] Helga imagines that her feelings of dividedness are the source of her intellectual power and of her potentially new ideas about race and knowledge. This recognition, however, does not come easily. After sharing a long-awaited and much-desired kiss with Dr. Anderson, formerly the principal at Naxos and now Anne Grey's husband, Helga considers whether she should have an affair with him. Her first instinct, as always, is to continue "exploring to the end that unfamiliar path into which she had strayed" (134). She reconsiders, deciding that despite her desire, "she wasn't, after all, a rebel from society" (135). While this conventional moment may seem false, considering her willingness to reject one form of social interaction after another and given the fact that she has desired Anderson for so long, it reflects Helga's effort at "exploring" her own internal divisions. At this heightened moment of feeling Helga finds herself still trying to discover a way to bridge the distance between two opposed desires without eliminating the intellectual usefulness of a sense of dividedness.[42]

Helga's contradictory personality eventually leads to her rejection of Harlem and her unexpected return to the South. While her statement on leaving Naxos at the beginning of the novel was that she hated the South and would never return, it is fitting that she goes back and that she seems to stay there (at least that is where she still is when the novel ends). Although Helga believes in progress, in exploration, in education, and in racial pride, she also rejects every single one of these things at various points in the novel. It is in keeping with her ideas about resistance that, by staying, her last act is to reject the act of rejecting.

Critics who take issue with the final section of the novel (beginning with the day that Helga stumbles into the Reverend Green's church in Harlem), as her failure to live up to her ideals, ignore the facts of her "conversion."[43] Waking up the morning after Anderson rejects her, Helga is dizzy and disoriented and can feel "her staggered brain wavering" (137). By the time she finds herself pulled into a church, she is too weak to reject the strange scene in front of her. She makes "one last effort to escape" before falling still against a railing in front of her. The fall, however, does not indicate an end or a death, as is often suggested, but rather an opening into another experience, because "in that moment she was lost—or saved" (142). This bizarrely imagined conversion to both a state of loss and gain occurs under the influence of a black preacher in Harlem and seems to be the antithesis to her initial experience at Naxos, when she rejects the white preacher; Helga temporarily stops resisting until she discovers that she has unwittingly joined exactly the same world that she initially escaped. She marries the Reverend Green, moves back to the South, and becomes a mother. Helga, who finally has the family, relations, and connections that she thought would free her in the past, discovers that she is perhaps even more entrenched and hidden than ever before. She also learns that no conventional form of resistance will work in this new environment (that is, she cannot easily leave, in part because she is pregnant). At first she tries to resist her new life by descending into a dreamlike state that frees her mind to travel in any direction it chooses, leaving her momentarily unencumbered by the constraints of her environment. Later, however, she resists the desire to resist, at least temporarily, because she does not want to leave her children.

The usual analysis that this decision to stay is Helga's final failure misses the larger point about resistance that the novel repeatedly makes. The novel suggests that the desire for individual and intellectual freedom requires the will to undertake unlimited resistance. It requires resisting all institutions, all systems, and all statements (even one's own).[44] Thus, the seeming contradictions at the end of the novel (the succumbing to religious ecstasy, the return to the South, the acceptance of marriage and motherhood, and the willingness to stay) are necessary steps toward the greater goal of freedom that Helga never abandons. That the novel ultimately suggests this goal can never be reached, however, is neither a failure of the novel nor of Helga Crane's quest. Helga learns that the freedom and happiness she desires, which she imagines as not only an experience of greater knowledge and insight but the articulation of it, can only be realized by participating in the process of trying to realize it. As a result her "final" destination in the novel, which includes the South, marriage, religion, motherhood—all the things she has previously rejected—is as important a part of her quest and as necessary a part of the process by which she learns as all of her previous rejections and resistances.

Although the novel seems to end where it began, on the cusp of a new set of rejections and resistances, it also includes within it the recognition that this understanding is an essential part of the process by which one learns to reorganize experience. Helga's disappearance into this world will never be mentioned or acknowledged by the white preacher, Mrs. Hayes-Rore, Anne Grey, or the Dahls, all of whom claim to have racial pride—but whose analysis for what that means is limited by their other prejudices (of class, of sex). Their racial attitudes are determined by particular categories of thinking about what it means to be black. Mrs. Hayes-Rore is no more willing to countenance the story of Helga's past than her uncle's overtly racist new wife. Helga is married, pregnant, and in the South by the end of the story, and no one who has narrated the experience of black life throughout the novel has anything to say about it. Helga is even an outcast within the Alabama Christian community she has joined; they think of her as an interloper. Helga's dissolution illustrates the degree to which lives and ideas are constantly being classified, hierarchized, and marginalized even by the very people who most loudly claim to want to help undo those categories when applied to race. Helga recognizes that her own life remains hidden to everyone except herself. This realization gives the novel's conclusion—particularly the odd use of the term "began" (162) to describe Helga's fifth pregnancy in the novel's final sentence—its unfinished quality. Larsen has demonstrated her knowledge of how ideas become classified and institutionalized and her own project of reclassification through writing about a woman's struggle to subvert existing and identifiable categories of experience. Although Helga fails physically in this scene as her consistent efforts to rise above her experiences and explain them have nonetheless resulted in a kind of death, the language of the novel is unable to stop the process of wanting to begin again and to leave open the possibility of some alternative ending to her life.

Knowing How to Pass

Larsen argues in *Quicksand* that knowledge is produced not through the mending of divisions but primarily through feelings of conflict, rejection, and uncertainty—all of which represent a resistance to mending. Helga's search for knowledge and answers occurs first in educational institutions—Naxos and the library—but eventually she recognizes that her most heightened moments of perception occur at the moment she rejects these institutions (because these are the moments that she can most clearly perceive a system at work). *Passing* goes even further in arguing that any system of knowledge is also a system of exclusion. While Helga is an intellectually curious and analytical woman who questions whatever she encounters, Irene Redfield, her seeming counterpart in *Passing,* is the opposite. As much as Helga resists statements, Irene embraces them. Helga believes freedom comes from not belonging and real knowledge can arise powerfully from feelings of uncertainty and disorientation; Irene wants routine and certainty, overuses the word *know,* and is constantly afraid of looking or feeling "foolish."

Larsen's second novel charts Irene's fraught relationship to knowledge and her increasingly tenuous hold on everything that she has ever felt certain that she knew. The wife of a doctor, Irene is an upper-middle-class woman who lives in a large house in Harlem and spends most of her time shopping and volunteering for race-related functions. She and her husband, Brian, clash most often on the issue of the education of their two sons. He believes that the boys should be told the truth about everything, particularly about sex and race; she believes that they should be protected from any knowledge that might disturb or upset them until they are older. Her desire to keep her life free from unpleasantness upsets her husband, but she feels justified in protecting her family from what she perceives as threats against their safety and security. Ironically, her husband's dissatisfaction with the details of their lives in Harlem makes him periodically want to flee, and, every so often, he suggests that they all move to Brazil; but Irene feels certain that they belong in America. Her tight hold on her family, however, is derailed when an old school friend, Clare Kendry, who passes for white, insists on entering her life again.

Irene's certainty that Clare is someone she should not allow into her life is, not surprisingly, borne out in the novel. What actually happens between Clare and the Redfields is unclear because the story is told only from Irene's quite limited perspective of the events, but she believes that her husband has begun an affair with the beautiful Clare: "Ah! The first time that she had allowed herself to admit to herself that everything had happened, had not forced herself to believe, to hope, that nothing irrevocable had been consummated! Well, it had happened. She knew it, and knew that she knew it" (267). Irene's absolute certainty about this event (after fearing for so long that something terrible might happen to her) is so strong that it is powerfully believable, but it becomes more suspect when put into the context of her other questionable moments of equal certainty. Since certainty is more important to her than truth (she never openly makes this claim, but her choices consistently make this hierarchy clear), she might be willing to know about an affair in order to feel that sense of security that she gets from knowing, the positive feeling that she "knew that she knew," even if that information disappoints her. Her determination to know, however, even without facts or evidence, puts her definition and use of the word into serious question.

In pitting Irene Redfield's certainty about knowledge against her rival Clare Kendry's equal uncertainty about it, the novel makes these choices about knowing literally life and death decisions. The first words that Clare speaks to Irene in the novel on the Drayton rooftop, where both are passing for white in order to enjoy a cool breeze and a glass of iced tea, are, "I think I know you." Clare's hesitation and uncertainty (and the way her words modestly echo what Irene's will be) are, unsurprisingly, not at all appreciated by Irene, who is later sorry that Clare spoke to her that day. Irene's first thought when Clare walks over to her table at the Drayton is that she has been found out and that the woman approaching her knows that Irene is passing and that "before her very eyes on that roof of the Drayton sat a Negro" (178). A moment later she convinces herself that this is impossible. Her reasoning, however, is incorrect; she convinces herself that she cannot have been discovered because "white people were so stupid about such things" (178). Irene argues that the woman walking over to her could not "know" her race because the woman is white; it is Irene, however, who does not know. Because she does not recognize that the woman is Clare Kendry, Irene does not realize that Clare is also passing and that Clare (who remembers her) *does* know her race. Clare's "I think I know you" is a more accurate statement than Irene's imagined certainty about "knowing" the differences between races. Despite this evidence of her misjudgment, Irene still believes in her system of judgment and is certain that black people can correctly tell a person's race whereas white people cannot. She even states this theory to Hugh Wentworth, the character who functions in this novel as a stand-in for Larsen's close friend Carl Van Vechten, to whom the novel is dedicated. Irene often uses Hugh as a sounding board to try out her theories of race. At the National Welfare League dance Irene explains to Hugh that "'it's easy for a Negro to 'pass' for white. But I don't think it would be so simple for a white person to 'pass' for colored'" (237). Hugh is the perfect foil for Irene because he claims to be surprised by her ideas; he often acts as though he has never thought about issues of race at all, which is what Irene already believes to be true of white people in general. His reply to her, "'Never thought of that,'" supports exactly what she already thinks. Irene's claim that black people can pass for white (but not the other way around because blacks would know) extends the individual certainty she feels about "knowing" to an entire race.

Irene's attitude toward Hugh Wentworth reinforces her sense of herself as an expert on issues of race. She views Hugh as "sincere" (237) and somewhat simple, and she is flattered by their friendship, given his fame, but never defers to him at all. In fact, in their exchanges she usually acts a little bit condescending toward him, viewing his trips to see and experience Harlem as evidence of his belief in her superior culture. Hugh doesn't disappoint. He sits with her at parties and tries to describe and to help her describe the characteristics of racial distinctiveness. In fact, part of Irene's attraction to Hugh Wentworth is that he classifies and catalogs people, races, and ideas as endlessly as she does (and he usually agrees with whatever classification system Irene has already set up). Nella Larsen was well aware that Carl Van Vechten was a serious classifier of books, ideas, art, people, and races. His recent controversial novel, *Nigger Heaven* (1926), had been about a female librarian (and though not necessarily Larsen, she would have recognized certain traits the protagonist and she had in common). Although Larsen wrote to Van Vechten praising that novel and helped him to collect clippings and reviews about it, she would also have recognized their very different conclusions about the role of the library in promoting and understanding ideas about race. While

Quicksand argues for ways to break down systems of categorization, *Nigger Heaven* served to reinforce them and explore their usefulness for making claims to black racial superiority.[45] In *Passing* Irene's use of Hugh Wentworth as her classifier-friend seems to underline Larsen's perhaps less entirely positive reading of Van Vechten's novel than the one she admitted to having. Irene argues lightly that Hugh must " 'admit that the average colored man is a better dancer than the average white man' " (235). Hugh admits this point, but he takes the comparison even more seriously, arguing " ''S something else, some other attraction. They're always raving about the good looks of some Negro, preferably an unusually dark one' " (235–36). Hugh's effort to articulate these ideas about race do not bother Irene because they coincide with her own. She repeatedly wants to prove the racial superiority of blacks. Their friendship develops over their mutual interest in explaining these points to themselves. Irene's devotion to Hugh, however, only extends to his willingness to see her in the superior light in which she demands to be viewed, and as her control over her life and her marriage begins to slip, she drops Hugh the moment she recognizes that he has seen this side of her (254).

Irene's feelings of certainty, however, ebb slightly in the presence of Clare. Something about Clare's interest in "danger" and her genuine curiosity make Irene more open. Even at the Drayton rooftop, just after that first accidental meeting with Clare, Irene, unusually, feels some "hesitation," and she almost asks a question: "The truth was, she was curious. There were things that she wanted to ask Clare Kendry. She wished to find out about this hazardous business of 'passing,' this breaking away from all that was familiar and friendly to take one's chance in another environment. . . . But she couldn't. She was unable to think of a single question that in its context or its phrasing was not too frankly curious, if not actually impertinent" (187). This moment is one of the few when Irene acknowledges to herself that she might not know something yet and want to learn more. And in this moment of curiosity, she defines passing (as she never defines it again) as a stepping away "from all that was familiar." Passing becomes, at this moment, something courageous and related to feelings of curiosity—a very different definition of passing than the one she uses later in the novel to explain self-righteously that she would never "pass" out of "loyalty" to her own race, one of the more crucial rules she sets up to function safely within a system (even if it is of her devising). For Irene, "reason" (190) is the term she uses to describe functioning within a clear set of social, racial, and even class-determined behaviors, a complicated project since various competing loyalties (to friends, to family, to motherhood, to marriage, to her gender and class) constantly threaten her abilities to feel that she acts with, above all, her reason. Despite the brief searching feelings that arise occasionally in the presence of Clare, Irene's need for "fixity" is stronger, and she clings to this desire that much more as she feels it slipping away.

Clare Kendry, however, becomes increasingly likable and insightful as the novel progresses, despite Irene's bitterness toward her. Beautiful, disarming, and intelligent, Clare flatters Irene at their first meeting on the Drayton rooftop by her seemingly innocent desire to "know": "Clare drank it all in, these things which for so long she had wanted to know and hadn't been able to learn. She sat motionless, her bright lips slightly parted, her whole face lit by the radiance of her happy eyes. Now and then she put a question, but for the most part she was silent" (184). Clare's face, with its childlike eagerness to learn about all that she has missed in life since leaving Chicago after her father's death, convinces Irene to relax and feel sympathy for her old schoolmate. Clare's personal tale, however, of those intervening years of "passing" as white, and thus moving freely among races, cities, and even buildings (such as the Drayton), makes Irene defensive about her own choice not to do so and reminds her of Clare's "having" way (182). This idea, meant to be a dismissal of Clare's intellectual powers—she does not have a "knowing" way but rather a "having" way—is mocked by Brian when Irene finally says it aloud (248). This moment is one of the few in the novel when a character openly challenges Irene's thought processes, and she recoils from the rebuke. Clare, however, also challenges the easy conclusions that Irene wants to reach (assuming, as Irene does, that Clare could not be both materially and intellectually aware); Clare increasingly attracts the interest of the intellectual group from which Irene tries to exclude her. Clare shows up one day at a tea for Hugh Wentworth that Irene does not wish her to attend. Not only does Irene discover that others want Clare there, but she also becomes aware that no one but herself sees Clare as less intelligent.

Despite these challenges to her system of ideas, Irene clings to her sense of "rightness"—Clare mocks her use of the word (225)—until her need for safety and quiet briefly overpowers her desire for certainty. She becomes aware of this thought just before leaving for the party at Felise Freeland's apartment, and it shapes her plans for her family's future: "She was aware that, to her, security was the most important and desired thing in life. Not for any of the others, or for all of them, would she exchange it. She wanted only to be tranquil. Only, unmolested, to be allowed to direct for their own best good the lives of her sons and her husband" (267). Irene's admission that "security," not "certainty," is "the most important and desired thing in life" reflects a change from earlier statements. This reversal occurs when Brian defends Clare's intelligence, and Irene sees these comments as further proof that their affair is serious.

For Irene, however, this displacement of terms is only temporary. At the party, in front of a large window on the sixth floor that Irene opens for air, Irene overpowers her rival, Clare Kendry, both physically and psychologically. She probably pushes Clare out the window but manages to accomplish the act without knowing (or anybody else knowing for sure) that she did it. For a brief moment afterward she behaves the way she perceives that Clare (who never feels she knows anything with certainty) behaves and that Irene has lately felt undone by. Irene's professed confusion surrounding the mysterious circumstances of Clare's sudden death from a fall out of the open window—even as she states rather directly that she touched Clare's arm in some way to hasten the fall—ultimately leaves her free not to know certainly whether or not she killed her. She feels "wonderings" and "questionings" (273), sensations she has never felt comfortable with, in the immediate aftermath of Clare's fall. This moment of uncertainty and confusion, however, does not last long; after learning absolutely that Clare is dead, Irene's last words before fainting are that she is "certain" that Jack Bellow, who had just arrived at the party to confront his wife with the discovery of her race when she mysteriously fell, did not murder his wife.

Through Irene's indeterminate and unpleasant elimination of Clare at the party, and her confidence in aligning herself intellectually with that great classifier Hugh Wentworth (who Irene assumes finds Clare unintelligent, too), the novel elicits the reader's participation in reexamining exclusionary systems of knowledge and their aftermaths. As critics have noted, the reader becomes increasingly aware that despite the fact that the novel is told in the third person, the story appears to come from Irene's own perception of events; her attitudes about knowledge are such that she can present her own beliefs as facts rather than opinions, and her understanding of the events of the story simply may not be true.[46] As a result, the reader's certain knowledge of every person who is seen from Irene's eyes becomes increasingly suspect, Irene's interpretation of the meaning of every event must be questioned, and the reasons for questioning (since it is not always necessary) must also be examined and weighed against the evidence that the novel offers for the truth of each episode. The question of what might be excluded from Irene's consciousness becomes the most important tool the reader can use to analyze and examine the belief system that drives the choices made in her or his understanding of the story. The characters' preoccupations with "knowing," therefore, become the reader's as well. *Passing* incorporates more than Helga

Crane's resistance to systems into the experience of reading the novel. It tells a story that does not just resist but rather openly defies interpretation, and it requires an investment in unpacking someone else's entrenched system of knowledge (in this case, Irene's) in order to determine what she left out.

Authorship and Librarianship

Larsen's desire for knowledge is the simplest explanation for her choice to train as a librarian, and her disappointment in her experience as a librarian provides the most straightforward explanation for why she quit.[47] She began her librarianship by bragging about how much she studied and the languages she practiced for the library's required examination, and after she left the library permanently, she worried about having to return to a job that did not "suit" her.[48] The daily logs that she carefully filled out for several months as the 135th Street children's librarian (fig. 6) show evidence of both these feelings: while Larsen initially filled in details about what books she read to children in nearby schools and other evidence of her community outreach work, she later included less information on the forms.[49] Her attention had turned by this point to beginning *Quicksand,* a new outlet for learning and, as her letters to Carl Van Vechten attest, an effort that she was certain would yield nothing but the persistent feeling of not knowing what she was doing—her favorite kind of challenge.[50] Yet even in this admission of uncertainty Larsen's consistent attempt (even after finishing the novel) to create new ways of talking about race can be found. It is well known that through Van Vechten's introduction Larsen wrote to Gertrude Stein, praising her depiction of the black voice in "Melanctha."[51] Written in 1928, two years after the letter she sent to Van Vechten claiming writerly inexperience, Larsen's letter to Stein suggests that in reading her own novel after the fact she was finding patterns of meaning and possibilities for thinking that she was not initially sure were going to be in it. Unlike Larsen's library job, which became less interesting the more completely she understood its systems of meaning, her novels continued to surprise her.[52]

Readers of Larsen's novels confront her ideas about knowledge and systems not only in her life and work but in considering questions about her diverse body of writing. From her first publications, examples of Danish games and songs written for *The Brownies' Book, Crisis*'s short-lived monthly children's magazine edited by Jessie Fauset, to her final letter to the readership of *Forum* defending herself against charges of plagiarism, Larsen's idiosyncratic ten-year writing career forces readers to ask questions about the categorization of writing, the professionalization of an author, and the relation-

6. The 135th Street branch children's reading room (c. 1926), where Nella Larsen worked. Photo courtesy of the New York Public Library Archives, New York Public Library, Astor, Lenox and Tilden Foundations.

ships between authors and archives.[53] As her training in library school and in the Dewey classification scheme had made increasingly clear, the professionalization of an interest with its emphasis on shared technique, common vocabularies and goals, carried with it certain unpalatable requirements; that is, to be professional was to be an expert or an authority over something.[54] Since she had come to understand through her work as a librarian that all systems needed to be resisted because they carried within them limits and exclusions that could be institutionalized in other models of thinking, she had to include within her body of work her resistance to even her own achievements.

Larsen's archive resists completion; always and admittedly incomplete, it challenges readers of her life and work to ask what they believe about her work and why, as well as to consider their own knowledge and systems of beliefs in relation to hers. Because Larsen's opus is so small, critics tend to consider seriously all of her published works (including letters to the editor, games for a children's magazine, reviews of others' works), and they have to analyze and categorize their own values about these seemingly lesser works in comparison to her published novels. Because Larsen used many pseudonyms (and variations of her name) during her career, it is possible (and, some argue, likely) that not all of her published stories have been found, and critics writing about her recognize and openly admit that their knowledge of her is incomplete.[55] Because she stopped publishing and returned to her former job as a nurse, she did not participate in any collecting or cataloging of her own work at all. The process by which her work has been discovered and analyzed must involve the works, thoughts, and ideas of others, thus ensuring that her thoughts and beliefs do not stand alone. While becoming increasingly fed up with librarianship as a career in the late 1920s as she became more successful as a writer, Larsen considered the connections between the two professions—what librarians and libraries *do* to writers (and vice versa) and the social and cultural consequences of collecting and classifying works. As much as aspects of these ideas must have appealed to her, she resisted the desire to make any final statements about what she knew and how she had come to know it. Her novels, a few letters, her name and library examination scores listed in official New York Public Library records, and her signature on 135th Street Library logs serve as the principal records of her complex understanding of the dual experience of being a librarian and writer in 1920s Harlem.

4
Accidents Happen in Marianne Moore's Native Habitat

Elizabeth Bishop's "Invitation to Miss Marianne Moore" (1948) imagines Marianne Moore in her native habitat—museums and libraries. This vision of Moore ascending the steps of the New York Public Library or gliding past an austere museum entrance fits her persona as a poet at home in the rich cultural life of the city:

> For whom the grim museums will behave
> like courteous male bower-birds,
> for whom the agreeable lions lie in wait
> on the steps of the Public Library,
> eager to rise and follow through the doors
> up into the reading rooms,
> please come flying.[1]

Bishop has fun with the relationship between Moore and these public institutions, giving Moore's museums and libraries magical qualities. "Grim museums" become "courteous male bower-birds" when Moore walks by, and the massive lions outside of the New York Public Library (the spot where Moore first agreed to meet a college-age Bishop) become "agreeable" and "eager" to follow her into the reading rooms.[2] Moore, however, does not notice that the museum is "grim" as she enters nor that the lions in front of the library "lie in wait," a mildly threatening image; she passes by, entirely focused on her own expectations for what will happen inside. Bishop's stanza, like the entire poem, is admiring of Moore's originality and wit and affectionately critical of her entrenched beliefs and institutional affiliations. While Moore has a modern and idiosyncratic courtship with museums and libraries, she is also seemingly oblivious to the way "grim" museums and libraries usually behave around others. Bishop's poem offers a rather quaint vision of Moore's relationship to museums and libraries (they cower and change shape as though in a fairy tale), but it also advertises the extent of Moore's devotion.

In this chapter I examine the close intellectual connections museums and libraries helped to forge between two seemingly disparate moments in Moore's writing career: its beginning and its end. Moore's first official book, *Observations* (1924), and her final decision on where to sell her archive belong to the same processes of thinking and questioning. Perhaps the primary reason this argument has not been made before is that so few of Moore's published poems directly mention the museum or the library. Yet in the background of *Observations* is not only Moore's simultaneous engagement with her job as an assistant librarian in the Hudson Park branch of the New York Public Library but also her readings on museum ideals and two drafts of "Museums" (1919), a poem she left out of *Observations*.[3] She draws on these and other early work experiences in shaping that volume, reflecting on her developing ideas about the ideal character and goals of modern American museums and libraries. The questions about poetry she asks as she contemplates museums and libraries as a young writer lead her to discover answers in the process of finally choosing a shelter for her archive in 1968.

Unlike Edith Wharton and Nella Larsen, both writers who saw the necessity to educate themselves primarily outside of universities and largely through studying paintings and books in museums and libraries, Marianne Moore took advantage of increasing opportunities for women to go to college and graduated from Bryn Mawr with high professional expectations for her future. Moore and particularly her mother, however, expressed frustration and impatience when her college degree did not immediately result in significant opportunities for intellectual work at a high salary. In the fifteen years following her college graduation, Moore took several positions directly connected to museum and library work. Mary Warner Moore found teaching to be acceptable employment for a college graduate, but she tried very hard to dissuade Marianne from staying in library jobs because she believed her daughter ought to do better professionally.[4] Despite these personal discouragements, Moore approached these positions with enormous energy; she chose to work as an assistant librarian at the Hudson Park branch despite her mother's misgivings because she believed that working in an intellectual space, close to home, and surrounded by books would help her writing career. In fact, Moore's interest in museums and libraries informed her approach to continued education and her professional plans. She never sought graduate school as an option, as Ruth Benedict would do. Instead, she saw a potential writing career as largely possible because of her ability to educate herself in museums and libraries. As the idea of a poetic career strengthened in her mind, so, too, did her trips to museums and libraries increase in frequency and intensity, suggesting her assumptions about the ways one learns or practices the processes of thinking and writing creatively.[5]

Moore's extremely aggressive revision of *Observations* in her later books—*Selected Poems* (1935), *Collected Poems* (1951), and *Complete Poems* (1967)—however, might suggest that she abandoned these earlier concerns and ideals she sought in museums and libraries. Most critics of Moore's work, in fact, have argued that her style and even her interests radically change in her later volumes.[6] Certainly, she significantly changes the order and choice of poems she includes from *Observations* in these later texts (from 1935 on, she uses *Selected Poems*, not *Observations*, as the basis for each volume), rendering that first book almost obsolete as a result. In recent years critics such as Catherine Paul have discussed how Moore's close connection to museums, at least, continued during the 1930s as she built poems such as "The Jerboa" from visits to the American Museum of Natural History, but even Paul suggests that this interest had peaked by the early 1940s.[7] I argue, however, that although she seems to leave *Observations* behind, she does not abandon that volume to the extent that she appears to; revisiting the process of her creation of that first volume in light of her early work in museums and libraries clarifies this view.

From her initial visits through her decision to deposit her papers and other items, museums and libraries provide Moore with a complex and unexpected vocabulary through which to discuss and understand her new ideas about poetry. Beginning with her first job with Melvil Dewey, the great systemizer, and through the end of her life, Moore had access to and interest in the systems developed to organize and display not only art and books but almost any products of knowledge. While in her initial discussions of systems of organization in letters home from Dewey's Lake Placid Club, her writing and ideas suggest that she is attracted to demonstrations of precision, completeness, and exactness, her serious grappling with the "purpose and ideals" of museums and libraries over the next three decades leads her to explore the aesthetic (and organizational) possibilities for "miscellany" and "accident." Although critical works on Moore's poetry overwhelmingly suggest that she is a writer more inclined toward precision than miscellany and toward formality than accident, Moore's engagement with museums and libraries illustrates her commitment to these less-discussed ideas and concerns. With *Collected Poems* and continuing through the late 1960s with her final collection, *Complete Poems*, Moore clarifies and deepens the aesthetic conclusions that she provocatively reaches in preparing *Observations.* In 1968, when she sells her archive to the Rosenbach Museum and Library in Philadelphia and creates her own museum and library plans, Moore's initial analysis of museums and libraries, as told through the creation of and subsequent revisions of *Observations,* becomes crucial to understanding the consistency of this final gesture in terms of her entire poetic career.

Preparing *Observations:* Moore's Professional Development

Shortly after she graduated from college, Moore developed a crush on the library. Taking a job at the Lake Placid Club as an assistant to Melvil Dewey, the premiere organizer and system-maker of late nineteenth-century thought and the man most famous for creating a classification system for organizing books, Moore discovered that Dewey had a great deal to teach her. She shared her excitement with her mother:

> Mr. Dewey is an HM* (*HM = handsome man) a Dream or anything favorable that you wish to call him. He called me in before dinner to give me some letters. . . . He was in a flannel shirt and slippers. Explained his attire said he couldn't stand the slightest restriction about his neck or across him. He talked to me a little while said I wasn't to be worried if I got things wrong at first. He said he knew shorthand was a thing which required years of practice and he would try to go slowly and spell the names but that I wasn't to be frightened etc. if I didn't get them. He asked me what my specialty was in college said that Miss Seymour said I had done very well in the work she had given me—got everything very accurately and was very promising. He didn't use that word but conveyed the idea. Mr. Dewey's room is ideal.[8]

It is not necessary to imagine Mary Warner Moore's response to this pronouncement. She writes back immediately, reminding Moore of her education and social accomplishments and encouraging her to come home if she is not being treated properly. Moore will eventually succumb to these entreaties, but for now she is inspired by the ways Dewey seems to wear his philosophies so handsomely: everything in its place but without causing the "slightest restriction about [the] neck."

Moore's desire to please Dewey is connected to her equally strong desire to forge her own intellectual life and her initial uncertainty as to how to do that. Her observations of Dewey suggest that his systems of organizing things and ideas instinctively appeal to her:

> Mr. Dewey has the walls lined with files . . . an engraving of a rebellion or school romp. I hadn't time to look at it. He has revolving bookcases of files, neatly labeled, perhaps only one bookcase and an extent of deck along the wall in front of the windows . . . and just in front of his chair in the corner where the windows stop, a bookcase set on the desk full of ordinary books. He has a wonderful command of English. He has a horror of Britticisms [*sic*] (MCT) [M. Carey Thomas, Bryn Mawr president] kind and yet the most finished individual style I have ever heard. Hence, contact with him is liberalizing. He is very droll. . . . He certainly is a dream as far as personality goes. He might be unpleasant, self-contained but very drastic and I am pleased to know that he has the idea firmly in his mind that I wish to please him. He gave me half a dozen letters tossing over the originals from the authors to be filed when I had copied his letters in carbon on the backs. They are very liberal and have every device imaginable to facilitate work and yet are economical.[9]

Moore appreciates this combination of neatness, efficiency, and economy.[10] She describes Dewey's spare office decorations as a match for his ideology of efficiency; Moore's admiration for order (defined here as a kind of neatness) is evident. She sees a connection between Dewey's ideology, his aesthetic, and his "wonderful" use of language. Dewey had been part of the movement that created "a growing belief that knowledge itself should and could be used more efficiently."[11] For Moore, contact with Dewey is "liberalizing"; she delights in his contradictions because these oddities make her think about ways that neatness, order, and economy can enhance self-expression.

Mary Warner Moore, however, who viewed Moore's work with Dewey as professionally and personally beneath her, implored her daughter to think more carefully about her prospects for advancement. After receiving warnings in letters from her mother, Moore began to complain about her job: "I missed a concert and had to work till 6 today and am so mad I don't know which way to stand. They don't mean to overwork anybody and provide for pleasures and emolliements [*sic*] but they certainly do have 'seasons of pressure.' I also made mistakes and was switched metaphorically so that nettled me. . . . If I can't turn out enough work to be paid more than $50 a month I will be justified in quitting. I don't intend to quit however under any circumstances."[12] Moore's mother, upset by what she perceives as unreasonable work requirements, sends her daughter a letter explaining to her precisely what she sees as the problem: "Your situation is entrenched on every side; and while others are less favored I cannot see that you need disregard your advantages, just that you might put yourself into the place others are in. To begin with, your equipment, socially and by education, makes it possible for you to have a position that pays enough for you to live properly."[13] Mary Warner Moore says that given past "advantages"—and implied here is that Moore has had a college education—she deserves a better class of work. This series of letters also shows that what Moore hopes to accomplish in her job is very different from her mother's goals for her. Moore's fascination with indexes and ways of listing and ordering information is made more and less legitimate by the time she spends with Dewey.[14] For Moore, her job with Dewey is exploratory; whether Moore yet realizes it or not, seeing in Dewey a vision of the aesthetic principles she seems to believe in at that moment allows her to try on those she might want to investigate and use in her poetry.

While her initial letters home suggest how impressed she is by him and the ideas he promotes, she also outgrows her crush. In her unpublished autobiography, written in the 1960s, Moore's memory of the early development of her working career is equal parts irony and pride, but her thoughts offer an intellectual explanation for her growing disenchantment with the job as well:

> After college, some kind of lucrative employment seemed necessary; Mr. Melville Dewey who invented the Dewey Decimal Classification for libraries was burdened by my inexperience for part of a summer in the clerical department of the Lake Placid Club. The Club was luxurious and abounded in opportunity for canoeing, dancing by frequenters of Wall Street, fashions and exports. But I was not seeking something connected with fashion but a publishing house. Instead of any exciting literary opportunity, an urgent demand was made from the . . . Carlisle Industrial Indian School. My brother . . . reminded me . . . why speculate on something of a literary sort when I could immediately take the place of a commercial teacher who had without warning resigned from teaching at the Indian School for work as a salesman of I think Smith typewriters in California? The salary was $2000 a year and it seemed self-evident to accept it. With misgiving I did.[15]

Although Moore's mother and brother support the move from working for Dewey to teaching at the Carlisle school because it seems to suggest actual professional and economic progress, Moore's willingness to leave the Lake Placid Club has to do with her growing intellectual disillusionment with the place. In this later account she dismisses her job with Dewey as uninteresting because unrelated to literature, but even these comments belie that argument. She writes that the club was "luxurious" and "abounded in opportunity," rather wry ways of underlining its snobbish attitudes and exclusivity (it excluded Jews and divided guests into classes).[16] The tone of the paragraph is mocking, as though making fun of herself as a young woman for not yet fully understanding the obvious concerns of her position there and Dewey's very problematic practical applications of his classificatory systems at his club.

Before Moore leaves the job with Dewey, she already begins to replace her initial attraction to order and neatness with a new set of aesthetic principles. In a letter home a few weeks later, Moore writes: "I am not much of a stenographer. My value is miscellaneous."[17] Her odd use of the term *miscellaneous* to describe herself at this point in her professional career suggests some new attachment to the ideas and values embedded in her definition of it. She uses the term to describe both her uncertainty as to what she is capable of achieving and her confidence in her abilities to do more than one thing. More than a decade later Moore returns to this term in a *Dial* essay touching on the character of museums and libraries, and it serves as an apt summary of one of the primary goals for the recently published *Observations.* She says that she is attracted to "miscellany" as a term describing systems that order thoughts in unexpected ways to inspire heightened levels of thinking: "Academic feeling, or prejudice possibly, in favor of continuity and completeness is opposed to miscellany—to music programs, composite picture exhibitions, newspapers, magazines, and anthologies. Any zoo, aquarium, library, garden, or volume of letters, however, is an anthology and certain of these selected findings are highly satisfactory. The science of assorting and the art of investing an assortment with dignity are obviously not being neglected, as is manifest in 'exhibitions and sales of artistic property,' and in that sometimes disparaged, most powerful phase of the anthology, the museum."[18] Moore argues that the seeming disorder and lack of completeness in "miscellany" can be "highly satisfactory" in certain contexts, including museums and libraries that help inspire the essay.[19] She remarks that "investing an assortment with dignity" is a kind of art that, thankfully, is not being neglected. She provocatively considers that "miscellany"—that seeming scourge of the organized—can, in the right hands, contain a kind of dignity.

Museums and Libraries

Moore continues to explore these initial insights into the complexities and problematics of systems of organizing knowledge as she contemplates museums and libraries and her own plans to publish a book of poetry. Robin Schulze has argued that around 1916 Moore began to think about publishing a book of poems. Although Moore recognized Bryher and H.D.'s generously funded and nicely crafted publication of *Poems* (1921) as a kind gesture and gift of friendship (despite their choice to produce the volume without her formal consent), it did not satisfy her desire for her own first book. She resisted requests for publication until she finally—although suddenly—agreed to one of Scofield Thayer's repeated requests for publication in 1924 along with the *Dial* award.[20]

Moore's intellectual excitement over the ideas she encounters in museums and libraries begins to resonate with her developing ideas about what a book of poetry ought to accomplish. In ten pages of preparatory notes in her reading notebook that she takes on Benjamin Ives Gilman's *Museum Ideals of Purpose and Method* (1918), in two drafts of the unpublished poem "Museums" (1919), and later in two versions of an unpublished review-essay of a recent Museum of Modern Art exhibition "Art and Interpretation" and "Concerning the Marvelous" (1937)—all of which build on Gilman's arguments—Moore studies the "ideals of purpose and method" behind contemporary museums and libraries. Even in her reading notebook Moore finds herself thinking about the concerns of museums and libraries together, reflecting on both spaces and moving between them. On the back of the page in which she begins to copy down Gilman quotations she jots down a poem on the library.[21] Through this research Moore focuses on ideas for discovering ways to organize knowledge consciously and carefully without resorting to a system that limits the possibilities for a visitor to discover something unexpected or unknown within it. This search is driven by both her intellectual interests in the organization of knowledge and her very personal desire to produce a book that participates in this process positively.

In "'Discovery, Not Salvage': Marianne Moore's Curatorial Practices," Catherine Paul argues that the serious development of Moore's museum ideas between 1916 and the early 1940s can be largely traced back to her initial recognition of (and agreement with) Gilman's ideas shortly after she reads his book. Paul argues that Gilman's work enabled Moore to understand quickly how specific groupings work to inspire thinking, or simply, how "collections afford discovery," and that this realization helped her to think about groupings within her own poems.[22] Paul focuses on the period when Moore wrote two poems using information from dioramas at the American Museum of Natural History, and she argues that Moore's interest in the organization of objects in museums helped to develop her sound curatorial instincts along the lines that Gilman advises.

Moore, however, seems to struggle with some of Gilman's ideas more than Paul allows for, and ultimately Moore seems to use his work somewhat differently—to think about the purpose of poetry broadly—than Paul suggests. Moore never publishes any of the work that Gilman's book inspired and that she completes on museums or libraries over the next two decades (although she flirts with the possibility), in large part because in thinking about these cultural spaces, she is doing preparatory work for her publications of books of poems. This work strengthens her vocabulary through which to discuss museums and libraries, and she discovers even more usefully that these terms and ideas are necessary to her clarifying her thinking about her own plans for a book of poems.

Moore vacillates between her view of museums as educational spaces and her view of them as recreational spaces. She copies into her reading notebook Gilman's comment that "by no liberality in the definition of the word education can we reduce these two purposes[,] the artistic and the didactic."[23] Yet Gilman goes on to say that "they are mutually exclusive in scope, as they are distinct in value." His wholesale argument against the "didactic" point of view is quite different from her less strident approach and her genuine interest in ways that didactic information can be made to seem enjoyable and inspiring if expressed in the right way. In her 1937 essay on an exhibition at the Museum of Modern Art, Moore offers several different literary terms and phrases to describe the ideal combination of necessary impulses behind a good museum or exhibition. "Throughout the rooms, one felt the tendency to multiple thinking; that is to say, the prevalence of innuendo and humor, effected often by paradox and the pun. As in books, these two literary devices work for and against the product, depending on the craftsman—cheapening or tending to a dazzling compactness."[24] Moore is thinking about how a good exhibition comes together; her conclusion is that certain means of disrupting orderly systems actually enable a greater vision of the ideal order of a group or a collection. How does one keep a spirit of spontaneity and casualness in a place that relies on careful systems of measuring and ordering? For Moore this question is as much a poetic one as an institutional one.

Moore's "Museums" asks even more bluntly whether it is possible to learn inside a museum, how that might occur, and whether learning is a good enough reason to visit. These questions were Edith Wharton's as well, but Moore's thoughts in this unpublished poem, though equally reflective, are less disappointed than Wharton's. Moore's poem is unusually descriptive about the feelings and thoughts that arise during a visit to a museum, and she reflects on the experience from moment to moment. In one draft a description of objects and collections is scattered throughout an analysis of the experience of visiting, and the section ends with a statement about learning:

The museum is
not a repository for clothes, jewels, circumstance, a place through which
to drag one's self in museum-tourist fashion. It exists
for those who are able to enjoy what they

see, at the same time as well as afterward: its half a limestone lion—advance-
ing troutlike through the architectural alphabet, one sees
it—set high on a piece of graveyard stone, the

eyes contorted to form triangles, the shaved plateau between the cars, white with
ivory dust and tinged with red as if a cloud of iron-rust
had been raised around it. It is not going

anywhere; it need not walk about to prove that it is formidable. One
may learn in a museum that the characteristic form
of the emerald in its raw state is a

six-sided prism—that there were two distinct breeds of dog in ancient Egypt. The information is there but there is there, something more mellow
than information—something which has widened

the mental horizon for men of a good many different ages. One
takes a horse from the stable for the purpose of visiting
a customary scene; one follows a stream,

every turning of which is a foregone conclusion; it is similarly
that one goes to a museum to refresh one's mind with the
appearance of what one has always valued.[25]

The two critical stanzas describing a museum's exterior lead the speaker to reflect on the possibility of gaining not only information but "something more mellow than information" on a visit to the museum. Moore develops this idea of something "mellow" as something less precise than information and very positive. The next sentence seems at first to critique the museum and the museum visitor, suggesting that the reason one goes to a museum ought not be to discover what one already knows, but this critique is undercut by the way "mellow"-ness participates in "refresh[ing]" the mind. The idea of a museum as refreshment, both reminding one of something that one knows and offering something newly inspiring and enjoyable, is important to Moore. Is a museum a place for enjoyment—a "more mellow" structure—or a place that has the power to impose its will on objects or subjects? Is it a place to gain information, or is it a place to reinforce already existing attitudes about the value of things? Is it a place of recreation and entertainment or a place of education? In her essay "If I Were Sixteen Today" (1958) Moore suggests (to her sixteen-year-old self) that she "give 'culture' the benefit of the doubt; don't look on art as effeminate, and museums as the most tiring form of recreation there is."[26] How does it change one's expectations of a visit to call a museum a recreational space? In the poem Moore suggests that the museum is "not a [mere] repository," indicating that there are organizing principles at work. There is also something oppressive in any idea of a museum as a permanent "formidable" structure, complete within itself. The poem suggests that the sense of a museum's authority (revealed, in part, through its formidable architecture and its system of organization) negates the learning process, while the promise of enjoyment and refreshment prolongs it.[27]

Moore suggests that missing from most museum visits is exactly this quality of enjoyment, informality, and spontaneity. In *Observations* she will ironically work very carefully to produce that sense of spontaneity; she demonstrates an interest in how this combination of seemingly contradictory impulses (carefulness and casualness) may not only work together with but improve the experience of seeing an object in a museum. She will include in *Observations* a self-made index, the ultimate organizer of information, but created with some obvious whimsy. That unexpected index, which emphasizes small and seemingly unimportant words and ideas in poems and ignores major ones, will do its organizing of the text's information in a most casual, nonexclusive, and seemingly accidental way. As she claimed in writing "Museums," one's enjoyment will increase and one will get more out of the experience of visiting an object or work of art if the experience of learning is "mellow."

If Moore gains insight into the intellectual and organizational pleasures of "enjoyment" from the museum, in her job as an assistant librarian at the New York Public Library Hudson Park branch (figs. 7, 8), she discovers the importance of what she will eventually describe as the pleasures of accident. Mary Warner Moore again had strong misgivings about her daughter's taking the library job, and Moore's mature voice details both her own annoyances about this position and a clear sense of what she gains from it:

> I worked as a secretary for a Miss Chairs who had a school, gravitating presently to Hudson Public Library across from our house. The library I used constantly and one day Miss Mary Leonard, the librarian, called on my mother and asked if I would like to work as one of their staff. My mother felt not. She felt that shoemaker's children never have shoes. But when I came home I said, "The very thing; if I could work half a day I would like to do it." I could run across the street without putting on a wrap. And it was arranged that I could come mornings, if possible, sometimes longer. I was to report to the Main Library on certain books given official B-slips about 3″ wide concerning the value as subject matter and as entertainment of books presented to the library. I enjoyed this work though it interfered with chosen reading. I was not paid and asked "why not literature or art"; out of the question as I had no pedagogic record or special credentials . . . I liked anonymity, had taken a required course of Library Economics. Mr. Frederick Hopper was in charge of the library at 42nd Street. Miss Anne Carol Moore was in charge of children's books and I liked the routine in the library, yet could not see that I needed a special course of instruction to tell boys and girls to read John McGraw, "How to Play Baseball," and Christy Mathewson, "Pitching in a Pinch." I liked youngsters and the grown public. Asked one regular reader how she liked "A Pair of Blue Eyes" by Thomas Hardy. She said, "It isn't anything like what I thought it would be but it is very gripping." I felt at home working for Miss Mary Leonard, the librarian, Miss Elizabeth Parker and Miss Carlton. I received $50.00 a month for half-days, $75.00 for half days extra on holidays.[28]

In this passage, from her unpublished autobiography, Moore compares her initial enthusiasm for working in the library to her developing annoyance at its rather authoritarian, somewhat undemocratic, priorities.[29] In the next paragraph Moore reveals how different her evenings were from her days: readings at the home of Lola Ridge where the future of modern poetry was being discussed and where her opinions were sought often and freely. Many years later she still sounds rather bitter about the extent to which she was not allowed to express an opinion at the library because of her lack of proper library-training credentials.[30] At the same time, this passage reveals what Moore was learning through the library job: the seemingly accidental bit of insight, the random piece of conversation that she could remember and collect. Some fifty years later, Moore still remembers the delight she felt by a reader's comment about a first encounter with a Thomas Hardy novel. Moore

7. The Hudson Park branch of the New York Public Library. Photo courtesy of the New York Public Library Archives, New York Public Library, Astor, Lenox and Tilden Foundations.

develops this faculty for remembering these unexpectedly fulfilling moments of thought, and she learns to hoard them, in part in resistance to what she perceives as the library administration's undemocratic lack of interest in anything said by the imperfectly degreed. Just as in all her previous work experiences, Moore sees value in listening and responding to the casual visitor.

Moore harshly criticizes the character of the library in her unpublished novel as well. Her opinion that the library, for all its supposed intellectual freedoms, is actually a rather rigid place to work and too bureaucratic in its conception of its own future appears again in "The Way We Live Now." She describes librarians quite bitterly as people who behave like policemen and who hide behind organizational systems instead of creating original ideas or genuine analyses of history: "A sightsee-er's decision between Pembroke first or Christ Church, might seem to an Oxonian scarcely more serious than the altered map of Oxford in Mr. Verdant Green's post-matriculation dream. But the proximity of the two Colleges in this instance reconciled differences of intention, and 'tramping from college to college in search of the University—that thing so difficult to find,' one encounters suggestions of it in spite of

8. Story Hour at the Hudson Park branch. Photograph by Lewis Wickes Hine (1874–1940); courtesy of the New York Public Library Archives, New York Public Library, Astor, Lenox and Tilden Foundations.

oneself, collegiate Oxford being a society where librarians truly seem more than policemen, and nomenclature may be history."[31] The library is both a place of remarkable intellectual freedom and a prison. Librarians behave as authorities, an act of self-aggrandizement that Moore generally does not admire. Although Moore gravitates toward libraries as places for freedom and learning, her professional experience inside them suggests the administration is often antithetical to that ideal. She wonders if "mellow"-ness is a possibility in the library and in a book of poems: is it possible to sustain efficient and fair methods for learning while still allowing for the pleasures of enjoyment?

Producing *Observations*

In 1935, when T. S. Eliot praises Moore as one of the great modernists by describing her poetry with phrases such as "an unusual awareness . . . like . . . a high-powered microscope," "control," and "precise fitness of form," he offers future critics a clear set of terms through which to consider her work. Descriptions such as precise, exact, and aware become crucial terms through which to identify a Moore poem.[32] Yet Moore's *Observations* is not only importantly charged less by goals of "control" and "precis[ion]," as *Selected Poems* insists, but also concludes with an attack on the very systems for enabling precision that Eliot will later use to praise her poetry and ideas as modernist. *Observations* is animated by other terms and ideas much more on her mind at the time of her production of that early volume—"enjoyment" and "accident" (terms that will appear in the poems) and the overarching aesthetic principles of "miscellany" (investing an assortment with dignity) and "mellow[ness]" (something more than information)—ideals for a book of poems that Moore had recently recognized as culturally crucial in her thinking about museums and libraries.

As Robin Schulze has chronicled, by the time Moore agreed to publish her first official book of poems for Dial Press in 1924, she had been flirting with the idea of publication of a book since 1916. In writing to Eliot to let him know (but also to complain) about the Bryher and H.D. version of her 1921 *Poems,* Moore explains that one reason she does not like that volume is because it does not include "any contribution of labor on my part in the production."[33] Moore is particularly interested by this point in her career in aspects of the "production" of the book—by which she means the choice of title, choice of poems, versions of and order of the poems, and the potential inclusion of author's notes and index. Whether she had always planned to include those for her first volume of poems is a matter of speculation, but certainly by the late summer of 1924 the inclusion of those framing devices became an enormously important part of her final production of *Observations* before it went to print.[34]

Although Moore had published most of the poems that would appear in *Observations* in little magazines (the earliest version of a poem—"A Talisman"—appeared first in 1912, the latest publication was "An Octopus" in *Dial* magazine, December 1924) and continued to revise them, her actual compilation of *Observations* occurred at an extremely rapid pace—in about a month.[35] In that period Moore put her newly established principles of order into play in organizing the collection of poems; she did not, as she could have, publish the poems simply in chronological order from oldest to most recent poems. Nor did she ignore all of her early poems, keep poems originally published in pairs or groups together, or cluster poems with overtly similar subjects (for example, her growing collection of poems in response to the outbreak of World War I).

Instead, Moore shifted the focus from each poem's initial publication purpose to achieve something quite new in *Observations.* Her interest in allowing the poems to build an argument—and one that she had not made before—over the course of the entire book was exciting to her. By means of her idiosyncratic index, the notated poems, and through the development in subject and idea of the carefully organized order of poems, Moore was able to give poems that had already been published a new, more fully developed, context. Moore ignored Ezra Pound's offer of his expert services in the organization of manuscripts; she had her own ideas. Her recent study of museums and libraries had given her a new intellectual vocabulary in which to think about her own principles for society, culture, and collection and to use those to achieve exactly what she wanted. The book would display an unexpected mix of ready wit and serious argument that highlighted both what she admired about the process of displaying books and art in museums and libraries and what she felt was problematic about the development of the character of those institutions.

Scofield Thayer, Moore's friend and champion, in his comment on *Observations* in *Dial* magazine, made special effort to discuss Moore's idiosyncratic index and to draw readers' attention to this important inclusion. Thayer thought that the index and notes were particularly interesting aspects of the book, and he encouraged her to include them.[36] In this odd index Moore includes minor terms and phrases and often ignores seemingly major subjects and ideas, underscoring her argument for a nonexclusive way of viewing information. For example, in her famous poem "Poetry," Moore chooses to index "elephants pushing," "tireless wolf," "business documents," "imagination, literalists of," "toads, real," and "genuine, the" (although in the poem the *the* is absent)—an odd mix of the seemingly ephemeral and crucial. While the usual discussion of Moore's changes to her 1925 edition of *Observations* centers on her radical revision of "Poetry" into a thirteen-line free-verse poem, in fact not only were individual poems changed in this revised edition, but so were the notes and index. Moore not only changed these seemingly ancillary texts to reflect changes in content within the poems in this new edition, but she also continued to play around with comma placement within the index. Moore's efforts after accuracy are no different within the index than within the poems themselves since she often meticulously played around with commas, suggesting not only that she sees the parts of volumes that supposedly only order, note, or catalog ideas as important as the poems but also that her idea for her first official book emerges as much from her creation of the individual poems as from her sense that with the right title, order of poems, and framing materials, *Observations* would emerge more completely as a reflection of the cultural world she had come to understand and wanted her book to participate in.[37]

Within this frame Moore's volume offers a history of the development of American cultural institutions, locating the beginning in the period of the Civil War, and explaining how this cultural process evolved awkwardly out of often mistaken assumptions about how to share what one knows. Out of the fifty-three poems in *Observations,* only thirty-three were included (some with revisions) in *Selected Poems,* and almost all of the poems not selected were the short poems from the first half of the 1924 volume.[38] To look at *Observations,* however, is to see the poems build—literally in that they become increasingly longer (with the obvious exception of the short poem "Silence," which purposefully breaks up this seeming system and appears third to last)—to the poems that conclude the volume. The poems also build by repeating certain images, words, and phrases throughout to emphasize aspects of her final, longer, and most recent poems and thinking. The big poems such as "Marriage" and "An Octopus," in the final section of the volume, have tended to stand alone as solitary achievements in subsequent volumes; but to return to their place in this 1924 volume and see them in the context of her brief, early poems is to see the big poems quite differently.[39] In their placement in this volume these final poems are inextricably tied to the narrative that the short poems initiate.

Moore introduces both the historical landscape of the volume—which encompasses the debates leading to the Civil War viewed through scenes from contemporary American life—and its witty tone in the first brief poem. "To an Intra-Mural Rat" explains what will happen in the rest of the volume:

> You make me think of many men
>   Once met to be forgot again
>   Or merely resurrected
> In a parenthesis of wit
>   That found them hastening through it
>   Too brisk to be inspected.

Although these men might have at one time been "too brisk to be inspected," suggesting their importance, the speaker has, in fact, "resurrected" them in order to "inspect" them. This opening, biting poem suggests that this volume—this "parenthesis of wit"—will chronicle this inspection. The title word, "Intra-mural," which literally means "within walls," suggests how this inspection will be accomplished. By placing these so far unspecified but "resurrected" men within her book, a space with clear boundaries, Moore can observe them, just as she might study the movement of rats in a zoo or objects in a museum case.

By not initially identifying these resurrected men individually, these first few poems address the impact of authority figures in general. The ghosts of Dewey-like men—creators, self-appointed authorities, cultural leaders—are found in most of the poems. Poems that at first seem to be simply about bodies that can transform their shape—wizards and chameleons—soon become more explicitly about how to resist strong forces and "men long dead" (the phrase that ends "A Talisman," the fourth brief poem). In "To a Prize Bird," which follows "A Talisman," Moore offers more details about these men:

> You suit me well; for you can make me laugh,
> Nor are you blinded by the chaff
> That every wind sends spinning from the rick.
>
> You know to think, and what you think you speak
> With much of Samson's pride and bleak
> Finality; and none dare bid you stop.
>
> Pride sits you well, so strut, colossal bird.
> No barnyard makes you look absurd;
> Your brazen claws are staunch against defeat.

The subject may be a bird, but it is a "colossal" bird that is such an unstoppable force that "none dare bid you stop." Yet the line "Pride sits you well, so strut, colossal bird" is by no means a clearly positive command; it is superfluous to say so in a poem about a bird so powerful that it can act independently of the forces that surround it. Moore's very short note to this poem—"Bernard Shaw" (originally part of the title)—cryptically glosses the poem. Certainly this poem could function both as a description of that irreverent writer and thinker and as an explanation for Moore's admiration of his originality, strength of thought, and humor. But these initial poems have underscored their admiration for the ideas and remarks of powerful men with some irony, suggesting that these ideas must be identified, understood, and—crucially—tested and resisted.[40]

These opening poems not only ironize "great men" who rose to prominence through the Civil War, but they begin to describe the culture the men produced. Although in its initial publication in the *Egoist* in April 1915, critics viewed "To Military Progress" as one of Moore's first lyrics on World War I, its new placement and context in *Observations* results in a shift in its emphasis and meaning.[41] This poem offers a narrative of men successful in war, though not without significant cost:

> Till the tumult brings
> 	More
> Black minute-men
> To revive again,
> 	War

The "minute-men" who had pledged themselves to fighting the Revolutionary War are now back again to fight. This poem is no triumphant ode; rather, it is a poem that questions the "prize" (the poem echoes the language of "To a Prize Bird") that came out of the Civil War and the money that it cost to win it. At the center of the poem is a body that is in pieces. There is a torso and a head, but rather than an upsetting image of a dismembered body, the pieces seem more like parts of a sculpture than of a human body. Is this poem a reenactment of the experience of history through art? Is this broken body a sculpture in a museum? The poem pointedly suggests that American art emerges from the culture of the Civil War, perhaps, at first, developed simply to commemorate that historical process.

As this poem begins to do, the next few poems will not only describe the kinds of aesthetic objects created but will focus on the process through which they are created, questioning whether this process matters in responding to art. "An Egyptian Pulled Glass Bottle in the Shape of a Fish" is the first poem in the volume to use the word *art,* a term that appears in the first of its two stanzas:

> Here we have thirst
> 	And patience from the first,
> 	And art, as in a wave held up for us to see
> 	In its essential perpendicularity;
>
> Not brittle but
> Intense—the spectrum, that
> 	Spectacular and nimble animal the fish,
> 	Whose scales turn aside the sun's sword with their polish

The poem is about the appearance of an art object. For Moore, the "Spectacular and nimble animal the fish" is a beautiful image; in fact, she repeatedly returns to the "fish," a favorite word, as an example of something beautiful. Its companion poem, which appears on the facing page, "To a Steam Roller," reflects on the process by which such beauty is created. This poem is about a machine that can crush glass, the kind of unstoppable force that was also present in "To a Prize Bird" and will recur in "An Octopus," and is frightening but impressive. The poem at first seems to celebrate this big piece of machinery that is able to crush glass down to so fine a point that it is hard to distinguish from the street underneath it. Moore asks about the relationship between an industrial tool and art, but she also resists sentimentalizing the connection:

> The illustration
> is nothing to you without the application.
> You lack half wit. You crush all the particles down
>   into close conformity, and then walk back and forth
>   on them.
>
> Sparkling chips of rock
> are crushed down to the level of the parent block.
>   Were not "impersonal judgment in aesthetic
>   matters, a metaphysical impossibility," you
>
> might fairly achieve
> it. As for butterflies, I can hardly conceive
>   of one's attending upon you, but to question
>   the congruence of the complement is vain, if it exists.

Moore initially suggests in the poem that it is in the completeness with which the steamroller crushes glass that it also achieves a certain aesthetic quality. The poem, however, undermines this idea at the end by imagining this machine next to a butterfly, a fragile image of beauty. Moore recognizes that she is attracted to the single-minded intensity of the steamroller, but she also understands that something gets lost in its singleness of purpose. The end of the poem observes two opposing images of beauty together: a steamroller and a butterfly; it does not attempt to hierarchize them, underscoring a less exclusive view of power. Moore asks in this poem whether there is an ideal process of creating and exhibiting a work of art.

In Moore's search for a potentially new image of beauty, she turns briefly to look at the development of the American language in "Poetry" (and later in "England"), which appears in the middle of the volume. Moore's choice to place "Poetry" in the middle of this volume might seem odd given both its intensely public message and the way William Carlos Williams had already trumpeted it as a central modernist tenet (through his editing of the final issue of *Others*). This choice, however, makes sense given the way the rest of the volume develops the poem's primary insight into the possibilities for finding new forms of beauty if one is not already prejudiced toward what might qualify as beautiful. In multiple and significant revisions of this poem, the one constant is the phrase "business documents and schoolbooks" from a quotation by Tolstoy. While T. S. Eliot uses the term *genuineness* as one of Moore's crucial modernist terms in introducing her poetry to the public in his introduction to *Selected Poems,* in fact in the 1925 second edition of *Observations,* Moore left out the term *genuine* completely from her radical rewrite of "Poetry" into a thirteen-line free-verse poem. Because of the absence of "genuine," the Tolstoy quotation becomes more central to the poem. Because she juxtaposes these two items—business documents and schoolbooks—Moore presents them as though they are two versions of the same thing: the sorts of things *not* currently considered to be part of poetry. The poem suggests that to recognize "business documents and schoolbooks" as both potentially important possibilities for poetry, not only ideas of what beauty is but ideas about the process by which something beautiful is created need alteration.

Moore, however, also is torn between what she sees as worth including as beautiful and her open disgust at the processes by which these beautiful things are created. In "Reinforcements" she returns to the language of "To an Intra-Mural Rat," and the poem makes the strongest statement yet about what these "resurrected" and industrious men might be working on and how this work simultaneously creates and destroys:

> The vestibule to experience is not to
> be exalted into epic grandeur. These men are going
> to their work with this idea, advancing like a school of fish through
>
> still water—waiting to change the course or dismiss
> the idea of movement, till forced to. The words of the Greeks
> ring in our ears, but they are vain in comparison with a sight like this.
>
> The pulse of intention does not move so that one
> can see it, and moral machinery is not labeled, but
> the future of time is determined by the power of volition.

These men "advanc[e] like . . . fish through still water," an image of both beauty and ambition. The poem does not completely celebrate the men or the work they have done. The men are single-minded, "waiting to change the course or dismiss the idea of movement, till forced to," and they are hungry to succeed. The speaker admires this fortitude but suggests that there is a moral price to pay in the future for such overwhelming displays of power and will.

"The Fish," which faces "Reinforcements," explores the evidence of man-made power, and the poem is Moore's most biting depiction and most direct assertion that even such a morally problematic process can still result in something beautiful. In its formal qualities, its measured syllabics and balanced, deeply reflective descriptions, "The Fish" stands out in the volume as a beautiful poem describing a searching after beauty. In the last three stanzas of the poem the cliff or wall of this dark underwater world suddenly reveals itself to be the victim of some kind of abuse:

All
external
  marks of abuse are present on
    this
    defiant edifice—
  all the physical features of

ac-
cident—lack
  of cornice, dynamite grooves, burns
    and
    hatchet strokes, these things stand
  out on it; the chasm side is

dead.
Repeated
  evidence has proved that it can
    live
    on what cannot revive
  its youth. The sea grows old in it.

This poem offers the stunning and mysterious world of fish and a critique of the defacement of beauty. The men, who were "advancing like a school of fish" in "Reinforcements," do so in "The Fish" in order to destroy the cliff for their own use. They drill and use dynamite in the cliff as they search for, perhaps, the oil that will make them both wealthy and powerful. In the sad last line—"The sea grows old in it"—"The Fish" offers a rather terrifying image.

The "it" can only describe the cliff. This recognition leads to the disheartening thought that the natural world grows old inside the human-marked world. What humans have not killed, they have taken possession of by inscribing through the use of tools that mark and change the face of the cliffs. Moore breaks up the words describing those marks—"the physical features of / ac- / cident"—abruptly enough to underscore her ambivalence about her intense reaction to them. While in "Reinforcements" Moore says that "moral machinery is not labeled," "The Fish" offers the physical "evidence" that suggests the opposite. The "label," however, is simply not visible to everyone. The fact that the artful world of the fish is the one being marked suggests an attitude of anger toward these powerful men who dominate their environment. Building on the questions raised in "Reinforcements," "The Fish" considers whether it is possible to create an artistic world, and exhibit the "evidence" of one's work there, that is still both moral and nonauthoritarian.

"Dock Rats" responds to her moral and aesthetic concern by giddily grappling with what a writer can do about it. Written about a shipping dock from the perspective of the rats that inhabit it, it is a poem excited about the spectacles that financial and industrial success can create. The speakers "we"—located at a site that is man-made and devoted to commodities and to world trade, want to enjoy the view of a dock where "the square-rigged Flemish four-master" testifies to its access to "the finest shipping in the world." The rats find this location a terribly entertaining place to observe "a parakeet from Brazil" or "a monkey—tail and feet." The accidental discoveries they find in a place such as this are celebrated here. This poem delights in the unexpected awareness of the degree to which spontaneity can be a highly engaging means to organize experience. As in "The Fish," "accident" may be something unwanted and even immoral, but it is also highly inspiring. The poem ends on a high note, in a celebration of the location:

> . . . One does
> not live in such a place from motives of expediency
> but because to one who has been accustomed to it, shipping is the
> most interesting thing in the world.

Moore wrote the poem shortly after her brother married and she and her mother moved to Manhattan. She remembers a friend's comment that her new St. Luke's Place apartment was a wonderful place for writing but a place from which Moore would often try to flee the heat by going down to the dock to watch the boats.[42] Wittily, from the point of view of the rats (and Moore, by this point, called herself "rat" in letters to her family), the poem translates this sense of the excitement about the place as connected to the excitement of writing in Manhattan.[43] While others may work at the dock for financial gain, these speakers simply stay there out of excitement and interest. Can one reconcile the fact that a world economy, an unstoppable force, a history of power leads to a man-made view (in the poem, "A Grave," Moore berates one man who is "taking the view from those who have as much right / to it as you have to it yourself") and the best view in the world? In "Radical" Moore suggests that the "secret of expansion" in the world economy leads to a willingness to believe the world is merely "a circumstance" in which to live, not a natural space with lands and resources to protect. Despite earlier poems that attest to her realization that gains (spectacles such as this shipping port) are made through corresponding losses—losses to the environment, to origins, to ancestors, and to "moral machinery"—Moore wants to have it both ways in "Dock Rats": mourn the losses, but still admire the view.

Moore responds to her writerly conundrum in the final group of poems (all fifteen of which would be included in *Selected Poems*) by considering issues that she had recently come to see were at the center of the development of modern cultural institutions. In later volumes these poems—particularly her two biggest poems, "Marriage" and "An Octopus"—seem more vague in their references to the historical process that each poem participates in describing. Moore was willing to have these poems read this way in the future, eliminating her idiosyncratic index (another level of potential for specificity) in later volumes, shifting around the order in which the poems are introduced, and, most crucial, removing the early poems, which provide a shared vocabulary and set of concerns with these later poems.

Returning to the conclusion of her unpublished poem "Museums," in "When I Buy Pictures" she suggests that "Too stern an intellectual emphasis upon this quality or that / detracts from one's enjoyment." She defines *enjoyment* in this poem, explaining why this term has become so important to her. "Enjoyment" is a way to modulate learning in order to discover truth and create literature, so that intellectual curiosity has an end beyond simply being intellectual. She pursues this line of thinking further in "The Labors of Hercules," which expands the discussion of enjoyment to creativity in general. She writes that "one detects creative power by its capacity to conquer one's detachment," again suggesting that a feeling of enjoyment is a sign of inspired thinking. She explains this idea further in her review of an exhibition, "Art and Interpretation," by suggesting that for a good exhibition—or good poetry—to work, it needs to undermine the very system that it relied on to organize it, explaining that "imaginative organizing" in a museum exhibition or a book of poetry leads to an "enlargement [of] knowledge."[44]

In "Marriage" and "An Octopus" Moore explores how to use imagination to enlarge knowledge. She begins "Marriage" in the present, but the poem eventually shifts back and forth between different periods in American and world history, lingering on the political and personal decisions that led to the seemingly odd conjunction of the Civil War and the loss of Paradise. Just as she promises in the early poems of the volume, Moore's "resurrected men"—Daniel Webster and Adam are two of them in this poem—mingle and behave ridiculously in the present. Moore connects these two seemingly unrelated stories through the behavior of the men in them, suggesting that while commitment to ideas and ideals is admirable in certain ways, one must always be allowed to change one's mind. Intellectually, Moore wants to leave open all possible avenues for creativity:[45]

> This institution,
> perhaps one should say enterprise
> out of respect for which
> one says one need not change one's mind
> about a thing one has believed in,
> requiring public promises
> of one's intention
> to fulfill a private obligation

Moore navigates this space intellectually and personally. Bonnie Costello remarks that one can see Moore working out her thoughts about the subject of marriage in her passionately argued letters about Robert McAlmon's marriage to Bryher in 1919.[46] Moore refers to her negative feelings about the marriage but states her most personal and pointed objection to it in a letter to Bryher: "I felt that your daily intellectual formula and Robert's were not the same."[47] Given that their letter exchanges are primarily about poetry and related activities, Moore coins "intellectual formula" to describe the process by which one can continue to be creative. The question of what kind of institutions enable that state to continue is not only a personal issue of whether or not one should be married but also an important question about the kinds of institutions that exist and the way in which they help to support an "intellectual formula" that can result in artistic achievement. Moore raises these questions in the context of offering a history of the development of American institutions in general. She begins by asking how the development of enterprise led to the achievement of institutions. The poem offers an answer by way of a long discussion on men and power.

Early in the poem Moore suggests that to feel power is often a prelude to an absurd act. The poem begins with a vision of Eve's knowledge, intelligence, curiosity, and beauty. She has a complex character that is obvious and radiant to those who are close to her, and she is also difficult. Adam and Eve have an argument. Adam feels "alive with words"—angry, argumentative—because he has "prophesied correctly," but instead of continuing to argue with Eve, he lectures her "in a formal, customary strain," which he cannot help doing, since he imagines that she looks at him as "an idol." Once Adam believes this about himself, the poem suggests, he is lost and has lost Paradise. Whatever version of Paradise they have at the beginning of the poem—a sort of intellectual environment where Eve's quickness and intelligence are its central features—is dismantled when Adam sees himself as her intellectual superior. Moore calls Eve's fall "that invaluable accident / exonerating Adam." She certainly does not idolize Eve, either, but is willing to admit that Eve's "invaluable accident" is ultimately more valuable for Adam than for Eve. Moore's focus is not on how Paradise is lost, or on how Eve falls, but on how Adam manages to avoid blame. He is "a force," a power that for the most part he claims for himself and that no one takes away from him. After Paradise is lost, Adam—arrogant, forceful, fortunate—continues to lecture. Eve begins to disappear from the poem. This bleak view of marriage treats the loss of Paradise as the loss of a central space for the expression of a woman's intelligence. If Paradise is treated as a kind of institution—it requires an adherence to a certain set of beliefs—this section of the poem suggests that one of the problems with institutions having been created initially as authoritarian male spaces is that women's voices tend to be lost in them, even if women have something important to say.[48]

This central power relationship, treated as a bad marriage ("he stumbles over marriage"), is compared at the end of the poem to the tumultuous process of creating a unified America. Moore takes Daniel Webster's cry, "Liberty and union, now and forever," from the end of a speech he delivered in the Senate in 1830.[49] The speech was delivered to try to end the nullification controversy and to keep South Carolina in the Union. The series of debates about these issues, though held thirty years before the Civil War, was a clear prelude to the issues that eventually resulted in the war. By linking a retelling of the Adam and Eve story as an early example of a power struggle in a bad marriage to a fragmented reference to an attempt made to save a breaking Union, Moore suggests that institutions can only become institutions if all parties recognize and adhere to the power that they wield. Moore's point is that skepticism and doubt can be remarkably effective means of undoing power structures. She makes this point most clearly in the poem when Adam assumes he has a degree of power that Eve does not recognize, so "he stumbles"; the Constitution can only wield the power that it potentially has if all of its subjects recognize it as having that power. By threatening to secede from the Union, South Carolina threatens not only the Union but also the idea of the future for all potential American institutions, the Union itself being the first and most necessary institution. Webster recognizes this reality and in another famous passage from the same speech, he defends the institution of the government more than the particulars:

> Unjust suspicions and undeserved reproach, whatever pain I may experience from them, will not induce me, I trust, nevertheless, to overstep the limits of constitutional duty, or to encroach on the rights of others. The domestic slavery of the South I leave where I find it—in the hands of their own governments. It is their affair, not mine. Nor do I complain of the peculiar effect which the magnitude of that population has had in the distribution of power under this Federal Government. . . . I do not complain; nor would I countenance any movement to alter this arrangement of representation. It is the original bargain, the compact—let it stand; let the advantage of it be fully enjoyed. The Union itself is too full of benefit to be hazarded in propositions for changing its original basis. I go for the Constitution as it is, and for the Union as it is. But I am resolved not to submit, in silence, to accusations.[50]

Webster's rhetorical phrase, "I go for the Constitution as it is, and for the Union as it is," is simultaneously an argument for upholding the Union and the Constitution to give it the power that it needs in order to work, and a defense of its inviolability. The contradiction in this idea becomes clear when Webster directly addresses the subject of slavery. He argues that he is willing to overlook slavery in the South in order to save the Union, claiming that "Congress has no authority to interfere in the emancipation of slaves" and that he will uphold this idea; he makes it clear to South Carolina that the South will not have to fear any kind of encroachment if it remains in the Union. Moore knows that Webster's speech did not keep the Union together, that by not addressing one of the central issues of concern between the North and the South, by declaring that "liberty and Union" could coexist with slavery, he merely stalled the inevitable—the breaking up of the Union and its reconstituting after the Civil War.

The issue of the need for a Union is also an anxiety that the more land there is, the greater the need for a centralized power to withstand the increased possibility for threats against it. In the poem Adam equates marriage with owning property. In his first attempt to explain what marriage is, he compares it to cultivated land. Marriage is a Paradise, he says, but this Paradise is not a wilderness but rather an "estate of peace." The image of marriage as an "estate" conjures up ideas of gentility—expense, expanse, cultivation, and privacy. Adam admires the cultivation and wealth—in other words, the type of man-made beauty—that results from industry. Eve, the author of the "invaluable accident," remains a critic and skeptic; she does not offer an alternative ideal of beauty, but she undoes Adam's static thinking enough to make him wonder.

Like all experiences for Moore, marriages (or unions) are mediated by language. Just as Adam begins making formal speeches at the moment that he feels most powerful, so does the "archaic" Daniel Webster. The word *archaic* is a mild critique for this speech-making man, and in the final lines of the poem Moore mocks Webster's self-important pose:

> which says: "I have encountered it
> among those unpretentious
> protegés of wisdom,
> where seeming to parade
> as the debater and the Roman,
> the statesmanship
> of an archaic Daniel Webster
> persists to their simplicity of temper
> as the essence of the matter:
> 'Liberty and union
> now and forever';
> the book on the writing-table;
> the hand in the breast-pocket."

The poem has earlier suggested that lecturing is the result of some feelings of superiority and a lack of creativity. Here the writing desk (which functioned as an image of the potential for writing and remembering in Wharton's *The Age of Innocence*) is instead an image of finality—the closed book, the finished task. The image of the breast-pocket that ends the poem suggests wealth and social custom, and it is connected to Daniel Webster's use of archaic language. Just as Adam's desire to lecture was the prelude to an assumption of his own power and superiority over Eve, Moore suggests that Webster's speech-making is also a sign of some desire to dominate. The poem ends by rejecting this use of language as being inspired by the same impulses that seek to harness the waterfall for industry and to try to turn land into an estate. From the earliest poems in this volume, Moore has identified the Civil

War as the point from which America began its awkward cultural life. In this poem she compares the descent into the Civil War to the loss of Paradise. She knows that something goes wrong and pinpoints this problem initially as a cultural one, an issue of the way people use language. Eve mocks Adam's speech-making just as the poem mocks Webster's. Although Eve's "invaluable accident" is useful, it only begins to offer an alternative possibility for language to counter Adam's limited imagination. Moore's poem "An Octopus" will take this idea of what language can do much further.

If "Marriage" tries to define what an institution is in a world of words and language, "An Octopus" goes much farther in trying to suggest how language can be a force of change by itself. Moore had described hearing news of Bryher's unexpected marriage to McAlmon as "but what an earthquake."[51] In "An Octopus" it is an avalanche instead of an earthquake that shakes things up, but the effect is quite similar: "An Octopus" *moves.* It is a poem about the necessity of motion and the benefits of changing thoughts, but this ending comes at the expense (literally) of the exactitude and precision in the opening of the poem and of the volume. Initially, the glacier is so slow-moving and unchanging that it can actually be measured. The poem ends with a frightening image of an avalanche, a natural force that is, in this case, man-made. While Moore deplores the ways human beings have marred the landscape, she also appreciates the way these changes force her to confront the fickleness of fact.

The poem begins with facts. The glacier has definable characteristics and it can be measured:

An Octopus

Of ice. Deceptively reserved and flat,
it lies "in grandeur and in mass"
beneath a sea of shifting snow dunes;
dots of cyclamen red and maroon on its clearly defined
        pseudopodia
made of glass that will bend—a much needed invention—
comprising twenty-eight ice fields from fifty to five hun-
        dred feet thick,
of unimagined delicacy.

Although the glacier's look is "deceptively reserved and flat," its surface can be "clearly defined" and accurately measured. This opening to the poem is structured so that the most lyrical phrase used to describe the glacier—its "unimagined delicacy"—offers some relief. The specificity of the number modifying "unimagined delicacy"—"twenty-eight ice fields from fifty to five hun- / dred feet thick"—suggests that again accuracy and precision are crucial, but the fact that the delicacy cannot be imagined suggests that these measured terms are not the end point but a point on the way to understanding some alternative way of seeing.

Before this stately opening can be undone by the end of the poem, Moore further explores the landscape. Margaret Holley describes the progression of the poem as that of a catalog: "The steady movement and concentration of the catalogue's procedure through the world of the mountain from glacier to firs to the minerals, animals, and vegetation, to the human implications of the place, and finally back to the glacier itself."[52] The poem does begin with the steady beat of facts, but even by the middle section, the natural exuberance of the animals interrupts the measured rhythm:

> What spot could have merits of equal importance
> for bears, elk, deer, wolves, goats, and ducks?
> Preempted by their ancestors,
> this is the property of the exacting porcupine,
> and of the rat "slipping along to its burrow in the swamp
> or pausing on high ground to smell the heather";
> of "thoughtful beavers
> making drains which seem the work of careful men with
> shovels,"
> and of the bears inspecting unexpectedly
> ant hills and berry bushes.

At first this vision of a democratic Paradise where curious and insightful animals share resources seems consistent with the early images of the glacier as powerfully untouchable; the natural world seems to be the only world. As Moore develops the poem's close observation of the wilderness, however, she identifies the marks of human intervention, which (just as in "The Fish") change the shape of the landscape. Beavers simply notice that their homes look "as if whole quarries had been dynamited." Soon businessmen arrive not only to use the resources but also just to see them; the local trappers become mountain guides. The forbidding glacier is turned into a national park: our natural museums.

This process is one that Moore participated in when she visited Mount Rainier National Park as a tourist. The park's history as a piece of land enjoyed by animals, transformed (and then preserved) by human beings, is similar to the historical process Moore describes in the poem. Environmentalists fought with the government over the question of how much of the land to preserve: "Thus Mount Rainier National Park itself can be interpreted as an example of scenic preservation designed to the specifications of big business and frontier individualism, not the needs of the environment."[53] Arguments between environmentalists and the government revolved around the question of "monumentalism," the desire to turn natural resources into national monuments. The heyday in its development occurred in the 1890s, just after the beginning of the museum boom, and Moore's curiosity about the place (including the tourist brochures she culls for notes) emerges from the same concern over its development into a place people visit to learn about nature.

Moore's poem attacks the static notion of nature as monument by unleashing a more powerful force of transformation: a literary avalanche. The sound of the "crack of a rifle" at the end of the poem is the sound of the avalanche barreling down the mountain with its tremendous forcefulness. This avalanche that ends "An Octopus" by destroying everything in its path is not unlike the flattening machines in "To a Steam Roller." The avalanche flattens the trees (and everything else that has grown on the glacier, a difficult process in itself, as Moore has explained) with such force that they are no longer trees or even like trees, and, like Moore's steamroller, the force of the avalanche creates some kind of new fragmented art from the pressure it exerts. While critics such as Bonnie Costello argue that Moore's avalanche purifies the environment through organizing and finishing it, the logic of the volume suggests that the avalanche actually undoes the precision and exactitude that enables accurate measurements in the first place, transforming both nature and monuments as part of a necessary process that will recur even after the poem ends.[54]

By beginning this poem with statements of fact about the glacier that she will undo by the force of the avalanche at the end, Moore underscores her attraction to her own experimental modes of reordering experience. In this gesture she argues for the aesthetic and cultural benefits of seeming disorder and lack of completeness. She resists leaving a final statement. There can be no final measurements. The poem releases a battle cry just before the avalanche unleashes its full force on the landscape of the glacier and the poem:

> damned for its sacrosanct remoteness—
> like Henry James "damned by the public for decorum";
> not decorum, but restraint;

it was the love of doing hard things
that rebuffed and wore them out—a public out of sympathy
with neatness.
Neatness of finish! Neatness of finish!
Relentless accuracy is the nature of this octopus
with its capacity for fact.

While this famous passage shouts "neatness," it does so ironically as it resists its own impulses toward reveling in "neatness," "finish," or "fact." This resistance to neatness is finally also a reply to Moore's early attraction to Melvil Dewey's philosophies (as represented by the man whom she described at the time as having "the most finished individual style" she had ever known). Dewey represented completion, exclusiveness, and totalizing systems. Henry James, whom Moore describes as "big" (physically and literarily) in a *Dial* magazine essay and whose ideas of beauty she admires but criticizes in her 1916 poem "Diogenes," also gets swept up in the avalanche at the end of the poem.[55] She admires him, just as she admires Shaw in "To a Prize Bird," but she must resist both writers' potential intellectual authority over her in order to continue to have the energy to transform her own thinking, to discover new ideas of beauty in a resistance to the very ideals she seems to want to admire most but does not want to get lost in.

While she was working on this poem, Moore copied down quotations on the behavior of octopuses into her reading notebook. She noted that "during periods of liveliness the tentacles are held closely packed together so as to offer no resistance to progress."[56] Moore's poem becomes like an octopus—not a reaching, grasping figure but one that offers no resistance to progress at all. This idea of progress, however, is of a different kind than the vision of the destructive marking of the cliff in "The Fish." In that poem the cliff is permanently marked as evidence of industrial progress; in "An Octopus" the avalanche undoes the implied permanence of the glacier as monument by transforming its shape and measurements, ultimately reminding all people (as Moore reminds Eve) that falling is not a mistake but an "invaluable accident." "An Octopus" offers an alternative to Adam's unrelenting lecturing and system-making: continuous transformation. Just as the glacier begins the poem known by its measurements, by the end of the poem the avalanche has completely transformed the glacier's size and shape, revising all of those earlier statements of fact.

Through these two big poems Moore revisits the story of the growth of industry and the development of an artistic response to what that progress enabled. Her discussion of art is also a discussion of women since she suggests that Eve's "invaluable accident" is, however accidentally, ultimately what enables real progress. By the end of *Observations* Moore replaces her "resurrected men" with women and accident. In her early jobs at libraries and schools, which led her to ask questions about the relationship between authority and creativity, and in her poem "Museums," Moore tried to understand the relationship between organized collections and the inspiration one gets from them. Art, Moore suggests through her vision of Henry James becoming undone by his proximity to the avalanche, can be a force by creating movement that undoes fact and resists permanence. In this state of energy and motion, art has forcefulness without authority and creates unexpected ideals of beauty without claiming permanence.

Revising *Observations: Collected Poems* and *Complete Poems*

Once Moore published *Selected Poems, Observations* retreated into the background. The revision of the volume was so thorough in 1935—eliminating almost half the poems—that it seemed as if Moore herself wanted to move on. Although some critics continued to read *Observations* as a whole, the force of T. S. Eliot's name and stamp on *Selected Poems,* the degree to which she seemed to have rewritten *Observations,* and the increasing difficulty in even finding copies of the text as it went out of print helped to encourage critics to move on as well.

In recent years, however, annoyance over Moore's complex and unrelenting sixty-year revision process has been replaced by increasing efforts to explain exactly what she changed and offer explanations for why she made some of the revisions that she did. Andrew Kappel and Robin Schulze offer two related and dominant theories. Both argue that Moore radically revised her poems for her final two collections, *Collected Poems* and *Complete Poems,* in ways that reflect primarily two crucial facts: the postwar world and the devastating effect that her mother's death in 1947 had on her. Because her mother advised excision and compression, Kappel argues that most of Moore's significant cuts to poems reinforce her commitment to these principles, a passion that had nonetheless existed from very early on in her career—in fact, was already evident in a 1916 poem, "Holes Bored into a Workbag by Scissors," in which she admitted her desire to cut and worried over it too. Kappel argues that *Complete Poems,* which includes the now-famous epigraph that "omissions are not accidents," shows her "new desire to advertise rather than hide the omission" process.[57] Both Kappel and Schulze maintain that Moore's poetics of excision, which is always present in her thinking from her earliest poems, becomes central to her work and thinking in the early 1950s and through the end of her life.

I offer an alternative, though complementary, explanation for Moore's epigraph and aesthetic philosophy. Moore's intellectual and practical thoughts about collections in museums and libraries were clearly equally strong forces, driving her thinking about the process of revising earlier work. In *Collected Poems* the idea of "collection" is foregrounded not only in the title but in the fact that the recent death of her mother (while the event might have made Moore cling to the ideals of compression and concision that her mother advocated, as Kappel and Schulze suggest) also certainly caused her to reflect on the practical aspects of death that directly involve issues of collection. What does one keep and what does one throw away when someone dies? The idea behind a collection, which had always been both an intellectual and aesthetic issue for Moore, became during this period a very personal and practical one as well. In 1965, during the period between *Collected Poems* and *Complete Poems,* Moore also finally moved out of her longtime residence in Brooklyn to a new apartment in Manhattan. At the same time, Moore was courted by various university libraries before finally selling her archive in 1968 to the Rosenbach Museum and Library in Philadelphia.[58]

This significant period helps to characterize her inclusion of the epigraph "omissions are not accidents" in *Complete Poems* quite differently than the statement has generally been read. In viewing Moore's revisions in *Complete Poems,* critics have leapt on the word *omission* as the important term of her final epigraph. Although her revision practice clearly had a great deal to do with the term *omissions,* as Kappel and Schulze have discussed, her thinking about collections, acquisition, and the organization of ideas and things suggests that the term *accidents* was equally, if not more, important to her intellectual and aesthetic principles.[59] The idea of a collection coming together through a series of "accidents" was one that Moore was already flirting with early in her career when she wondered whether *miscellany* might be the most apt term to describe an ideal collection. In pointing to her future archive in *Complete Poems,* Moore's focus on "accidents" suggests the incompleteness and unexpectedness of even an archive—undercutting and ironizing that title for her final edition of her poems.

The term *accidents* connects her early work with her final archive in other ways as well. In a 1929 interview she admitted disliking "acquisitiveness."[60] In a *Women's Wear Daily* 1965 article, "Dress and Kindred Subjects," however, she finds a way to resolve this crisis when she writes that "I am not a collector, merely a fortuitous one." The idea of "accidents" is here connected to her denial of her role as a collector, a comment that she feels is true since most of the objects that she has amassed are not the result of purchase but of accident—gifts from friends, hand-me-down clothes, things she has made and not purchased. Through the term *accidents* Moore is able to supply herself with a term that suggests that her life as a collector is not in conflict with her moral principles concerning acquisition, a tension that she had always felt anxious about.

Complete Poems points both forward to the creation of her archive at the Rosenbach Museum and Library and backward to her early work in museums and libraries in order to understand Moore's aesthetic philosophy at this point in her career. Kappel sees *Complete Poems* as ending Moore's career very much as Eliot wanted her to end it, and he reads Eliot's gesture (in rearranging Moore's poems so that "Silence" is the last poem in the 1935 *Selected Poems*) as having reshaped Moore's thinking about the meaning of her poetic output, emphasizing concision and compression as premier modernist terms: "[Eliot] makes the silence that follows the last poem speak feelingly. It was a brilliant editorial gesture that Moore was never to forget. She was to repeat it on her own, as we shall see, to an even greater moment at the end of her career, when of course silence would perforce be more resounding."[61] By focusing on the word *omissions* in the epigraph, Kappel sees *Complete Poems* as the final statement Moore makes on poetry; in doing so, however, he ignores the ways in which the word *accidents* points to her creation of her archive as the next step in understanding her particular take on modernism and her response to Eliot. By viewing *Complete Poems* as participating in Moore's thinking about museums and libraries, and as part of Moore's contemplation of the relationship between aesthetics and the organization of ideas, that final edition becomes more closely linked to her work preparing *Observations* than it does to Eliot's editing of her work in *Selected Poems.*

Moore makes her own, different, equally modernist gesture, pointing beyond "silence" or compression as the ultimate modernist principle, to her poetry in the archive as her final comment on her principles of order. This gesture away from silence and toward miscellany and accident is her revision of Eliot's rearrangement of her poems in 1935 and her revision of Eliot's definition of her modernist principles. It is also a return to her original thinking about order and arrangement in *Observations*, where she initially explores those terms.

Looking back from the vantage point of the 1960s, her interest in collecting and her thinking about the philosophy behind it developed for more than fifty years. One could say that her first job working for Melvil Dewey, the great classifier, her intensive study of museum ideals, and her work at the

Hudson Park branch of the New York Public Library, where she complained that her colleagues were sometimes more interested in systems of order than genuine learning, were crucial in helping her think about what an ideal collection might be like. Where would it be located? What would it look like? How would it be organized? After posing these questions in abstract forms for five decades, she found a way to answer them directly for herself.

Designing a New Institution: The Rosenbach Museum and Library

In her will, Moore's final written work, she designed her own institution. In poems such as "To a Snail" she had first imagined different kinds of shelters; she wrote about animals that carried around their own houses, and she praised these animals for having homes that are movable and aesthetically pleasing. In choosing a place to deposit her papers, Moore created a shelter not for herself but for her possessions. In 1968 Moore declined an offer from the University of Texas to buy her papers. Moore considered donating her things to Bryn Mawr, but shortly before her death she instead sold her papers to the Rosenbach Museum and Library in Philadelphia and signed a codicil to her will that established the possibility for a museum:[62]

> *Re: Estate of Marianne C. Moore*
> "I GIVE, DEVISE AND BEQUEATH to THE PHILIP H. and A. S. W. ROSENBACH FOUNDATION such of my furniture, furnishings and objects located at my apartment at 35 West 9th Street, New York, or stored in said building, as it, in its sole and absolute discretion may select, to be used by it for display in a 'MARIANNE C. MOORE ROOM.' The balance of such furniture, furnishings and objects not so selected by it, shall be distributed and disposed of by my Executors, by gift or otherwise, to such person or persons as they in their sole and absolute discretion may determine."[63]

Moore's will creates a new space for the "Marianne C. Moore Room"—the objects taken from her 1960s New York City apartment—to be placed inside the Rosenbach building, a privately owned townhouse built in the 1860s near Rittenhouse Square (figs. 9, 10); another section of the same building would hold her manuscripts and other papers. She wills a new institution (her own museum) within a modest building on a street of private homes. In her unpublished poem "Museums" Moore had criticized the formal city museum for its "formidable" power that is "not going anywhere" and its gothic archi-

9. The Marianne C. Moore Room at the Rosenbach Museum and Library. Photo courtesy of the Rosenbach Museum and Library, Philadelphia.

tectural style. As a response to these criticisms much later, Moore creates a museum at her death and picks an utterly antimonumental, unformidable type of space in which to exhibit.

In the often anthologized painting *The Artist in His Museum* (1822), Charles Wilson Peale sees the early museum as a place where the artist stands in the center, looming over his pieces even though he blocks the visitor's view of them. Moore's poem "A Grave" in *Observations* offers a critique of this early image of the museum and the artist. Her anxiety that it is part of "human nature to stand in the middle of a thing" seems an especially apt epigraph for this image of Peale's rather authoritarian pose. The museum seems to be more about him than the art; certainly the rational, painstaking organization and classification scheme and the multiplication of images Peale is so apparently proud of in his museum celebrate human rationality in organizing meaning more than anything else, since one cannot see clearly what is behind him. This image of museums as authorities, of museums and libraries as celebrations of the human ability to stand in the middle of a thing, is exactly what Moore does not want to create in any one volume of her poems

10. Marianne C. Moore's Greenwich Village living room at 35 West 9th Street, March 23, 1972. Photo © Nancy Crampton; courtesy of Nancy Crampton and the Rosenbach Museum and Library, Philadelphia.

or in her archive. Moore's choice of the Rosenbach, her choice to will her things into different rooms and spaces, and her insistence that so much of what arrives there is by accident guaranteed that if she created a museum and library, there would be no clear center, but learning about the work and author would require movement among different rooms and spaces.

The seeming antimonumentality of Moore's museum space is reinforced by its mobile nature. Although the townhouse does not move, Moore's possessions inside of it do. Despite her many comments to the contrary, Moore had an enormous number of possessions. In an interview with Moore in the 1950s, a writer detailed the enormous clutter in her apartment in Brooklyn:

> Miss Moore's apartment . . . includes a tremendous array of books. . . . It includes a walrus tusk from the Greely Expedition to the Arctic in 1881, countless porcelain and ivory likenesses of tigers and elephants, and a mass of bric-a-brac in less readily identifiable shapes. And it includes paintings, drawings, and etchings, as well [as] pictures that Moore has cut from magazines and framed—a display whose sheer square footage threatens to overflow the limited wall space that is not occupied by bookcases. . . . The subjects of the whole informal gallery are pre-

> ponderantly animals—elephants, kangaroos, alligators, chickens, mice, hermit crabs, and very nearly all the rest. . . . Occasionally, though, the encroaching multitude of her possessions drives her to the verge of impatience. "I never want to own anything any more," she told a visitor not long ago. . . . However she has never been able to bring herself to discard any of her remarkable accretion. Even in her most exasperated moments, the mere mention of some old coin or bit of porcelain in her collection will prompt her to dig it out and show it off with undisguised affection.[64]

Almost all of this massive number of objects went to the Rosenbach building. Some remained so miscellaneous as to be somewhat unsortable, including clippings and ephemera.[65] The objects were divided among the museum, the archive, and the library. As a result, objects that inspired poems (Elizabeth Bishop's gift of a paper nautilus that inspired the poem of that name) or were inspired by poems (both E. E. Cummings and H.D. gave Moore artistic renderings of a yellow rose after she wrote the poem "Injudicious Gardening") are in the Marianne C. Moore Room, while the various working drafts of those poems are in the archive, and the versions in the published volumes of the poems are accessible on the shelves of the library.

The space resists any kind of easy identification; it is neither a library, an archive, nor a museum, and it is also all of these things. The necessity to move among the rooms (to understand her work) encourages questions about what the differences among them might be, and it discourages treating any one object, work, or idea in any one space as a finished product. In "Of Other Spaces" Michel Foucault writes: "The idea of accumulating everything, of establishing a sort of general archive, the will to enclose in one place all times, all epochs, all forms, all tastes, the idea of constituting a place of all times that is itself outside of time and inaccessible to all ravages, the project of organizing in this way a sort of perpetual and indefinite accumulation of time in an immobile place, this whole idea belongs to our modernity. The museum and the library are heterotopias that are proper to western culture of the nineteenth century."[66] Moore chooses a nineteenth-century space but reinterprets it through a twentieth-century perspective. She does not treat the library or the museum as an immobile place or as a place set apart from other spaces (the townhouse does not stand alone on the street or the neighborhood; the library does not stand alone from the archive or museum). Rather, she gives to the building attributes of modern movement by creating necessary (and natural) movement within it. This mobility, this continuous loop of information, is the finest example of Moore's philosophy of order, and it serves as her final mode of resistance against that master narrative of progress and expansion that *Observations* had sought first to retell and undo. Moore, writing her final work during the civil rights movement and the women's movement, during a period when she also believed that interest in poetry was declining, created a mobile, flexible, sociocultural space that will continue to circulate among systems of thought and experience without ever settling into one model of expression.[67] She admired the spectacle of grand spaces such as the museum and the library (enough to create one), but she also managed to include within that space enough evidence of miscellany and accident to sustain in the physical world the very ideals that she had discovered in the process of creating her first book of poems.

5

Finding Freedom from Museums and Libraries in Ruth Benedict's Poetry

For Marianne Moore, becoming a modernist poet involved a process of enthusiastically embracing and learning from the opportunities and even annoyances that New York City museums and libraries afforded her; for Ruth Benedict, becoming a modernist poet involved initially exploring but later turning her back on those very same experiences. For Moore the best record of her attachment to those spaces is her creation of an ideal museum and library to house her life and her poetry; for Benedict the best record of her attachment to those spaces is an insistence on assessing her professional career in terms of her escape from working in them.

Shortly after the successful publication of *Patterns of Culture* (1934), at a moment when Ruth Benedict might reasonably have thought that her professional prospects were becoming assured, she instead sat down to take stock of her career and to reflect on her concerns about women and work. In her autobiographical essay, "The Story of My Life . . ." (1935), she narrates her career by suggesting that her choices were shaped at a very early age by her observation of her mother's poor treatment in her job as a librarian. Benedict explains that her reaction to watching her mother's professional experiences was to reject the possibility of a library job despite her interest in it. When she later decides to work toward a position in a university, her familiarity with her mother's story leads her to recognize the similarities in the way these educational institutions treat the professional prospects of women who work in them. She repeatedly faces the same prejudices against women that her mother did, yet she initially explains her choice to pursue a job in the university not in terms of her own ambition but in terms of her realization that she must look for professional and personal fulfillment outside of more traditional places that women work: "From the time I was eleven we were very poor. . . . Mother elected to take the position of librarian in charge of the large staff because of its greater security as compared with the teaching jobs she had had in the Middle West. Library salaries could be depended upon to advance at a regular amount each year, and the job was permanent until retirement age. She went on a salary of sixty dollars a month—fifteen dollars a week for a family of four."[1] Benedict's mother (fig. 11) has to choose between fair pay and job security in her library job, and she has no chance for professional success even at an institution that needs her skills. Benedict interprets the low pay and limited possibilities for advancement in a particularly negative light: as a lack of professional respect and an assumption that female employees are not ambitious.

As Benedict continues her studies, she discovers that this personal realization can serve equally as an intellectual one. She becomes aware of new research that increasingly supports her growing discontent with women's professional prospects and helps shape her desire for other kinds of work in terms of modern necessity. Elsie Clews Parsons, Benedict's teacher at the New School for Social Research, had recently argued that the professionalization process did not change much for women.[2] In two books, *Social Freedom* (1915) and *Social Rule* (1916), written shortly before she met Benedict, Parsons remained extremely skeptical of the claim that the professionalization of women did anything for women other than "remov[e] the vast numbers of women from the class supported by men to the class working for them" (53).[3] Parsons saw cultural institutions as not only products of cultural knowledge but also central reproducers of it, and she believed women needed to be especially careful as they used these spaces to professionalize.

Parsons's course gave Benedict the vocabulary to place her anger over her mother's library salary (which she had initially viewed as a personal issue) in broader terms—as part of a more general disappointment in the historical development of cultural institutions. Parsons describes the history of museums and libraries in terms of their relation to the simultaneous development of classification systems that organize the world in ways of which users are not always aware. Explaining that "scientists have long been aware of the dangers latent in classification, of the arrest to thought its rigidity causes" (*SF*, 8), she explores how a systemization of thoughts and ideas occurs through the creation of classification systems that necessarily standardize and simplify ways of thinking—often ways of thinking about race and gender. Parsons argues that to resist these entrenched and often invisible systems for understanding the world, one has to understand how they develop and how they then operate in the minds of individuals. Benedict would eventually generalize, clarify, and deepen these ideas in *Patterns of Culture*.[4] Benedict's opening chapter forcefully tries to replace the belief that culture is somehow a

11. Ruth Benedict's mother, Bertrice Shattuck Fulton (1860–1953), a former librarian. Photo courtesy of Vassar College Libraries Archives and Special Collections.

"biologically transmitted complex" (*PC*, 14) by recognizing that "behaviors which we had always assumed to be innate and beyond our control were, in fact, determined by the nature of our social institutions."[5] She encourages the realization that even "a very little acquaintance with other conventions, and a knowledge of how various these may be, would do much" (*PC*, 10). At the heart of Benedict's statements is the suggestion that knowledge and awareness are the first steps toward discovering a place in which it is possible to feel greater freedom.

Benedict's particularly intense concern over her mother's treatment in the library and the ways that lack of regard reflected a flawed professionalization process for women was fueled by her own serious uncertainties about her career path. Even after she chose anthropology as a profession, she continued to think about the links between the library and her developing professional life as she worried over the deadening effect of her graduate school work in a library. She writes: "Class at nine—Library—Lunch with N. Kellner—Class—Back to Seminar room; exhaustion." And: "Worked in Library 10–6. Missed lunch till too late. Weary." Or: "The longest day I ever remember. Holiday—Worked in locked-up Barnard library on art all AM."[6] Although Benedict clearly is proud of what she accomplishes by being so disciplined, she also criticizes this library work in complaints that underscore her concern about whether certain kinds of intellectual sacrifices are a necessary part of the process of pursuing an anthropology degree (or any academic degree). She will expand on these arguments against library work in her anthropological and autobiographical writings during the next ten years. Her experience writing a dissertation, which she prepares entirely through library research (rather than ethnographic fieldwork) as is still the custom for anthropological projects in this period, leads her to suggest that intellectual reliance on the library contributes to a loss of curiosity.[7] She criticizes the old-style anthropologist reading in the library:

> The usual library-trained comparative student works with standard versions from each locality; in primitive cultures, usually one from a tribe. This version arbitrarily becomes "the" tribal tale, and is minutely compared with equally arbitrary standard tales from other tribes. But in such a body of mythology as that of Zuni, many different variants coexist, and the different forms these variants take cannot be ascribed to different historical levels, or even in large measure to particular tribal contacts, but are different literary combinations of incidents in different plot sequences. The comparative student may well learn from intensive studies not to point an argument that would be invalidated if half a dozen quite different versions from the same tribe were placed on record.[8]

She associates a kind of intellectual laziness with anthropologists who develop their thinking primarily through reading uncritically. Benedict's argument reiterates Ralph Waldo Emerson's much earlier concerns about libraries as places that encourage a belief in the authority of texts, resulting in a corresponding loss of critical skills, yet she updates his concerns to help provoke methodical transformations within the new discipline of anthropology.[9]

Both Benedict's personal experiences and her intellectual studies suggest to her that writing might function as just this kind of hoped-for escape (or certainly as an outlet) from these pressing professional concerns. In her books and courses Parsons had argued for this idea, offering Benedict the possibility of doing exactly what she already loved to do—write—as also the primary mode by which (in Parsons's terminology) to resist forces of authority or power without being engulfed by them. Parsons argued that as women matured in their awareness, so would they increasingly recognize that pursuing creative work would expand their understanding of how to undo or resist systems that oppress them (overtly or not). For Parsons, genuine knowledge cannot result unless these systems are recognized and resisted:

> From such a rigid classification the mind as it matures seeks escape. So a maturing culture struggles against its categories. At first it aims for mobility within them and then, as in these latter days, for freedom away from them. The time comes when it will drop its crude scheme of classification altogether, letting the facts, so to speak, take care of themselves. . . . No more segregated groups, no more covetous claims through false analogy, no more spheres of influence, for the social categories. And then the categories having no assurances to give to those unafraid of change and tolerant of unlikeness, to those of the veritable new freedom, to the whole-hearted lovers of personality, then the archaic categories will seem but the dreams of a confused and uneasy sleep, nightmares to be forgotten with the new day. (*SF*, 104–6)

She considers what damage might have already occurred to minds ("rigidity") as a result of being systematized. Yet she argues that eventually a woman—part of the "maturing culture"—will want to escape from these kinds of limits on thoughts, ideas, and emotions, and when that happens, there will be a greater possibility for social freedom and creativity for all of society (not only women). Benedict shares or easily adopts Parsons's philosophy (since she already loves to write and seems to view writing as one way to secure a place from which to consider other parts of her life), believing on some level that a writing life enables a certain freedom from the anxieties and limitations that she has observed in the professional sphere.

At the moment that Benedict is thinking about what necessary professional steps she needs to undertake to become a professor of anthropology, the discipline is also taking steps to become central to university studies. Susan Hegeman explains that by the late nineteenth century, Benedict's future teacher Franz Boas had already started to transform the structure of the discipline by objecting to the method that the Smithsonian's National Museum of Natural History used to display objects. Hegeman explains that "arguing that different types of objects should be displayed together, not according to function, but to their sites of origin," Boas's reorganization "has been seen as both a rejection of the evolutionary biologism that undergirded the older curatorial practices, and as the creation of a new ordering principle."[10] By the early twentieth century, the results of this rethinking are not only the reorganization of display cases but also the reorganization of the discipline—as "the transition from museum to university, from 'amateur' to 'professional' identities and practices, from artifact collection to participant-observer fieldwork" takes place.[11] Benedict's *Patterns of Culture* would popularize many of these intellectual concepts reflected in structural changes within the discipline.

While Benedict's critique of the usefulness of a career in the museum seems in keeping with this process already under way within the discipline of anthropology, it also reflects her careful observation of the professionalization process that began with her analysis of jobs in the library. Boas's critique of the Smithsonian display organization prompted a rethinking of the ethnographic museum's relationship to twentieth-century anthropology. While the initial result was a sense of separation between museums and universities, this institutional divide was often bridged as museums reorganized displays and continued to learn from anthropologists. Despite Boas's resignation as a curator from the American Museum of Natural History in 1905 (apparently a result of personality clashes with colleagues), he continued to devote attention to the space. By the 1920s, Columbia University anthropology students generally viewed a position at the American Museum of Natural History, where Boas had revolutionized display organization, as a necessary step for developing their careers. In her early years as an assistant to Boas, Benedict was required to teach courses at the American Museum of Natural History. She never became a curator there, however (as Franz Boas, Robert Lowie, and Margaret Mead had), and she also rejected opportunities for a dual appointment.[12]

Benedict's unwillingness to participate in this common museum practice suggests both her personal resistance to professional trends and her desire to carve out her own idiosyncratic approach to the discipline.[13] The reason she offers for not pursuing a museum job (alongside a university position) is because it interferes with her hope to develop a different way of thinking through writing, a belief that lasted at least until the late 1920s. In a reference to an impromptu discussion of poetry at the museum, Benedict gives a clue to her attitude. At a lunch with Dr. Goddard, who was then director of the museum, the discussion turns to poetry: "Lunch with Goddard and meet his daughter of FPA [Franklin Pierce Adams] verse fame. Dr. Boas joined us for dessert—He'd rather have written a good poem than all the books he'd ever written—to say nothing of a movement in a symphony. It was his answer to Goddard's veiled attempt to betray my poetic inclinations—whereat he guesses merely."[14] Benedict suspects that Boas reveals artistic inclinations to out her as a poet, suggesting the degree to which she feels the need to protect her imaginative life from the grasp of her colleagues. Margaret Mead interprets Benedict's protective attitude toward her own poetry as insecurity about her artistic promise, but Benedict's comments more likely suggest her desire to protect her imagination from those people she believes do not respect it.[15] Benedict's professional development at this time follows the cultural trajectory of the period—women were beginning the slow process of moving professionally away from museums and libraries and toward what they perceived as more prestigious work in universities.[16] Her personal sense of this journey, however, holds creative work, as Parsons argues and Boas seems to consider as well, as falling outside the grasp of this professionalization process.

Given her critique of libraries and museums as problematic professional spaces, Benedict's diaries reveal that she instead pursued a job at Columbia University, a place she initially viewed as distinct from and preferable to these other cultural institutions. She sometimes felt, however, that her ambition was greater than her ability, and she frequently worried that she did not deserve a college job. In a 1923 diary entry she writes: "worst sick headache I've had in years. I know my subconscious staged it—But really I suppose it's hanging on to the idea that I can teach at Barnard—which my conscious self has known I couldn't do—always."[17] In 1924, when informed by a board of university professors that her application for a grant was rejected because she was too old to apply, she initially accepts the setback as further proof that she cannot succeed at a career in the university.[18]

As her career progresses, however, her insecurities are replaced by annoyance at the way the university treats her. She kept records that show that she was frequently asked to do work for which she was not paid or paid a considerably lower amount than her male colleagues. For example, in the period between May 1926 and June 1927 Benedict is listed as a "Lecturer in Anthropology," and it is recorded that she received no salary for her work. She was asked to teach extension courses, and Benedict was suspicious that this request was another way for the anthropology department to use her to teach graduate students without any official position and at a much lower salary, something the department repeatedly tried to do. In 1930 she was made an assistant professor with an official salary, but in 1932 she was still teaching at least one extra extension course without a salary. While a recent biography of Columbia University describes Benedict's position in glowing terms as the "first woman to hold a full-time faculty position,"[19] in fact Benedict was earning, and quite aware of earning, significantly less money than less successful and less published male colleagues. Even after the success of *Patterns of Culture* in 1934, she was not promoted within the department. From 1933 to 1937 she remained an assistant professor of anthropology at a salary of $3,600. Only in 1937 did she finally receive a promotion to associate professor and a salary increase to $5,000, but her excitement at this promotion may have been dampened by the fact that Duncan Strong, the other associate professor in the anthropology department, was earning $6,000 and Ralph Linton, who had been brought to Columbia as a visiting professor and who Benedict disliked, was earning $7,500 for the same period.[20] By 1940, busy on the lecture circuit and working part-time in Washington, D.C., Benedict withdrew from departmental matters with negative feelings about the place.[21] There was a fight for the chair of the department that Ralph Linton won. Although she was eventually promoted to full professor, she withdrew from the department even more between 1940 and her death in 1948.

Unwilling to work in libraries or museums, in part because they did not offer her a sense of possibility for advancement and prestige that she believed a university offered, she found herself instead discriminated against for her age and gender at Columbia University. Benedict's professional and intellectual frustration—in the records she keeps, as well as the timing of her autobiographical essay—is evident. The usual story of the professionalization of anthropology argues that the Columbia anthropology department (under the leadership of Franz Boas, a Jewish immigrant) embraced other marginalized people, transforming the field by altering the makeup of a discipline that had formally included primarily "gentlemen explorers and military men."[22] Hegeman has argued that Franz Boas's "conception of himself as an autonomous and activist scholar was in some sense predicated on his position within the academy"[23]—and against the older model of ethnography whose conception of human cultural evolution he had opposed. Yet Benedict experienced the university as instantiating the same kinds of prejudices she first encountered in observing her mother's job in the library. Within this new, more open system, Benedict recognized old prejudices about women and work that had never gone away.

During this period of professionalization and difficult transitions in the 1920s, Benedict turned to poetry as a purer, that is, less institutionally sanctioned, practice—a view that she was both naturally inclined to believe and one that had been given increasing intellectual weight in her discussions with Parsons and Boas. She hoped to find in art a space in which to think outside of institutions. She found something else instead. Benedict, who idealized poetry and believed that aesthetic works were potentially a necessary escape from expectations for professional progress, had to reconsider these conclusions as she faced multiple rejections of her poems. She never entirely abandoned her idealism, but her unsuccessful efforts to publish suggested to her that the dissemination of those aesthetic ideas was possibly more difficult—at least as controlled and limited—by modern poetic professionalism as by anthropological professionalism. These investigations—what I call her ethnography of modernism—helped her to generate anthropological theories in response to the realization that poetry was just as exclusionary a field—with its own set of terms, rules, and roadblocks—as a professional life in the cultural institutions from which she sought escape.

Becoming a Poet: An Ethnography of Modernism

As a practicing poet, Benedict was—at least temporally—a high modernist. She wrote the vast majority of her approximately 150 poems in the fifteen-year period between 1919 and 1934. During those years she published only a small portion of them (about twenty) in a mixture of little magazines and mainstream publications such as *The Measure, Palms, Poetry, The Nation,* and the *New York Herald Tribune,* and she tried to publish many more. Her files include frequent rejection letters from editors. Her achievement and her failure as a poet culminated in 1928 in a rejection letter she received from Harcourt Brace for *November Burning,* the volume of poetry she had recently submitted at the urging of Louis Untermeyer. Despite these repeated and often harsh dismissals of her talent and effort, she struggled to produce a significant volume of poetry, rewriting and reorganizing this volume of poems for the next twenty years.

Benedict was not only temporally a high modernist, but she tried to publish like one as well. She respectably made her debut as a poet in the August 1926 *Poetry* magazine, publishing the short poem "Toy Balloons" under the name of "Alice Singleton," one of her pseudonyms. In fact, this appearance was not Benedict's first in that publication. She appeared slightly earlier, in the January 26 issue in which her good friend the linguistic anthropologist Edward Sapir (fig. 12) dedicated his poem series, "Foam-Waves," "To A.S." Sapir's use of her pen-name initials was a sign of his respect for Benedict at the time because he later made it very clear that he was personally against her use of pseudonyms. Just as Ezra Pound served to introduce Hilda Doolittle to the establishment by signing her poem "H.D." in a 1912 issue of *Poetry,* Sapir's choice of initials seemed at least an ambivalent nod in the direction of that radical and splashy dedication (of which he would certainly have known and likely disapproved).

12. Edward Sapir (1884–1939). Photo courtesy of Vassar College Libraries Archives and Special Collections.

Despite Sapir's initial championing of her work, ultimately both he and the anthropologist Margaret Mead—her closest friends during the 1920s—criticized it without fully appreciating Benedict's artistic and intellectual process. As a result of their strong and frequent critiques, it is no longer possible to encounter her poems without first encountering what others, particularly Sapir and Mead, negatively have said about them. In fact, although her 1928 manuscript was Benedict's primary achievement in writing during the 1920s, its future was entirely in the hands of Mead as Benedict's literary executor. Mead eventually chose to publish only a small portion of poems from Benedict's unpublished volume, a group of poems that Benedict copied out for her as a present in 1941.

Mead argued that the majority of Benedict's poems rightly remained unpublished during her lifetime because they were poor imitations of the work of more accomplished contemporaries. She pointed out that Benedict's poetry was influenced by other more successful modern poets (several of whom she personally introduced to Benedict) such as the lyricists Louise Bogan, Léonie Adams, and a wider circle including Elinor Wylie, Edna St. Vincent Millay, and Amy Lowell. In the context of these other poets that Mead admired, she discounted the effectiveness of Benedict's style, encouraging a rather cursory reading of the poetry:

> Chief among these relationships which, for the first time, made her interest in writing poetry a lively, shared preoccupation was her friendship with Edward Sapir, which began in formal anthropological terms but soon overflowed into an interchange of poems and discussions of poetry. As she came to know Léonie Adams and Louise Bogan and Eda Lou Walton, she had their poems, too, to enjoy in manuscript and as part of the lives of people she knew. Many of our poems grew out of our relationships to one another, and the intensities of the contemporary human plots were discussed and rediscussed against the background of the childhood experience and special temperament of each.[24]

Only occasionally would Benedict also admit that she was a lesser poet than those in her wider and more well-known circle. Mead writes that "each of us made a different contribution. The poems of Léonie Adams gave [Benedict] pure delight and a measure of her own slender gift. Long, intricate discussions with me marked the self-awareness."[25] Mead slyly suggests—almost as proof of her own conclusions—that when confronted with the work of a superior poet, Benedict understood that she had a rather "slender gift." Mead chose to publicize Benedict's poems as not only less established versions of the work of these other poets but also as the products of "childhood experience" and "special temperament."[26] By linking Benedict's poetry to her personal feelings, Mead simplified the poems into reflections of temporary moods. Mead dismissed her own efforts at poetry, but she compared her realization that there were better poets to Benedict's less complete understanding of her own limited poetic talent.

Mead's evident annoyance at Benedict's attachment to her own poetry (despite her repeated publishing failures) underscores a major difference in their attitudes toward the relationship between writing and culture. In editing *An Anthropologist at Work: Writings of Ruth Benedict* (1959), the first major collection of Benedict's work to appear after her death in 1948, Mead argues that Benedict was a far better anthropologist than she ever was a poet. Prepared from Mead's intimate and long-standing knowledge of Benedict—Mead was initially Benedict's student, then friend, and later colleague—the volume opened up to the public some of Benedict's work that was previously unpublished or unknown but simultaneously closed off certain approaches to this work by offering primarily autobiographical readings of the poems.[27] Mead revealed Benedict to be a searching, thoughtful figure whose experiments with language were alternately immature and almost good and who finally understood that she must abandon her untutored aesthetic ambition and focus her approach in anthropology. Mead's authoritative view of Benedict permanently stamped the way her writing, and her poetry particularly, was received while at the same time actively promoting recognition of its existence in anthropological circles (a fact that Benedict kept rather private).[28]

While both Mead and Sapir offer different explanations for Benedict's lack of success as a poet, both showed frustration at what they viewed as Benedict's naive attitude toward the relationship between writing and culture. For Mead, Sapir's influence on Benedict was perhaps not profound enough, but it was mostly positive: "it was in the vivid, voluminous correspondence with Edward Sapir that her own poetic interest and capacity matured. Only one side of their correspondence—his letters to her—survive. . . . Each planned a book of verse. . . . In 1928, Harcourt Brace turned down her manuscript of verse in an unsigned letter."[29] Mead suggests that Benedict learned something important from working so closely on poetry with Sapir. Benedict's missing correspondence with Sapir is mentioned but not dwelt on; Mead sees Benedict's side of their correspondence as represented in Sapir's comments and ideas—again suggesting that she finds Benedict's poetry lacking in literary independence and originality.[30]

While Mead views Benedict's exclusion from modernist poetic publications in the 1920s as a fair assessment of her limited talent, Sapir interprets Benedict's lack of success as further proof of the exclusiveness of modernist poetic practices. In both of their views, however, Benedict is characterized as not recognizing that poetic practice involves its own set of exclusions and inclusions—its own cultural system (an issue of which she was acutely conscious in her anthropological work). Sapir often took it on himself to explain to Benedict how culturally problematic modernist poetic practice was. Although Sapir's preference for one style over another might have been a personal one, he argued fiercely against modernist attitudes and subjects through the philosophy that good poetry requires distance from contemporary experience:

> Do not make the cardinal mistake (for you) of essaying any but worthy themes. I am becoming still further convinced (I have just read "Our Task Is Laughter") that you will do well to give the sonnet a rest. You do it thoroughly well but its external prettiness does not quite go with good style of matter. Try severer forms—crisp, angular patterns that will drive you to your very best, sudden, and sardonic expression.[31]

> The last sentence [of "Genessaret"] is tremendously apt and gives that impression of reserved strength which your best verse always gives.[32]

He argues that good poetry must resist the poetic establishment's intent to modernize both its subject matter and its form. In an essay on rhyme that he published in 1920, he makes several comments that he repeats to Benedict in letters later on: "We like to think that form and subject matter are wedded from the beginning in an indissoluble unity. But all art is largely technique, and technique involves experimentation, rejection, selection, [and] modification of the originally envisaged theme."[33] For Sapir any issue of form is always also intimately connected to his feelings of rejection—his sense of not belonging to a particular modernist club. He views American modernism as an exclusive thing with its own set of geographical, experiential, and stylistic rules not always openly stated and often distinguished by allegiance to and frequent publication in particular little magazines. Perhaps it was Sapir's sensitivity to this point that spurred him to refer to Benedict so discreetly by initials in *Poetry,* since his choice succeeds in implying that Sapir is part of an exclusive club of his own. Despite his complaints about modernist cultural practices, he is not above invoking his own set of cultural concerns.

Sapir chafed under a sense that his writing was prejudged by a set of restrictions with which he claimed vigorously not to agree. Although he seemed to take every criticism of his work extremely personally, he responded to rejections (of his poems and, loyally, of Benedict's) from modernist publications such as Harriet Monroe's sensibility at *Poetry* and, beginning in 1925, Marianne Moore's desk at *Dial,* with a defensiveness that also served as an attack on modernist exclusiveness:

> "Withdrawal" is magnificent a fresh old English flavor that adds to the more modern feeling. But will Harriet Monroe or the current *Mea-*

> *sure* editor take it? I doubt it. Anything but passion. One must know how to write for cowards.[34]

> I attribute Harriet's reaction chiefly to her inveterate softness or sentimentality. Difficult or in any way intellectual verse gets past her only with difficulty. She prefers stuff about sweet love and my baby.[35]

> Seeing "The Dirge" in *The Dial* gave me a momentary feeling of being a poet, but scant reflection showed the unconvincingness of the argument. . . . The age and I don't seem to be on very intimate speaking terms. In the last number of "Poetry," for instance, I find almost nothing that remotely interests me. I think the ideology of a Hupa medicine formula is closer to my heart than all this nervous excitement of Hart Crane's. Can you tell me what he wants? You spoke of Mark Van Doren's excellence. I've not read his recently published book but the citations in the review in "Poetry" were not very alluring. They sounded more like keen cerebration in verse form than poetry. And I'm utterly sick of intelligence and its vanity. It's the arch disease of the time and the reason for its choking vulgarity and its flimsiness. . . . The experimental excitements of this great modern time do not rouse me, they chill me to loathing.[36]

For Sapir modernist poetry is both too detached and overly excited, both anti-intellectual and too intellectual, both extremely sentimental and anxious. Hart Crane and Mark Van Doren are both held up as examples of the same problem, though it would be difficult to discover two poets with greater differences in style or attitude. The obvious contradictions in these comments suggest that Sapir's primary complaint is that he feels his work is being misjudged. He "loathes" the "experimental excitements" in poetry, which he perceives as merely changing whims. Even his phrasing suggests his condescension toward those who are excited by current literary styles.

While Sapir trusts Benedict during the 1920s primarily because he believes that they share similar views about modern poetry, there are important indications that she recognized some truth in his critique of the exclusivity of modernist poetic professionalism without fully sharing his bitterness about it. After sending her the latest version of a completed manuscript, he responds to her comments: "Thank you very much for your very careful reading of the MS. As you may have noticed from my new table of contents, I followed all your suggestions in regard to order of pieces, exclusion and inclusion, and title."[37] He responds positively to her "suggestions" about which poems to keep. Sapir's comment shows that he trusts Benedict and is obviously interested in improving the order and look of his volume of poems. Yet his thinking also reveals that he views concerns about poetry—both personal ones (the look of a manuscript) and professional ones (acceptance in modernist magazines)—primarily in terms of a vocabulary of "exclusion and inclusion." Benedict, however, does not accept all of Sapir's suggestions about her poems, often leaving lines and stanzas exactly the same way she had first written them despite his criticisms.[38] Many of Benedict's poems are also directly written in response to contemporary experience, particularly to feelings of disappointment in her job at the university. In her papers at Vassar College there are also examples of poems and notes about poetry written on the backs of grant applications and academic letterhead.[39] Although none of her poems directly address her experience as a professor at Columbia, her poems do astutely express her uncertainty as to how to behave freely and feel free intellectually when evidence suggests that one's thinking is shaped by forces beyond the scope of individual experience. Unlike Sapir, who directed his anger at specific editors, magazines, and modernist ideologies, Benedict's struggle for respect and fair treatment in a career and her efforts to publish poems that ideally exist outside that conflict but still manage to comment on it emerge in her thinking within the poems.

Benedict's reaction to Sapir's sense of unfairness in the modernist poetry market was not to become as angry as he did but to use her experience to better understand an individual's relationship to culture. Thus, her personal experience of not publishing leads her to the specific and practical task of coming up with new methods for asking questions about how individual beliefs emerge within a culture. This attitude and practice illustrate, of course, that she was certainly not as naive as either Sapir feared or Mead accused. Benedict sums up her view in a 1938 lecture, explaining that "human nature for the anthropologist is just a special set of habits that have grown up in a special society, and it varies according to the institutions of that society."[40] Defining culture as the developing institutions within a society that shape human nature, she suggests that an individual should always be in a process of reflecting what a culture is through reactions to limited and constantly shifting frameworks—and she always believed that writing was one of the safest places to do that. For Hegeman the discipline of anthropology's new insistence that there are multiple cultural systems, that cultures are always in flux, and that individuals are often "estranged" from their experience within them is its most modernist quality.[41] Benedict, however, takes this recognition a step further. She does not stop at her recognitions of feelings of "estrange[ment]" from dominant cultures or the constant state of change within cultures to which individuals must adapt themselves, but she explores ways for individuals to respond to these uncertainties positively through efforts at awareness in art. For Benedict an idea of escape is a way to exist within something and acknowledge its forces while still protecting oneself from it.

Undoing the usual reading of Benedict's poetry as merely reflections of her moods and personal crises, I consider these poems instead as necessary parts of the process by which she expressed her understanding of how individuals are shaped by, try to escape from, and react to culture. One way to reconsider the meaning of these poems is by interpreting them not in terms of the order and date in which she initially wrote them, as most critics have done, but to consider them together as she planned them in her ultimately unpublished book.[42] Her 1928 manuscript and its subsequent revisions suggest that Benedict always held out the hope that there were some ways in which the individual (even the ambitious individual) could escape the demands of culture in order to obtain some sense of genuine freedom. In both her poetic and her anthropological texts during the 1920s, she championed close reading, comparative judgment, and analytical rigor as the kind of work necessary to becoming culturally aware.[43] Her insistence on these methods for understanding arose from her knowledge of both the writing and publishing processes.

Writing and revising her poems involved a kind of focus and attention that Benedict believed was missing from the old-style anthropologists' museum and library work. She also thought that the questions she had to answer in trying to write—about what it means to be a good reader, how to remain open to the possibilities for how a narrative might function, and whether rejection meant exclusion as Sapir and Mead argued—were the very questions that contemporary anthropologists needed to ask in undertaking worthwhile ethnographic fieldwork. Her investment in all of these techniques for improving cultural awareness and the freedom of the individual thinker ultimately led to her dedication to rewriting poems and revising and rethinking her poetry manuscript over the next twenty years, despite (though, in some ways, because of) her consistent failures to publish.

Cultural Awareness and Creativity in *November Burning*

Benedict's unpublished essay on Mary Wollstonecraft (composed just before graduate school) and her devotion to creating a poetic manuscript (which began during graduate school and continued to the end of her life) demonstrate how she increasingly understood ways that creativity and culture are closely linked in modern life. The most enduring aspect of the Wollstonecraft manuscript is Benedict's insistence on illustrating Wollstonecraft's thinking process as a prime example of twentieth-century American modernism. She argues repeatedly that not only Wollstonecraft's life and ideas "might all be clipped from our twentieth century," but her "pitiless thirst for understanding afresh" and the "experimental" quality of her intellect are thoroughly modern.[44] The essay captures Benedict's belief in thinking as a creative process and in thinking widely and wildly—"forever probing"—as exemplifying modern American possibilities for continuous study and discovery. The Wollstonecraft essay offers a clear sense of what Benedict hoped was the "spirit of the age" and what she also wanted to accomplish in her own work. Her poetic manuscript, which I read in its final archived form as *November Burning,* is a continuation of the ideas that Benedict set forth in the Wollstonecraft essay on the excitement of a probing, analytical, creative spirit, but it is also shaped by her related and recent efforts to move modern anthropology out of the library, to free researchers from long-held prejudices, and to enable them to become more culturally aware.

In *November Burning* Benedict demonstrates how difficult it is for human beings to become aware of themselves as both products and agents of their culture. The poems, however, are critical of people's desires to withdraw from or claim power over nature (and each other), in part because she recognizes that human beings depend on the very processes that they try hardest to control and sublimate. Benedict's manuscript celebrates creativity, and despite countless rewrites and consistent rejection, these poems reiterate the worth of any imaginative process as one that focuses thinking. Benedict argues that imaginative outlets are a crucial part of the process of becoming—as she put it in *Patterns of Culture*—"genuinely culture-conscious" (*PC,* 10). She demonstrates in this volume that the achievement of the creative process is both its ability to enable constant awareness of social experience's influences on thinking and an indefinable quality of making its practitioner feel more intellectually and physically free.

Although Mead and others have claimed that her writing slowed down after the book's initial rejection in 1928, there are convincing indications that Benedict continued to work on and rewrite these poems quite seriously through the 1940s. She submitted the manuscript in a finished form to Harcourt Brace in 1928, but drafts of this volume contain multiple names, pseudonyms, and addresses on the title page and on specific poems, suggesting how often and in how many different locations she continued to work on it.[45] She also still collected lists of magazines to which she could submit single poems in the mid-1930s, marking off possibilities on a 1935 list.[46] The final copy of this book was a short version that she handwrote and delivered to Margaret Mead in 1941. Mead included this version (with noted changes) in *An Anthropologist at Work.*

In the existing draft of this volume, deposited in Ruth Benedict's papers at the Vassar College Libraries Archives and Special Collections, the manuscript is organized with a prefatory "Dedication" followed by five sections, each consisting of between eight and eleven poems. Although she never resubmitted the entire manuscript after Harcourt Brace's 1928 rejection, she continued to revise the table of contents as she wrote new poems and changed her mind about older ones. The poems are no longer attached to their sites of origin in personal letters, journal entries, and initial publications (since certain poems published originally in magazines in groups are separated and reordered). In the new manuscript, formerly published and unpublished, accepted and rejected poems exist side by side, and the context of all of the poems becomes the building argument that the manuscript makes through its five sections.[47]

The straightforward, three-stanza opening "Dedication" suggests the direction for the five sections to follow: a project about a long process of enlightenment. Written in quatrains with understated rhymes, the poem chronicles a secret experience of learning to "see" properly and what that process might help an individual to achieve:

Haws when they blossom in the front of summer,
Snow breasted to the sun, and odorous
Of wind dissolved honey, flaunt their bodies,
Secret and quick, to eyes incurious.

Their fertile golden dust the wind shall scatter,
Surfeited bees maul yet one feast the more,
And all their dainty-stepping petals flutter
At last and publicly to grassy floor.

Still through their roots runs the most secret liquor
No wind shall tamper, no hurrying bee shall sip;
Let the haws blossom, let their petals scatter,
In covert earth wine rises to their lip.[48]

This opening poem explores the territory the entire volume will cover as it attempts to explore a "most secret liquor." At first, the poem describes simply a rite of spring, when "haws blossom." "Wind" and "bees" "maul" the flower, trying to reach its "liquor"; this process, though it looks harsh to the outsider, is a natural one that enables bees to live and flowers to grow. There are other, less obvious, threats to the flower's continued growth, however, and the poem suggests that the flower must be able to maintain some part of its "most secret liquor" in order to survive. The poem ends by acknowledging that threats exist, and the narrator asks how an object or a person can protect itself and its uniqueness in the face of potential defacement or extinction. In this poem the secret is buried deeply enough in the flower's "roots" that nothing can reach it. Once the threats diminish, the flower can "covert[ly]" drink the "wine." Benedict's entire volume follows the logic of this opening poem. Within the five sections and through multiple poems, Benedict shows how human beings suffer constant threats to whatever they view as most precious—often their creativity or their sense of freedom—but that through a slow and difficult combination of self-protection and enlightenment, they can (and must) learn to thrive even in a seemingly hostile environment. In the narrative the book offers, however, the desires to protect oneself and to gain enlightenment are often in direct conflict; in each of these short poems the narrator is sympathetic to, but also a harsh critic of, the conflict, generally arguing through each stanza that a need for new knowledge ought to override concerns for personal security.

Section 1 develops these ideas, describing the difficulties of feeling free enough to protect one's ideas while still being open enough to finding new ones. In the opening poem, "But the Son of Man," the speaker berates human beings for their willingness to exist without understanding their own environment.[49] Offering a comparison with the way foxes live, the speaker notes that people would like to exist in winter as foxes do, oblivious to difficulties:

> Foxes have holes, and in the wintry weather
> Save themselves warm at price of breath and bone;
> Playing to shortened strength a shortened tether,
> Taking to breast a stone.
>
> Their light feet tranced, their blood become as earthy
> As sodden marshes when the flood is gone,
> They sleep, not knowing bereavement, content, worthy
> The ecstasy withdrawn.
>
> So at the winter of the blood we straighten
> Our limbs to quiet, crying flesh to find
> Oblivion as the fox's, sun forsaken,
> Deaf and dumb and blind.

The narrator initially admires the way foxes can "save themselves" in winter. Foxes do not build holes to save themselves; they already *have* them, suggesting that they are animals always prepared to protect themselves if they need to. Though hungry and weak, the animals nonetheless know how to "play" to survive. Even in these conditions, they know how to comfort themselves, and the narrator's attitude toward them is straightforward and respectful.

In the second stanza, though, the narrator becomes more critical of this period of hibernation. Remembering how foxes behave when awake, the narrator traces the process through which "their blood becomes as earthy / As sodden marshes." They are, literally, one with the earth; this phenomenal process, however, which enables them to remain protected from the experience of loss, is equally a barrier from any experience of "ecstasy." While the narrator seems in the first stanza impressed by the foxes' ability to "save themselves," she suggests in the second that, as a result, they miss an experience of joy.

The speaker finally connects the foxes' experience to her own in the final stanza. In her quiet way she chastises fellow human beings who manage to remain in a state of not knowing, pretending as though it were a natural state. We all have "the winter of the blood" (also a title for the book that Benedict seriously considered), she suggests—a moment of quiet, when blood flows more thickly, slowly, and all the agonies of experience are quieted. This experience, however natural and pleasurable the earlier parts of the poem suggest, is one in which our senses become "deaf and dumb and blind." The volume considers physical experience both profoundly painful and absolutely necessary to a process of gaining real knowledge and enlightenment. And through this poem the volume begins in earnest its analysis of ways to resolve a perceived conflict between a desire to limit the experience of the body and a wish to explore the expansiveness of the mind.

Just as Elsie Clews Parsons had anxiously tried to explain in *Social Rule,* Benedict argues more metaphorically in these poems that individuals pay a high price for not being fully aware of what happens to them. Parsons makes the point both a critique of systems of control and a call for awareness: "The will to power and more particularly the will to power over other people is a more general character than we are quite aware of. There is an enormous amount of energy put to controlling or regulating human creatures, to keeping them in their place, to keeping them in order" (*SR,* 6). Parsons's critique of the systems designed to create a rational order suggests that she wants something other than order. Benedict agrees. Her poems idealize creativity as possibly the only tool in the individual's arsenal that offers the potential to resist a powerful force.

As Benedict establishes creativity as the primary means through which an individual can withstand her culture in this first section, it makes sense that she explores various experiments for accessing creativity in middle sections of the book. At first, the speaker is less confident that an individual will be able to be creative in order to feel free. In "Sleet Storm," the opening poem of the second section,[50] the narrator imagines a long and difficult night of reflection:

Dusk came grayly with an iron weight
That gathered from the unsubstantial air
Stilly upon the boughs. Upon their spare
And delicate limbs it laid its body straight
And inescapable, an old lust bare
Of joy, and terrible with hate.

All night there was no respite where they stood,
Broken with weight, brittle with agony;
And winds made plaything of catastrophe,
And, for their pain, smote laughter through that wood,
Wherein ice-shackled branches grievously
Cried out for interlude.

O terror of snapped limbs, and dread that night,
At quiet morning had the sun but looked
An hour from heaven, we had brooked
The night its torment. The valley lay to light
A blossoming paradise. And we have looked
In vain, until the night.

In this poem the process of reaching some light, some sense of relief, is described in detail but not yet realized. Again, as with many of her poems, Benedict transfers a human process of losing fear and gaining strength to a story of the landscape. In the first stanza the heaviness of dusk and its "inescapable" qualities envelop a tree with the awful nakedness of an "old lust bare / Of joy, and terrible with hate." The night that this tree must spend surrounded by its long ago passion is almost too much for it to bear "for there was no respite where it stood." As in other poems, natural events destroy—or try to destroy—the seemingly unmovable, staunch object. During the second stanza, the tree barely withstands the assault as the winds "made plaything of catastrophe" and its "ice-shackled branches grievously / Cried out for interlude." In the last stanza, however—as in many of Benedict's short lyrics—although the narrative concludes, the process the poem describes is far from over. Even though there is finally daylight, the light cannot fully relieve the pressure of the previous darkness or pain. The morning is "quiet" but reveals no "light." If there were light, the speaker could imagine that the valley would look like "a blossoming paradise," but this hope is "in vain," at least until another night passes. The poem ends inconclusively; though having endured a painful process of trying to reach the "light," the narrator indicates that her idea of a bright place of paradise is so powerful that it also serves as an indication that this process will be repeated until it succeeds.

Benedict uses religious stories in section 3 broadly and metaphorically to stand in for this cycle toward a fruitful process of imagination and creation.[51] These poems illustrate the degree to which this hope for enlightenment takes an astonishing amount of sustained effort. In "Annunciation" she writes:

Wide-eyed, O Mary, take the branching lily;
The slant light falls no otherwise today
Than all your quiet days, and if it blossoms
Most lover-like, this god shall disarray

No fold of your slight garments. Therefore go forward
Boldly, your inadvertent maidenhood
Unstirred as yesterday. Draw no curtain
Before this place lest any passing should

Spy on the coming of the holy lover;
In likeness of a dove, as casual
As any perching pigeon, he shall settle
In your blue-kerchiefed bosom. He shall dwell

In your girl's body as a prayer chastely.
Though you grow great with god, desire shall be
A song you know not, and sometimes you'll wonder
When, tending sheep, girls talk of ecstasy.

But after, when you have gone in to Joseph,
And borne to him, out of desire, a son,
Will you not pity us, a timid people,
Who confound so the god, the holy one?

In *Patterns of Culture* she also elaborates on the idea that in Western civilizations religion and art had a kind of intimate connection that was often not found in other cultures (*PC*, 38). In "Annunciation" the subject is less the religious experience of incarnation than the fact that "wide-eyed," innocent Mary intuitively recognizes that women have feelings and experiences beyond what she knows. Yet Benedict suggests that it is precisely Mary's ability to remain connected to, but apart from, broader experience that makes her a spiritual being and a source of admiration to the speaker.

"Annunciation" is also one of Benedict's longer poems, though like her briefer lyrics, it tells a story that does not fully resolve by the final stanza. Unlike Benedict's nature poems, however, which tend to treat flowers and trees as stand-ins for reticent and emotionally complex human beings on which the local environment enacts a certain kind of test or punishment, Mary exists outside these sorts of constraints and anxieties. Although she seems too innocent and untouched to fully understand the complexities of a population quite unlike her, the narrator calls on her to help. In the last stanza the narrator suggests that Mary might be better able to help this "timid" people than the god that so "confound[s]" them. In describing a Mary whose behavior is rather idiosyncratic, Benedict seems to signal beyond Christianity to a Mary she knows much better: Mary Wollstonecraft. In Benedict's analysis of this other Mary (for whom childbirth, also, is linked to the end of a life and a new beginning), an intellectual woman in the eighteenth century is illustrated as an ideal model and leader—a prophet—for the intellectual woman trying to find her way in the twentieth century and all innocent and searching figures like her.

The title poem, "November Burning," which opens section 4, reiterates the question that "Annunciation" poses—who will watch over human beings and pity them enough to lead them toward a state of greater knowledge and less confusion?—and it begins a process of trying to discover an answer.[52] As a short, ambitious poem that alludes to, edits, and critiques T. S. Eliot's *The Waste Land*, "November Burning" claims a central place in the development of the searching, plaintive mood of the entire volume. Just as in many of Benedict's other poems, its surface narrative describes a rite of fall:

> Meadows, the harvest done, the kernelled corn
> Filched for the granaries, are given to flame,
> To flame that fashions of dry useless things
> Brief flowers of no name.

The poem begins with the word *meadows*, which produces one kind of natural image, but that image is immediately undercut by the clauses that modify it. The meadows are, in fact, empty meadows as the corn has been hauled off the ground to store in a building for the winter. The meadows are being burnt, but this burning is useful; it gets rid of "dry useless things" to enable (much later) a new field of corn to grow. The poem ends: "let the dead find / Life's apotheosis" and suggests that it is through this ritual burning that something transcendent and visionary asserts itself. These rituals allow for something—possibly artistic and beautiful—to arise after necessary destruction. Just as in William Carlos Williams's brief "Farmer," on the farmer-artist who surveys the desolate winter land and can imagine exactly how he will do his spring planting, which appeared (without the later addition of title) in *Spring and All* (1923), Benedict's poem celebrates the ability of the imagination to help reorganize and rebuild in the face of nothing. As a kind of response to the "stony rubbish" of *The Waste Land,* Benedict's poem answers Eliot's and suggests more certainly and idealistically that the process of not growing can lead to growth.

She develops this idea of the potential usefulness of the creative process at the end of this section by suggesting that this process (more than its products) can function effectively as a mode of resistance against confusion and constraint. "In Praise of Uselessness," which reiterates Edith Wharton's anxiety about the pitfalls of committing to a philosophy of usefulness, offers praise for the creative effort, no matter how useless it seems:

> Let it be useless as the winds at dusk
> In river shallows, or the dalliance
> Of crimsons in the sunset. Know, this husk
> Men cast to careless winds, and lift no glance
> From their plowed, harrowed meadows, lovelier
> Than any mouldering kernel in the loam
> Shall lift on delicate breezes. Wherefore stir
> The earth to futile pregnancy for whom
> We know are futile, and cast forth the brief
> Plump grain our day shall grant no more of? Here's
> The surety shall garner-up of grief
> Its loveliness; of love, remembering tears.

The opening sentence confidently suggests that what seems "useless" is often as beautiful as "the winds at dusk." The next few sentences underline this thought, commanding the listener to recognize that what is thrown away or not even considered is often "lovelier" than what is kept. The poem continues considering these paradoxes, asking in different ways, Why work so hard to create something that will exist so temporarily or that will simply go unappreciated? The narrator wants to be convinced that "the brief / plump grain" is worth the "pregnancy" that it takes to conceive it, but she cannot fully give up the idea that the experience might be "futile" simply because it is brief. But the sounds of *g* and *l* that huddle around the last sentence (and the response to the narrator's question) suggest, at least, a sense of aesthetic unity in the answer: "Here's / The surety shall garner-up of grief / Its loveliness; of love remembering tears." The sonorous ending to the poem offers guarded optimism; there is no "surety," the narrator contends, but there really is "loveliness," something perhaps even better.

The fifth and final section offers hope about the role a creative process can play in mediating even the most difficult experiences of individuals.[53] In "And His Eyes Were Opened," Benedict retells the story of Adam's awakening from the point of view of his ancestors:

> Suddenly from the sky, lacquered with light,
> Light fell, a mask withdrawn, and the gold stars
> Stood fixed in austere heaven. It was not night,
> For still the jewel of the water lay
> Thick flawed with glitter, its more lovely scars,
> And sunshine splintered in the grass all day.
>
> He was not mad, for to his hands the bark
> Was harsh as always, and the low-hung fruit
> Dripped shadows to his eyes; only the arc
> Of heaven, letting fall its casual veil,
> Stood intricate panoplied, all its minute
> And jeweled loveliness his holy grail.
>
> After, he went so canopied at noon,
> His seeing loosed upon a tameless glory.
> He laughed that we, who know the stars, so soon
> Believe them shattered, day on day, or make
> Imponderable light an old wives' story,
> A glittering curtain that no eye can break.
>
> Secure in sight that held its level way
> To tangible barriers, he left to us
> The insubstantial fables, that, some day,
> No stone being shifted, will as then make bare
> The world new-minted, the sky luminous
> With stars at noontime, laughter on the air.

Like most of her poems, this one tells a story. The first stanza describes the sudden appearance of light from the sky. This description of creation is at first somewhat impersonal: "a mask withdrawn." From the syntax of this stanza, it is not clear if the mask is the sky's or a person's. Initially, the new light affects only nature.

Although never named, the "he" who appears in the second stanza is an Adam-like figure. Not unlike Moore's more specific depiction of Adam in "Marriage," this Adam also seems slow and confused by the sudden shift in what he can see of his environment. The narrator points out that, at first, he does not notice any changes, for "the bark" of the tree from which he picks fruit "Was harsh as always." The third stanza suggests that his new sight is limited and his awareness of new things to see remains limited also. Although "His seeing" is "loosed upon a tameless glory," he becomes almost immediately aware of the limitations of his sight, the fact that what exists is a "glittering curtain that no eye can break."

In her final thought about the story just told, the narrator suggests that Adam's legacy is a realization of these limitations of knowing. Once he feels comfortable—"Secure in sight"—and he knows how to look, he is able to leave his ancestors only "the insubstantial[ity]" of that kind of seeing and knowing. There is, of course, the promise still that "some day" a kind of seeing that makes "bare / The world new-minted, the sky luminous" will become still possible, but even in Paradise that kind of substantial knowledge only exists as a future possibility.

In "Eucharist" Benedict directly develops her ideas from "And His Eyes Were Opened," underscoring her final point that an individual's quest for knowledge is, in part, about a desire to gain creative freedom through knowing. Benedict is aware of what is potentially problematic about learning how to see clearly, but she believes the effort is worthwhile:

Light the more given is the more denied.
Though you go seeking by the naked seas,
Each cliff etched visible, and all the waves
Pluming themselves with sunlight, of this pride
Light makes her sophistries.

You are not like to find her, being fed
Always with that she shines on. Only those
Storm driven down the dark, see light arise,
Her body broken for their rainbow bread,
At late and shipwrecked close.

The poem's pithy first sentence—"Light the more given is the more denied"—summarizes the rest of the stanza, which reflects on the difficulty of being truly aware. "Eucharist" also reiterates the famous opening to Emile Durkheim's *Primitive Classification,* a work Benedict knew well: "When a person who has been blind since birth is operated on and given sight, he does not directly see the phenomenal world which we accept as normal. Instead, he is afflicted by a painful chaos of forms and colours. . . . Only very slowly and with intense effort can he teach himself that this confusion does indeed manifest an order."[54] Benedict had referenced Durkheim's ideas in *The Concept of the Guardian Spirit in North America* (1923) and would again use them in *Patterns of Culture.* Although this poem does not claim any direct connection to Durkheim's essay, Benedict's description of the confusion that arises with the experience of suddenly gaining insight and then beginning to recognize how one's thinking has been shaped derives directly from Durkheim's initial point. In both works the structure of the world is utterly overwhelming to those too intelligently skeptical or questioning to accept automatically what they experience as true, yet some improvements can be made simply by understanding the difficulty of maintaining one's consciousness.

Benedict ends the volume with the kind of modestly hopeful tone that she has tried to find throughout. "Resurgam," not quite a sonnet, efficiently sums up the argument of the volume:

> This is the season when importunate rains
> Rutting the graves unearth slim skeletons
> We buried to corruption, and strong winds
> Whip from the ocean where no passing suns
> Strike nethermost, the bones we wept beside.
> Now is the season of our mourning past
> And reek forgotten, the white loveliness
> Of ivory ours to play with. Now at last
> Our griefs are overspanned, decay played out,
> And nothing dead but it is perfected.
> Come, of the bones we'll make us flutes and play
> Our hearts to happiness, where worms have fed.

Again, Benedict struggles with Eliot's world of death and darkness but finds in it something hopeful. Benedict's optimism is muted by the final phrase, "where worms have fed," but the speaker is willing to admit that within this darkness "we'll make us flutes and play / Our hearts to happiness." Moments of enlightenment that result from experiences of creativity will preserve memories and promote feelings of freedom and "happiness." The volume ends with this opportunity not exactly to overcome the natural, decaying world, but to find a creative way to live within it.

Benedict's plans for *November Burning* did not succeed as she had originally envisioned them, since the volume always remained unpublished, but her work succeeded as a demonstration of the modernist intellectual ideals she had first outlined in her biography of Mary Wollstonecraft. The process of writing and failing to publish taught Benedict about the relationship between her intellectual passions and professional goals and also the distinction between literary and cultural histories. The rejection gave her insights both within the poems and in *Patterns of Culture,* which reiterates the necessity of understanding the distinctive (and not always obviously productive) creative process within each culture.[55] Her intellectual experience working on her own poems as she developed anthropological methods also suggested to her that new patterns for understanding could be revealed through a commitment to writing and thinking. Every effort to reorder or rethink her work gave her new opportunities to organize her ideas into a coherent whole in a single volume. The volume never could live up publicly to her hopes for its achievement, remaining unpublished and replaced in public memory by both the smaller, less ambitious group of poems that Benedict gave to Mead in 1941 and by Mead's criticism of her poetic efforts as purely emotional and personal.[56] Benedict's realization that failure to publish does not mean failure to learn meant that she could mourn the poems' lack of an audience and still believe them to be representative of the worth of an aesthetic and intellectual process. She could recognize the writing process (with or without publication) as one that also allowed an individual to function within a dominant, professional culture and still remain aware enough to feel free within it. This distinction between failure to publish and failure as a poet was one that Mead did not make in reading the poems so literally as the work of a failed professional poet. Benedict used her obvious failures to discover an intellectual through line connecting her thinking about women's professional lives with her thinking about poetry. This realization would enable her effective creation of a new anthropological method.

A New Method

To understand how Benedict thought about poetry, it is necessary to understand how she thought about her own culture, particularly her critique of women's professions beginning with library work; to understand how Benedict thought about cultures, it is equally necessary to understand how she thought about poetry. During the 1920s Benedict moved between the philosophies and practices of anthropology and poetry, not only looking for methodological connections between them but also considering whether one discipline might offer a more effective space to express ideas than the other. Benedict used her exploration of the poetry market and her process of learning about all facets of her writing life in her developing anthropological theories in major and minor ways, constantly thinking about the differences between the cultural registers of these different professions—so much so that the study of creativity became central to her anthropological theories about how to understand how cultures function.

In an early example of Benedict's interest in the interchange between poetic ideas and anthropological ones, Benedict sent Margaret Mead the poem "Patterns" by Amy Lowell when Mead left for Samoa to do fieldwork for the first time in 1925 (fig. 13). Benedict's growing realization within her anthropological essays was that effective fieldwork developed from "an understanding [of] the way in which 'pattern' shaped thought would affect our ability to think"; this argument examines the connection between the culture in which a person lives and the person's ability to think about the systems that enable the culture to function.[57] Benedict did not offer Mead an analysis of Lowell's poem, a work which considers two different definitions of *pattern,* but she did send it as part of a large packet of different excerpts on possible methodologies and examples of experiences in conducting fieldwork. Benedict's act suggests that the Lowell poem serves as a reminder of the ways imaginative work connects to fieldwork. Identifying "patterns" is a crucial process in conducting the new ethnographic fieldwork that Benedict champions (direct observation leading to an understanding of a particular culture); however, the experience of contemplating the contextualized meaning of every detail is an equally necessary step in becoming culturally aware. Since Benedict recognizes that improving analytical techniques is equally necessary in anthropological fieldwork and literary work, it makes sense that Benedict pushes Mead's thinking forward by sending a poetic "document" as an introduction to fieldwork.

Benedict further encourages a focus on creativity in what she views as a necessary interchange between processes of reading and ethnographic research and analysis during this period. Benedict casually referred to a more open process of reading in a proposal for her book of three short biographies, the first of which was the essay on Mary Wollstonecraft: "As you will see from the accompanying drafts—of a 'Foreword' and of 'Mary Wollstonecraft,' the first 'story'—it is a book to be classified with feminist literature without being concerned either with *pro* or *con.* A whole library of theorizing can't give half the real conviction that comes from adventuring through the life of one restless, highly endowed woman. It is from that conviction that I have written this book. Besides the lives of these three women are in themselves splen-

13. Margaret Mead (1901–78) on Manus (c. 1928). Photo courtesy of Vassar College Libraries Archives and Special Collections.

didly romantic human documents."[58] Benedict's book proposal resembles a nonfiction version of Gertrude Stein's *Three Lives* (1909); she sees her text as modernizing the genre of biography by focusing on what is necessary to pay attention to in "reading" a person. Her sense of a library's limitations, her flexibility as to what constitutes "documents" for analysis, and her belief that "conviction" and "adventuring" ought to substitute for bland "theorizing" all point toward a new, more open (and modernist) analytical and creative focus. By updating this idea of research to make any process of reading (whether a book, a person, or a culture) equally analytical—active, comparative, and challenging—Benedict illustrates the extent to which genuine understanding can result from a new process of thinking.

Benedict's critiques of the way anthropological research has been carried out in the past serve to shift thinking from a focus on a specific object or practice to that piece of knowledge always in the context of the process through which it was created and continues to function. Beginning with her 1922 article "The Vision in Plains Culture" (an essay that emerged from her work on her dissertation), Benedict consistently argues that early anthropologists are unable to understand the relationship between small details and an entire culture: "The classical anthropologists did not write out of first-hand knowledge of primitive people. They were armchair students who had at their disposal the anecdotes of travelers and missionaries and the formal and schematic accounts of the early ethnologists. It was possible to trace from these details the distribution of the custom of knocking out teeth, or of divination by entrails, but it was not possible to see how these traits were embedded in different tribes in characteristic configurations that gave form and meaning to the procedures" (*PC*, 48–49).

There are really two separate smaller critiques here, though Benedict merges them in her discussion. She suggests that "armchair anthropologists" were unable to recognize what traits were important within a culture because they did no direct observation; rather, they relied on existing ethnographies, often composed simply by enthusiasts. Benedict then argues that these "armchair anthropologists"—named, in part, as a result of their lack of direct experience of cultures—could not understand that similar-seeming behaviors might actually signify vastly different cultural systems. As the discipline of anthropology moves away from research based on existing ethnographies, anthropologists do new research using direct observation (such as Mead's work in Samoa). In a 1923 essay Benedict continues this argument, emphasizing that just as small details reveal larger cultural patterns if studied carefully, studying a culture as a whole can help explain what role an object, person, or idea—no matter how seemingly small—plays within it.[59] This relationship between details and cultural wholes she calls cultural patterning.

Benedict's work on the *Journal of American Folklore*—both as a writer and as an editor (1925–40)—enables her to extend this study of cultural patterns to include more direct discussions on creativity. Her interest is in both how creativity functions within different cultures and how specific creative works are interpreted inside and outside the communities in which they were created. Virginia Wolf Briscoe explains that Benedict's analysis of folklore enabled her to consider the creative process in new terms: "She therefore demanded of fieldworkers not only that they gather as much data as possible from all areas of behavior within the society, but also that they recognize and try to elicit explanations for discrepancies between observed behavior and that contained in narratives or songs. She . . . insisted that patterns and meaning could not be determined from the observation of a single event or institution, but rather from the relations between them . . . to provide evidence for the ultimate configurational patterns of the culture."[60] Benedict recognized that the creative process could do several things within a culture: shed light on the distinctions between observed behavior and artistic renderings of those actions, add a comparative component to an understanding of a culture, and encourage ethnographers to recognize a creative process within a culture. Benedict goes further in her discussion of creativity, explaining specifically the difficulty in studying narratives: "The literary problems which confront a primitive narrator are easily misunderstood. The gap between the traditionalism of primitive mythology and the emphasis upon originality in our own literature is so great that the reader from our civilization confronted by a collection of folktales is often led to false conclusions. Many students have assumed that the fixity of the tales is absolute or almost so, that the individual narrator has no literary problems, and that the tales originated in a mystical source called communal authorship."[61] This effort at encouraging readers to look closely at a text helps to distinguish not only what a creative work is (something that Benedict was trying to understand and successfully identify in her poetic efforts as well), but the extent to which one can interpret those works genuinely. While she uses this process to reflect back on the anthropologist's efforts to read and analyze material always comparatively, her interest also serves to refocus attention on her belief that studying the creative process (not only the products that result) is central to understanding how cultures function.

In 1928, the same year that she submits her poetic manuscript for publication, Benedict sums up the new anthropology by touting its new "method," a broad term that stands in for the very shifts in approach and analysis that she has pushed forward. The new anthropologist must recognize both that individuals "learn" their own culture in unexpected ways and through experiences they may not be fully aware of and that these small details need to be considered always in terms of the entire culture:

> The second sophistication of anthropological method during the last decade has been in the study of learning. It is a very different thing to learn to be a Dobuan and to learn to be a Zuni. . . . Even the smallest bit of learning teaches an individual not only that specific item but also expected sequences and sanctioned ways of seeing the universe. They are . . . learning of which no individual is conscious but which can be abstracted from detailed observation of his behavior. These sequences and assumptions are cultural and are necessarily what he operates with in political, economic, and family life.[62]

The "method" requires cultural analysis; it is the tool of observation that the researcher uses to recognize that "even the smallest bit of learning teaches" a person what to know and how to think. She explains that the most important recent shift in this "anthropological method" is the recognition that what builds a person's behavior and beliefs is the "expected sequences and sanctioned ways of seeing the universe" that individuals do not even realize they have absorbed from within their culture. This system is so powerful that it can lead an individual to act in certain ways and believe certain things without revealing any of its power. To uncover something that an individual may not even recognize as an influence, the anthropologist needs sharpened analytical skills, an openness to learning, and a heightened awareness of the creative process.

Benedict saw that both the new anthropology and the new poetry provided crucial ways to examine culture, and she looked for new methods to illustrate the ethnographer's (and, by relation, any narrator's) necessary recognition of her own limitations in telling a story.[63] One of the techniques she found to use was the self-consciously aware narrator of much of modernist fiction. As with the other women writers chronicled in this book, Benedict's recognition of and use of modernist techniques is often overlooked amid debate over whether her ideas and processes of thinking were modernist. Like the other authors as well, her poetry relied on her developing intellectual awareness of ways she could free herself from nineteenth-century cultural institutions and their professional realities. In fact, her very definition of poetry as providing—through its formal elements, its lyricism, and its uneasy separation from her career aspirations—a place that could protect her from cultural realities was thoroughly reflective of the concerns of the modern age.[64]

Benedict intellectually embraced literary modernism as these narrative experiments buttressed her new approach to ethnography and her excitement about the creative process. Despite these interests, the subject of Benedict's modernism is almost always introduced tentatively and with multiple defensive positions by her critics. Benedict was a modernist because anthropology came of age at a particular historical moment.[65] Or, Benedict's openness and skepticism are testimony to her modern spirit even though she also seemed to have an ideological foot in the nineteenth century.[66] Or, Benedict's poetry seems old-fashioned, but she was influenced by the lyricists, a group of modern poets embracing older formal elements often for subversive reasons.[67] Or, Benedict's interest in the self and modes of expressing the self is a modernist "hallmark."[68] Her overarching project—which could be summed up as a personal and professional effort to undo the biases that enabled Westerners to view their existence as unique—grew from her critiques of her own and her mother's professionalization processes.[69] She finds in this long-term study the kernel of her own writing process and resulting poems, and she discovers in her genuine curiosity of this process of navigating the modernist poetry market an ethnography of modernism and firsthand evidence that her anthropological ideas and her poetic efforts are necessary to one another.

Benedict emphasizes these views throughout *Patterns of Culture* and in her essays that follow. While the unpublished, autobiographical "The Story of My Life . . ." (1935) and her professional publication "Introduction to Zuni Mythology" (1935) might seem to have little in common other than their date of publication, in fact the two works share the same critical outlook. While she criticizes the late nineteenth-century library in the first essay, she criticizes its 1920s descendants—anthropologists still reading poorly in the library—in the second. Both essays, despite their seemingly unrelated subject matter, make the same argument: an individual can discover methods for becoming aware by first acknowledging ways they relate to the cultural world they inhabit. This argument underlines the enormous role the "cultural process" plays in the development of patterns of language, attitudes, and behavior.[70] In "Introduction to Zuni Mythology" the focus seems to be on folklore, but the argument is actually about reading and writing: "Even more serious misunderstanding of folklore is introduced by the outsider's inability to appreciate the fixed limits within which the narrator works. The artist works within definite traditional limits as truly in folklore as in music. The first requisite in understanding any folk literature is to recognize the boundaries in which it operates."[71] Benedict's observations on ethnography are not only reinforced by her critiques of the library and reading in general but also by her contemporary reading experiences. She recognizes that the ability "to appreciate the fixed limits within which the narrator works" is of central importance to the creation of modernist narratives as well. Modernist works as diverse as James Joyce's *Ulysses* (1922), F. Scott Fitzgerald's *The Great Gatsby* (1925), and Virginia Woolf's *The Waves* (1931)—all of which Benedict was aware of and had at least partially read—celebrated the overt incorporation of those limitations as not only a feature of but even the primary subject of the narrative.[72] Benedict similarly argues that a small misunderstanding of the narrator's position in relation to the ethnographic material discussed can result in serious misunderstandings of the primary data under investigation. She argues that for ethnographers to ask what might be their own limitations in understanding existing material and to have some sense of what the real answer might be is the beginning of a genuine understanding of a culture.

Benedict's recognition that her comments on the limitations of a single perspective are also central principles of modernist novels encourages her to emphasize the way *Patterns of Culture* participates in and adds to this discussion of a cultural ideology implicit in modernist writing techniques. Just before *Patterns of Culture* was published, Benedict's publisher asked for a descriptive blurb to include with the book. Benedict first asked Margaret Mead to do this but then decided to write it herself. She wanted to underline the way in which her anthropological text was reiterating a central realization of modernism in its use of small pieces of disparate cultures to reveal larger truths about the ways people think and what they believe. This writerly argument was equally conceptual, counteracting problematic broad generalizations about cultures that claimed some were sophisticated and highly civilized and others impossibly uncivilized and primitive. In writing the blurb, she wanted to underline two facets of the text of which she was most proud: the clarity of writing (for Benedict, style was never an issue of modernism, but belief was)[73] and the book's explanation of seemingly fragmentary aspects of a life as part of a larger and consistent pattern of living. The process by which she went about understanding this view included "her search for meaning within fragments" of a culture.[74] No detail was unimportant, and every detail reflected in some way on a particular patterning within that culture. Her essays in this period and the chapters that she included in *Patterns of Culture* reflect this new view: that genuine knowledge of a culture is discernible in incompletion or partial pieces but only as long as the recognition of the limitation of a partial view is always part of the discussion. If we apply Benedict's own principle to her complete body of work, then her efforts in anthropology become that much more apparent through examining the unfinished or fragmentary examples of her creative work. Certainly, her poetry remains her most unfinished, incomplete long-term effort. The poems add to this view of their importance in understanding Benedict's thinking about culture as they express her celebration of the means by which individuals find freedom from—or even within—entrenched patterns and cultural realities.

Finding Freedom

Up until the very end of her life Benedict demonstrated loyalty both to modernist literature and to the related vision of creativity she shaped outside of the museums and libraries from which she had sought escape as a young anthropology student. Shortly before her death in 1948, Ruth Benedict attended a poetry reading at the New School. Her old friend Louise Bogan described the event:

> The great "poetry festival" went off well at the New School. I read first (like the acrobats or trained dogs in vaudeville!); and then came R. Lowell (who is now quite pert); and then darling Marianne (who was in a cunning little Quakeress get-up). Then Allen closed the proceedings in his usual smooth way. A good largish audience. Sherry upstairs afterward . . . Djuna Barnes casting baleful looks around, from under a Paris hat. Many old friends. . . . O yes, Margaret Mead and Ruth Benedict in the front row: I hadn't seen them in years. Ruth looking old and beautiful; Margaret as "earth-bound" as ever. Such celebrities, yet![75]

The letter succinctly describes a late modernist poetry reading. A quartet of poets of various ages read in turn: Louise Bogan, Marianne Moore, Robert Lowell, and Allen Tate; Djuna Barnes appears almost ghostlike, haunting the event in the wings; and the two celebrity-anthropologists and formerly practicing poets Ruth Benedict and Margaret Mead are seated "front row" in the audience, a spectacle themselves, lending an air of dignity and respectability to the event.

The characters and the geography are similar to what they were a quarter century before, when Marianne Moore first excitedly and informally read her poems in Lola Ridge's living room, but Bogan's letter underscores some significant changes. The event still takes place in Greenwich Village but no longer in the private home of a fellow artist; instead, it is held at a school. The evening is no longer made up of unknown poets standing up to read new poems; rather, the four poets read in an established order. All of the poets have a "personality" at this point in their career—a "get-up" or a "usual smooth way" of reading. Even "R. Lowell," younger than the rest—referred to by neither the first name of the poets of Bogan's generation nor the full name denoting a kind of outsider status—is "now quite pert," suggesting that Bogan finds him a more polished, professional reader than she has before. Djuna Barnes also plays a role; she attends as a comparative reminder that this polished, institutionally sanctioned performance of American modernist poetry is a new achievement. Barnes still wears the "Paris hat" that marks her as part of an earlier avant-garde group that built up its aesthetic authority through its attachment with Europe at a time when Paris, not yet New York, and salons, not yet universities, were cultural centers. Barnes is back in Greenwich Village, but she is not invited onto the stage nor importantly seated. The audience space is reserved for the academic and thoroughly American counterparts to the poets onstage—that is, "such celebrities, yet!" Both Benedict and Mead, through their popular books on culture and their positions at Columbia University and the American Museum of Natural History, are well established as New York City intellectual celebrities. Even the epithets that Bogan attaches to them—Benedict is "old and beautiful" and Mead "earth-bound" in comparison to Moore's "cunning" performance—serve to reinforce the celebrity of each. The description of the "largish" event underlines the extent to which Bogan sees the academic and poetic circles of late American modernism as overlapping and reinforcing one another (one might think of "cunning" as a more apt term for an academic and "beautiful" a more likely description of a poet). Bogan's journal depicts an event in which there is no effort at distinguishing between cultural registers—institutional history and literary history seem happily intertwined. Benedict and Mead are not only welcome at the event, but they are key elements in describing the success of the performance.

If Benedict knows that Bogan believes her presence helps to sanction the event in any way, she might find the idea rather ironic since her attempts to be part of the poetic group on display were rejected so handily throughout the 1920s. To read through Benedict's exchanges with publishers, magazine editors, and even her close friends with whom she discussed her poems is to discover an enormous and consistent amount of rejection and only a small amount of encouragement. Mark Van Doren at *The Nation,* Ridgely Torrence at *New Republic,* and Harriet Monroe at *Poetry,* editors who eventually published some of her poems and to whom she sent frequent submissions, more often sent her poems back with mild encouragement that the poems were "better than your earlier things" but still not good enough for publication.[76] Benedict's poetic and professional path to her "front row" seat—as central a position as possible for a nonreader at a modernist poetry reading—is a long one, involving simultaneous rejection (as a poet) and achievement (as an anthropologist). There is no question that Benedict would have rather been reading her poems onstage than providing a mirror of authority in the audience to reflect its image back on the poets. Despite Bogan's sense of her serenity, Benedict's long-standing frustration with her career had never been (nor ever would be) fully resolved. Finally having reached the holy grail of a full professorship at Columbia after a long and unpleasant struggle for the position, Benedict may seem to provide an image of the beauty of the university, but her heart and mind are with the poets.

At a memorial service for Benedict in 1949, Clyde Kluckhohn, the anthropology professor, librarian, and curator of the Peabody Museum at Harvard, ended his eulogy by reading four of Benedict's poems and suggesting that more interest ought to be paid to Benedict's devotion to poetry. Margaret Mead seemed to echo that thought when she read one of Benedict's poems before the end of the event as well.[77] While many of Benedict's colleagues since then have acknowledged that there is a relationship between Benedict's poetry and her anthropological work, most echo the conclusions expressed in these eulogies that the relationship is primarily a personal one.

While writing poetry may have served as an emotional outlet for Benedict in the 1920s as she was trying to become a professional anthropologist, as many critics have argued, it certainly also provided her a sharp tool through which to examine how an individual reacts to possibilities for freedom. During this same period she was also analyzing what a culture was—and thinking about whether it was even culturally possible to have imaginative outlets. As she later explained, "the anthropological method of cultural study . . . is based on recognition that there is no other locus of culture than the habituated minds and bodies of men and women."[78] If, for Benedict, "culture" existed primarily as a belief system instantiated within an individual that the person might not always be capable of recognizing, then it might not be possible to step outside that system entirely.[79] Her intellectual interest in following through on this question of how to create awareness of one's culture while still functioning as a product of that culture—in short, what it means to be both a participant and an observer—is part of what led her to work on and try to publish a volume of poems throughout the 1920s. The rejection of individual poems and of her 1928 manuscript resulted in some disappointment (as critics have emphasized) but also a growing intellectual stubbornness. Regardless of responses to the volume, she continued to revise her work, showing a commitment to the very ideals that the poems imagine.

As late as 1948, the year she attended the poetry reading with Marianne Moore, Benedict was still trying to determine the best way to influence people's ideas about culture and to heighten awareness. She had spent the last few years working for the government, and it may have seemed to her colleagues that she no longer saw a conflict between the individual and cultural authorities.[80] She wrote in an essay for the *Intercultural Education News* that "we . . . know that cultural patterns can be directed" but also that "we just have not yet decided what is the best way or whether it is right in a democratic country to direct them."[81] Since her early pre-Columbia days, when she wrote not necessarily to publish but as a way to clarify her own ideas and processes of thinking, she had claimed that artistic work could transcend any other kind of achievement in thinking. A creative effort could "direct" culture from within yet without necessarily inhabiting the space of an authority. In a very early but undated essay, "The Sense of Symbolism," Benedict explained this idea: "All the tendencies of the modern world have been in keeping with this development—the growing emphasis on the active life, the spread of education, and especially the development of modern science. It is inevitable, however, in this effort after exact realism of detail that the sense of the large unity of things should be obscured. It is inevitable also in this restless inquiry into all things for the sake of complete understanding that the sense of reverence and awe should also be lost."[82] Benedict's poetry represents a seeking after "reverence and awe," in part through its continuous effort at trying to achieve a place from which to view and feel this possibility. Benedict never loses a measure of awe in the face of inspiring beauty, the kind that by virtue of its inherent power reorders experience in the viewer. In her final work, *The Roots of American Culture* (1942), cultural historian Constance Rourke reached a similar conclusion about the relationship between institutions and art: "It is doubtful whether the beginnings of any art are ever orderly, and when patterns have become sharply grooved they are usually lifeless."[83] This statement could serve as a helpful epigraph to explain Ruth Benedict's efforts at continuing to write and revise her volume of poetry despite her lack of success as a published poet. She gave a handwritten reorganized book of her poems to her literary executor, certainly understanding that act would guarantee not only its preservation but generate new interest in her unpublished 1928 manuscript and its subsequent alterations.

In 1948, the year that Benedict died, T. S. Eliot was awarded the Nobel Prize for literature. Over the next four years Marianne Moore would receive three big prizes—Bollingen, Pulitzer, and a National Book Award—and she would decide that her own contribution to art could not only be through her poems but through altering the experience of poetry in museums and libraries. Because Benedict was immediately distrustful of museums and libraries (and eventually universities), and because she recognized firsthand both how crucial these institutions were and believed they participated in instantiating negative cultural patterns through seemingly positive promises, Benedict's hopes consciously remained with the poets. In the 1940s, as she rearranged her poems yet again and copied down a few for her friend Margaret Mead, she still hoped that these poems would offer a check—a quiet, thoughtful act of resistance—to the seemingly successful professional career she had crafted.

Conclusion

On September 19, 2003, the *New York Times* reminded readers that museums and libraries, as well as the artifacts and books they house, "are the very things we count on to remember for us."[1] Such an observation betrays a post--9/11 anxiety, a newspaper worrying that if we do not allow our institutions to preserve and "remember for us," we—or our culture, our things—might disappear. As I have written this book on early twentieth-century women and American museums and libraries, I have watched these venues continue to undergo transformation. This development is perhaps due in part to the inevitability that the further we move away from 2001, the more our cultural perception of museums and libraries is changing. We expect different things from museums and libraries than we did even ten years ago, especially since the last fifteen or so years can unofficially be labeled a renaissance in museum and library building. Most libraries, even college libraries, now also include coffee shops, comfortable chairs, and places to eat and talk. Museums not only include fancy restaurants with celebrity chefs but also look different from the museums of the past. The Guggenheim Museum in New York City used to be a distinct architectural space, but now, in the context of newer museum buildings, it looks dated. Museum benefits are attended by the very same people who attend the Oscars; arrivals at the Metropolitan Museum of Art gala benefit are covered on television entertainment shows with similar giddiness. All of these changes suggest a new attitude about the present-ness of museums and libraries. They are not only there to preserve our culture but also to provide people with a place to meet and change it.

When I began this project, I wanted to prove that there were more women writers who ought to be called modernist than their male contemporaries would admit to. I wanted to show why women writers who were particularly singled out for seeming too entrenched in the nineteenth century deserved more respect from their twentieth-century peers. I didn't find exactly what I was looking for. I didn't discover a community of women writers beholden (albeit secretively) to the modernist principles held triumphantly by their male counterparts. Instead, I found women hanging around the museum and the library, looking worried, and writing about it. At first, their anxieties within and about these places seemed quaint, but a closer look revealed that these women were looking closely at these places, much closer than most of their colleagues and with a great deal more detailed knowledge about how the places functioned and why that kind of almost overly detailed, esoteric information about categories and systems even mattered.

Once their interests became clear, it was only a matter of recognizing the distinctions between that line of thinking and better-known modernist attitudes for me to see that these women writers were participating in a modernism of their own. Male modernists' intellectual lives were launched through the university (even if that means because they challenged, abandoned, or avoided it); these women writers had to carve out a place for themselves in museums and libraries and gained no clear sense of intellectual independence by refusing to participate; male modernists' formed writerly and publishing connections through their years at the university; these women never met (or knew of each other) within the libraries and museums where they worked; male modernists formed and participated in intellectual groupings, sometimes around an intellectual personality or teacher; these women writers came to their critiques and praise for museums and libraries entirely independently of one another or any primary figure. Because of the qualities of their experiences, women writers' concerns were so unique, and so difficult to perceive as a group, that they simply seemed too unfamiliar to be included in the larger tag of modernism.

Yet Edith Wharton, Nella Larsen, Marianne Moore, and Ruth Benedict were modernists. In all four of their careers the question of whether their writing constituted a fully modernist sensibility was raised at some point. More often than not, their institutional affiliations with museums and libraries and their femaleness were cited as evidence that the question was a reasonable one. Yet these women belong together as modernist writers through a recognition that their critical thoughts about museums and libraries were not only a source of great creative inspiration but shaped their intellectual inquiries and their skepticism about institutions in general. By virtue of these facts alone—even before knowing that they shared similar jobs and self-educational paths—their works can be viewed as revealing a neglected facet in the development of modernist literature.

In addition to their literary works, the legacy of the thinking of these women is in the very institutions they first analyzed and critiqued. Edith Wharton's former Lenox home—The Mount—has had many lives since she sold it, though it now functions as a refurbished museum, with tours, lectures, and discussions (even weddings) generally dedicated to Wharton's work and ideas. Nella Larsen did not keep personal papers, yet quite a bit of information about her survives through papers saved by her archive-savvy friend Carl Van Vechten (who deposited letters, clippings, and photographs at the Beinecke Rare Book and Manuscript Library and at the New York Public Library) and through records kept by the New York Public Library School and by the 135th Street Library (now the Schomburg Center for Research in Black Culture). Marianne Moore complained about her rather unkind treatment while working as a library assistant, but she is now the only former librarian mentioned on the New York Public Library Hudson Park branch Web site.[2] Through her own efforts, her papers and objects from her former living room are on permanent display in Philadelphia as part of the Rosenbach Museum and Library visitor's tour. Ruth Benedict, who kept records proving that she was always paid less and received fewer promotions than her male colleagues at Columbia, is perhaps still receiving some of the same treatment there: she is mentioned only as a graduate of Franz Boas's anthropology program, not as a Columbia professor, on Columbia University's Virtual Tour.[3]

Wharton, Larsen, Moore, and Benedict were idealists. As idealists, they might argue that this evidence of continued interest in their work by the very institutions where they learned to shape and question that material is a good thing. Nella Larsen might feel some pride that early steps she and her fellow librarians took to turn the 135th Street Library into a central research space for black culture have been realized. Marianne Moore might also enjoy how the Rosenbach Museum and Library has continued to wrestle with methods for organizing her papers and objects, in some ways duplicating her own questions about the relationships among poetry, museums, and libraries as it makes material available to researchers. Wharton, however, might be less thrilled by the ways in which her interests in museums have been interpreted inside the grand and glossy Mount. While she might have enjoyed the gift shop devoted to her work and life, and perhaps have appreciated the attention to detail in her beloved gardens, she might have rejected the choice to use her former home as the site of a rotating decoration of rooms (by local interior designers) as historically inaccurate or misleading. Benedict also might be less than thrilled at the wide variety of uses in which her name has been invoked in the service of Columbia University. Alternately promoted as one of the first female full professors and as a famous student of Franz Boas,

Benedict maintains a connection to the institution that is neither claimed consistently nor always accurately.

Wharton, Larsen, Moore, and Benedict were also moralists. For each of them the moral view was the inquisitive view. In each of their fictional worlds, to neglect to ask a question was a sin, and to challenge an idea or to offer a new perspective was an example of beauty or delight. Each woman tried to mediate her commitments to the social world through writing, and to write morally was a complicated process that involved exercising authority while challenging and questioning the very desire to be an authority. In several of Moore's poems, for example, the speaker studies a mark left on nature by some individual. This mark exists as a silent testimony to everything that has happened in history up to the moment of its discovery. The speaker is fascinated by what the mark reveals, and she is also repelled by the way the mark has defaced the landscape in order to gain permanence. All of these writers struggled with such contradictory desires—to give permanence to ideas by writing about them and to resist the notion of permanence, which necessarily involved an act of defacement (not just of the landscape, as in this example, but of ideas, of the past, and of the possibility for change in the future).

As idealists, they wanted cultural institutions to transcend the inherent conflicts of exercising authority and effacing history. As moralists, Wharton, Larsen, Moore, and Benedict were deeply concerned with interpreting the past accurately, and they understood museums and libraries to be the predominant public spaces involved in remembering and interpreting history. They viewed this role as an enormous burden and a powerful cultural responsibility. They also believed that any institution with such potential for power and authority demanded close scrutiny. They wanted these spaces continually to acknowledge and embody the discomfort that comes with being viewed as an authority. The genuine concerns of these women over the ways museums, libraries, and universities would try to resolve these difficulties in the future are still culturally resonant.

During the past fifteen years, newspapers and magazines have directly linked aspects of this historical moment with American writers of the late nineteenth and early twentieth century by declaring that we were in a new Gilded Age.[4] The last Gilded Age brought about the increase in private wealth that led to the creation and aggressive expansion of museums and libraries and subsequent methods of organizing those collections, including the Dewey decimal and Library of Congress classification schemes. This new one, which has brought about a similar rise in wealth and interest in philanthropy, has enabled the creation of new museums and libraries and the redesign of older ones. Spurred by innovations in technology, this new age of museums and libraries involves a rethinking of these traditional "spaces." The creation of new kinds of organizational systems such as the Google search algorithm has led to the creation of the Google Book Search Library Project and transformations in the concept of museums and libraries to include digitized, interactive, and virtual spaces. New systems being created to help visitors find and organize the information they need online have empowered individuals to revise and even reject older methods for physically organizing ideas, objects, and books (particularly the Dewey decimal classification system) in favor of more flexible systems.[5] While in the first Gilded Age, "order," "category," and "classification" were key terms underlying national efforts at organizing information in an overarching and rational system, "spontaneity" and "serendipity" might arguably be the key terms underlying the thinking of the new one, as individuals experiment with new systems to discover knowledge.

In reading contemporary debates about the creation, planning, and maintenance of these new museums and libraries, the concerns of Edith Wharton, Nella Larsen, Marianne Moore, and Ruth Benedict seem eerily prescient. These four writers provide the beginning of an unlikely but articulate contribution to early twenty-first-century anxieties about the organization and distribution of knowledge. When the *New York Times* ran a series of articles in 2005 stating that Google had finally surpassed Microsoft as America's "villain"—capping a year of almost nonstop coverage of Google's ambitious plans to become the world's most comprehensive library—it suggested we were in a new age of anxieties about knowledge and information. Two of the most important questions being raised about the future of the Internet—how is knowledge created or manipulated through methods of organizing information? and how do those systems change the way we think?—would be remarkably familiar concerns to these writers.

Modern American writers who reacted to the rapid late nineteenth-century development of institutions such as museums, libraries, and universities by reflecting on the growing power of those places recognized the expanding cultural institution as a force so great that it often overpowered individuals working within it. They exemplified a broad modernist response to Ralph Waldo Emerson's mid-nineteenth-century comment that the unexamined use of libraries and universities could lead to the loss of an individual's ability to think. Modernist women writers shared Emerson's fears that cultural institutions potentially exert too much control over the minds of individuals. Yet they also worried that these institutions were becoming too large and too powerful to control successfully the products of knowledge emerging from them.

These anxieties have resurfaced recently in popular books, magazines, and even in national reports such as the National Endowment for the Arts's *Reading at Risk* (2004) report. In his preface the then-NEA chairman Dana Gioia blames the Internet for exercising too much influence over minds by distracting them from real thinking and too little by not directing them toward a greater sense of civic commitment and responsibility. Underlying Gioia's comments are more general concerns about the potential loss of authority and expertise. Similar anxieties are voiced in the recent book *The Cult of the Amateur,* where Andrew Keen argues that reliance on the Internet has created a new reliance on the amateur and a loss of belief in the idea of expertise. Keen contends that—even worse—current trends make it seem increasingly unnecessary to differentiate between the expert opinion and the amateur one. David Weinberger takes the opposite view in his book *Everything Is Miscellaneous.* He writes excitedly that "the miscellaneous order is not transforming only business. It is changing how we think the world itself is organized and—perhaps more important—who we think has the authority to tell us so."[6] Weinberger argues that the new desire for systems that allow individuals to organize ideas and find information using nonhierarchical methods—unlike Dewey's scheme—indicates that a necessary revolution is occurring to shift the idea of authority and expertise away from one person and place it into shared hands. He praises Web sites such as Wikipedia, which models a system of knowledge that relies on multiple users to share information and check the accuracy of each other (rather than relying on a single expert in a field, as in the older encyclopedia model), as a very positive development in the history of knowledge. Weinberger suggests that those who claim to want more evidence of authority and expertise are looking backward, not forward.

As contemporary American writers react to the development of new technologies for the production of knowledge, early twentieth-century analyses of those older technologies—cultural institutions—will provide an increasingly powerful point of comparison. The *New York Times* quotation with which I opened this conclusion suggests the extent to which the concerns of Wharton, Larsen, Moore, and Benedict deserve to become a more integrated part of modernist discussions. All four women recognized the social desire to let a cultural institution think for them, and they resisted this desire in their writing. They feared the day when a newspaper would state, without a corresponding sense of horror, that museums and libraries "are the very things we count on to remember for us." The notion that any institution would be given such historical, cultural, and social authority without an obvious system of checks and balances was anathema to their ideas about learning.

Wharton worried that the kind of remembering that museums participated in was selective and ahistorical and that museums ought never to be relied on to replace other effective practices of remembering and inquiring. She would be dismayed, for example, to discover that the Metropolitan Museum of Art ultimately reinstated part of its original Cesnola exhibition with no mention of the objects' controversial histories.[7] This contemporary omission recalls both Cesnola's omission of the facts of his discovery and the museum's unwillingness to engage with the questions the disputed collection raised for the institution. Wharton's carefully chosen word—*time-blurred*—in the climactic museum scene near the end of *The Age of Innocence* described the consequences of historical omissions and repudiations of responsibility as a loss of or a "blurring" of memories. Much later, the modern museum is still playing a similarly complicated role in culture, obscuring history even as it claims to exhibit and explain it. This act of trading on its cultural authority while actually misusing it was what made these writers so fearful of the power to explain culture that these institutions were gaining.

Larsen's work also suggested that there were huge consequences for relying on museums and libraries for social memory, not least of which was an individual's loss of (or an inability to feel a sense of) identity. Museums and libraries might wish to remember, for example, as Dewey's system maintained, that black women have no historical or intellectual relationship to nineteenth-century American political history. For Larsen a passive acceptance of institutional memory could lead to a loss of self. Benedict also recognized the enormous responsibility institutions have over the cultural understanding of individuals; just as with all of these women, she personally experienced the effects of a misuse of this power, from her early observation of her mother's poor treatment in the library to her own similar experience in the university. Benedict's response to this recognition was to immerse herself in the creative process, searching for ways to awaken an individual to the relative nature of any seeming cultural truth.

For all four writers the consequences of such a purposeful act of cultural forgetting and of a passive reliance on the memory of cultural institutions were potentially serious: individuals without identity living in a troubled, unfeeling world. Wharton, Larsen, Moore, and Benedict tried to intervene to prevent the creation of such a world by writing about institutions and by offering models for inquisitiveness that they believed were antidotes to the potential for loss that this cultural reliance would produce. They repeatedly argued that the only way to turn knowledge into wisdom was to keep learning. Any kind of acceptance of information, any reliance on an institution to do the thinking or remembering for them, would result in a tremendous personal, social, and cultural loss. Paradise, for these writers, was whatever place enabled the learning process to continue. They believed that there was potential for Paradise inside institutions but only if these places were being perpetually challenged and their cultural authority and potential for pattern-making was being resisted. Each woman left a body of work that provides a model for the kind of questioning they believed necessary. Difficult, unwieldy, and contradictory, the writing of these women itself participates in a process of resisting the author's own authority and encouraging the discoveries of new processes by which to read and to think.

The enduring image of Edith Wharton ought to be a picture of her walking energetically through a museum with a curator-friend, an event she frequently noted in her line-a-day diary, rather than the usual image of her sitting stiffly in an expensive chair. The enduring image of Nella Larsen ought to be of her at work in the 135th Street Library—thinking, organizing, reading, and talking—all activities she pursued each day as noted in the records she was required to keep. The enduring image of Marianne Moore ought to be her efforts at organizing her postcard collection, adding an index to her reading notebook, or filling bags with miscellaneous items—items so miscellaneous that they have continued to defy categorization for the past thirty years—all of which she would eventually place in her museum and library in Philadelphia. The enduring image of Ruth Benedict ought to be her attendance at a poetry reading in Greenwich Village rather than—as she is usually pictured—standing up in her office at Columbia. I offer these images, unknown except in letters, yellowed records, or lines in an old diary, as an addition to better-known examples. These images suggest the impressive energy of this group of women. Each was able to offer a critique of these massive institutions through her creative works and to stand up to the institutions and casually remark that the existing systems for thinking about what knowledge is and how to use it are problematic and deserve further examination.

Notes

Introduction

1. James, *The American,* 5.

2. Woolf, *A Room of One's Own,* 7–8.

3. Some good recent examples include Newfield, *Ivy and Industry;* Gould, *The University in a Corporate Culture;* Lentricchia, *Modernist Quartet;* and McDonald, *Learning to Be Modern.*

4. Watson, *Prepare for Saints,* 12.

5. Page and Page, *The World's Work,* 580.

6. The only direct literary links among them are Marianne Moore's brief remarks in an essay and in two letters (one to H.D. and one to Hildegarde Watson) in which she praises Edith Wharton's work: "Mrs. Wharton's literary behavior, if one may be permitted the phrase, her uninflated accuracies, sudden sensibilities of statement, her feeling that the artist cannot ask too much of himself and must be prepared to pardon the public's 'lack of imaginative response to his effort' is a true guide, not so much toward becoming famous, as toward an essential discernment of values. Admitting flaws, such as the too mundane phrase in context that is reduced and aware, *A Backward Glance,* from which the present pages are taken, steadies fortitude, demonstrates the worth of self-discipline, and revives confidence in charm made profitable by sincerity" (quoted in Willis, *The Complete Prose of Marianne Moore,* 356; orig. published in the *Brooklyn Daily Eagle,* April 18, 1937, 15C). Moore mentions reading Wharton's *The Age of Innocence* and *A Backward Glance* in the two letters; see Moore, *The Selected Letters of Marianne Moore,* 139, 323. Ruth Benedict also submitted poetry to *Dial* magazine while Moore was editor. Although no direct link exists between Edith Wharton's work or life and Nella Larsen's, Larsen's friend Carl Van Vechten refers to Wharton's novels dismissively in his *Nigger Heaven* (107). Meredith Goldsmith notes Van Vechten's brief reference to Wharton's writing in an article that speculates on Larsen's literary debt to Wharton's *The House of Mirth;* see Goldsmith, "Edith Wharton's Gift to Nella Larsen," 3–5, 15. I also look at the few but significant moments when

their paths crossed, moments that have not been examined in the critical scholarship until now: specifically, Ruth Benedict's attendance at a poetry reading by Marianne Moore, and Nella Larsen's and Marianne Moore's overlapping library careers.

7. Some excellent examples include Conn, *Museums and American Intellectual Life, 1876–1926;* Sutton, *The Classification of Visual Art;* Battles, *Library;* and Van Slyck, *Free to All.*

8. In a *New York Times* article (May 21, 1904) chronicling a recent address on "the education of women," M. Carey Thomas (president of Bryn Mawr while Marianne Moore attended) explained that "we all either are ourselves college bred, or wished to be and were not permitted to by our parents." Thomas goes on to explain that college is becoming an increasingly accepted practice for women, particularly those in the middle class. Only the upper classes continue to dissuade their daughters from attending a school of higher education, a practice that Edith Wharton found especially problematic among her upper-class family and friends.

9. See *New York Public Library Minutes: Committee on Circulation, 1921;* Marianne Moore is mentioned on pp. 12 and 14, and Nella (Larsen) Imes on p. 378.

10. Benedict, *Patterns of Culture,* 16 (hereafter cited in the text as *PC*).

Chapter 1

1. See, e.g., Newsom and Silver, *The Art Museum as Educator,* 14. In their introduction they write that "it is probably no accident that both [Henry Watson] Kent [supervisor of museum instruction at the Metropolitan Museum of Art] and [John Cotton] Dana [director of the Newark Museum, 1909–29] began their [museum] careers as librarians. The practices and attitudes of the public library movement, which was becoming increasingly professional toward the end of the century (Melvil Dewey had proposed his decimal system in 1876), were an important influence on any who were into museum work. Francis Henry Taylor commented on the metaphor that called the museum and the library 'the two halves of the public's memory of the past.'" Connections between the museum and library are also discussed in Henry, *Babel's Tower,* 29.

2. See Stielow, "Reconsidering Arsenals of a Democratic Culture," 3–4. Stielow tells the story of Fisher Ames's famous 1809 public address that "condemned" American libraries, comparing them unfavorably to British libraries.

3. Reprinted in Wadlin, *The Public Library of the City of Boston,* 21 (italics added).

4. Ibid., 32, 35.

5. Harris and Spiegler, "Everett, Ticknor and the Common Man," 251–52.

6. Everett, one of Oliver Wendell Holmes's prime examples of men of "the Boston Brahmin caste," and a great orator, was less politically conservative than Ticknor. A Harvard president and professor of Greek, Everett was also Emerson's teacher, though Emerson later became critical of Everett's political ideas. See Varg, *Edward Everett.*

7. Emerson, "The American Scholar," 85. For a good article on Emerson and li-

braries see McMullen, "Ralph Waldo Emerson and Libraries." McMullen draws attention to Emerson's "The American Scholar" and "Quotation and Originality."

8. Emerson, "Quotation and Originality," 157–58 (orig. in *North American Review* [1868]).

9. Spofford's essay can be found in Small, *Handbook of the New Library of Congress*, 123–28.

10. See, e.g., Joint Committee on the Library, *Condition of the Library of Congress*, March 3, 1897, 179–298 (Google Books offers a full view at http://books.google.com/books (search on "condition of the library of congress"). Herbert Putnam answers a question about the employment of women: "They are less inclined to be effervescent than boys. I am speaking now of girls for this purpose. As runners we have to trust them in the stacks without supervision, and they are certainly less inclined to mischief, more satisfactory, more equable, more to be relied upon than boys would be" (200).

11. Coleman, *The Museum in America*, 1:16–17 (italics added).

12. "A Museum of the Fine Arts for Boston," *The Nation*, Jan. 27, 1870, 32.

13. Trachtenberg, *The Incorporation of America;* Trachtenberg describes the process by which he chose the title phrase in the preface (3–10).

14. Gilman's *Museum Ideals of Purpose and Method* will be discussed in more detail in chapter 2. Marianne Moore took notes on the text in her reading notebook, and it inspired her to write a poem on museums. Roger Fry, who was the curator of paintings at the Metropolitan Museum of Art from 1905 to 1910, eventually published a series of essays that reflected, among other things, on the purpose of art (see Fry, *Vision and Design*). Did art museums exist as educational spaces or as places for contemplation? And were these two desires as different as they seemed? Both these texts suggest that the museum's emphasis on education transformed the process by which objects were exhibited and displayed in terms of lighting, organization, labels, and other teaching materials used.

15. See Larson, *The Rise of Professionalism*, xiii (hereafter cited in the text as *RP*). Larson writes that "the ethics of disinterestedness claimed by professionals appear to acquit them of all capitalist profit motive" (xiii). Throughout the work she shows how professionals claimed "disinterest" by arguing that their status as experts was the result of their achievements in a meritocratic system of education. This idea extended to cultural institutions such as museums, libraries, and schools. These spaces were also able to claim a certain outsider status (existing outside of the marketplace) through their emphasis on education.

16. In the late 1920s and 1930s sociologists and anthropologists sought to explain in more detail the sociological observations that had helped to create their theories. These writers asked what kinds of thoughts became institutionalized and how knowledge was systematized and gained cultural power. Sociologists such as Charles Cooley, in *Social Organization: A Study of the Larger Mind;* W. H. R. Rivers, in *Social Organization;* and Floyd Allport, in *Institutional Behavior* turned away from the notion of institutions as analogies for "structures" and "machines." These and other

contemporary sociologists defined institutions as abstract sets of ideas, symbols, and beliefs that had crystallized and begun to exert power and influence, sometimes in subtle ways. They examined how this crystallization occurred, in part by trying to define exactly what an institution was. Were institutions simply the "outcome" of extensive human thought about the same problem (Cooley), an example of customs that had become "fundamental" to the social organization (Rivers), or simply all repeated human behavior (Allport)? These sociologists and others argued about how certain kinds of shared knowledge resulted in shared behaviors.

17. Dewey, "The Profession" (the *American Library Journal* became the *Library Journal* the following year).

18. In his influential essay "Storehouses and Workshops" John Cole makes much of Dewey's image of the new visitor to the library as a "workman among his tools," a phrase that suggests the library's new attitude about itself as a living, usable space. Cole's essay chronicles the library's development from a "storehouse," a space interested primarily in the accumulation of materials, to a "workhouse," a modern space invested in an idea of itself as an information center through the increased use of its materials by patrons. Cole (371) promotes the idea that the library became a more modern and useful space by the end of the nineteenth century.

19. Chandler, *Structure and Strategy.*

20. Joint Committee on the Library, *Condition of the Library of Congress,* March 3, 1897, 267–68.

21. Fox, *Engines of Culture.*

22. Koch, *A Book of Carnegie Libraries,* 7–8. Koch quotes extensively from two articles Carnegie wrote that discussed his gifts to the libraries. These articles were first published in the *North American Review* in June and December of 1889 and were eventually revised and republished in Carnegie's book *The Gospel of Wealth and Other Timely Essays.*

23. Although there were only six hundred museums on record in the United States in 1910, by the end of the 1920s there were more than two thousand (Coleman, *The Museum in America,* 1:3).

24. In their introduction to *The Art Museum as Educator* Barbara Newsom and Adele Silver explain this phenomenon in museums: "Americans were moved to seek out their own education wherever they could find it, including, most notably, museums . . . [even] before museums and other cultural agencies were relegated to 'leisure-time activity.' The drive toward self-improvement was so strong in the 1880s, in fact, that 10,000 persons signed a petition demanding that the Metropolitan Museum and its sister across Central Park, the American Museum of Natural History, be opened on Sunday, the only day of the week, said the petition, when the working man was free to visit" (14–15).

25. Dickson, *Sexism and Reentry,* 33.

26. Wire, "The Library Assistants of the United States."

27. Douglas, *The Feminization of American Culture,* 8. Douglas foresaw *The Femi-*

nization of American Culture as the first book of a trilogy (xiv). Her next installment, however, *Terrible Honesty,* which considers these questions at a later point, did not revise this thesis and consider the ways in which women writers of the 1920s offered a new perspective on the feminization of culture.

28. For helpful analyses of this period see Wiebe, *The Search for Order, 1877–1920;* Machlup, *The Production and Distribution of Knowledge in the United States;* Oleson and Voss, *The Organization of Knowledge in Modern America, 1860–1920* (esp. "The Application of Science to Industry," by John Rae [249–68]; and "The American Economy and the Reorganization of the Sources of Knowledge," by Louis Galambos [269–84]); Addams, *Philanthropy and Social Progress;* Hoogenboom and Hoogenboom, *The Gilded Age;* Tarbell, *The History of the Standard Oil Company,* vols. 1 and 2; Campbell, *The Human Tradition in the Gilded Age and Progressive Era;* Trachtenberg, *Democratic Vistas, 1860–1880;* and Zakaria, *From Wealth to Power.*

29. In *Education of Women* M. Carey Thomas detailed the changing cultural response to women in higher education (both college and graduate schools). Her data suggest that in the last few years of the nineteenth century women began attending private institutions, and the percentage of women attending college continued to increase as it had become increasingly accepted for a woman to continue her education.

30. During the late nineteenth century 21 percent of students in college were women. By 1900 that figure had increased to 36 percent, but then "the proportion of women students dropped during the 1920s" before rising again (Snyder, *120 Years of American Education,* 64).

Chapter 2

1. Woolf's vitriolic analysis of *Ulysses*—as the "illiterate, underbred book . . . of a self taught working man, and we all know how distressing they are, how egotistic, insistent, raw, striking, and ultimately nauseating"—has been used by critics as a shorthand to show that Woolf's upper-class consciousness left her unsympathetic to modern writing (Woolf, *A Writer's Diary,* 46). Only after Woolf became a preeminent modernist herself did her analysis get more attention as a valid opinion rather than a misunderstanding of Joyce's work. Wharton's seeming misunderstanding of the same work has also been taken to show her lack of connection with modernist writing in general. Wharton's letter describes *Ulysses* as "a turgid welter of pornography (the rudest schoolboy kind) and unformed and unimportant drivel; and until the raw ingredients of a pudding *make* a pudding, I shall never believe that the raw material of sensation and thought can make a work of art without the cook's intervention. . . . I *know* it's not because I'm getting old that I'm unresponsive" (Wharton to Bernard Berenson, Jan. 6, 1923, in Wharton, *The Letters of Edith Wharton,* 461). Wharton also mentions reading *The Waste Land,* the works of F. Scott Fitzgerald and Sinclair Lewis (who dedicated his novel *Babbitt* to her in 1922). In *The Writing of Fiction* Wharton

discusses Marcel Proust's work in detail and other modern French writers. She was an avid reader of modern fiction. Even critical works sympathetic to Wharton's way of reading consider her critiques of modernists (including Woolf) as writing self-indulgent "me-books" a testimony to her "curmudgeonly scorn" and old-fashioned writerly aesthetics. See Killoran, *Edith Wharton,* 10; Goodman, *Edith Wharton's Inner Circle,* 9; and R. W. B. Lewis, "A Writer of Short Stories," 10.

2. Though Wharton did not return to America from a six-year family stay in Italy and France until 1872, she would have known about the creation of the Metropolitan Museum of Art from her "Uncle Fred," as she called him (see Wharton, *Edith Wharton,* 283), who was her godfather (Lee, *Edith Wharton,* 75). He attended her baptism, and he gave her away at her wedding (Lee, *Edith Wharton,* 16, 75). He was a member of the Metropolitan's initial board of trustees and the executive committee; he served as treasurer and later vice president of the corporation. He served on several subcommittees including loan exhibitions, finances, and building. He became president of the Metropolitan Museum of Art in 1902 on the death of then-president Henry Marquand; he remained in that role until his unexpected death from a heart attack in September 1904. In her 1938 follow-up essay to *A Backward Glance,* "A Little Girl's New York" (published in Wharton, *Edith Wharton,* 274–88), Wharton notes that her youth consisted of drawing-room conversations in her parents' home about "my uncle Fred Rhinelander's ambitious dream of a Museum of Art in the Central Park" (283). In previous biographies of Wharton there has been some confusion over her mother's family (in part because so many of the men she was related to were named Frederick Rhinelander). R. W. B. Lewis's biography incorrectly identifies Wharton's uncle as "Frederick J. Rhinelander" (Lewis, *Edith Wharton,* 5), contributing to the confusion (Hermione Lee's recent biography leaves out any middle initial). No biography of Wharton discusses the very significant role that Rhinelander played in the creation and development of the Metropolitan Museum of Art. The New York Historical Society has published a genealogical history of the Rhinelander family that clarifies the lineage; see Rhinelander, *One Branch of the Rhinelanders in the USA—From 18th Century German Rotgerbers to 19th Century Old New Yorkers to 20th Century Dispersed Americans.* Winifred Howe's pioneering study of the creation of the Metropolitan Museum of Art contains the following analysis of Rhinelander's service: "Frederick W. Rhinelander, the third President of the Museum, had also known the Museum from its infancy. He was one of the signers of the original charter granted by the Legislature, one of the original subscribers, and continuously a Trustee. All his powers were enlisted in the service of the Museum, which became his chief pleasure and duty. He not only acquainted himself thoroughly with its collections and its needs, but also became familiar with foreign museums, that he might be better fitted to further the interests of his own museum" (Howe, *A History of the Metropolitan Museum of Art,* 1:281).

3. She began a line-a-day diary in 1920 that chronicles her visits to museums with friends and professionals, notes with whom she went, and gives a very brief description of what she saw and thought. The line-a-day notebooks that she used from 1920

until her death in 1937 are found in the Wharton Mss. Collection at Indiana University's Lilly Library, Bloomington.

4. Kenneth Clark asks to have the Royal Commission Report on Museums sent to him in order to prepare for an upcoming board meeting: "I should be glad to have a look at the Standing Commission report *before* I return, as it will give me more time to see what I ought to say. Would you be so kind as to mail it to me at the following address: c/o Mrs. Wharton, Pavillon Colombe St. Brice-sous-foret, France" (Kenneth Clark to his assistant, May 27, 1934, in *Kenneth Clark Correspondence as Director, 1934–1948*). Adeline Tintner considers the "not often closely investigated" subject of Wharton's "flair for art history" and her "inclusion of art in novels" (Tintner, *Edith Wharton in Context,* 5). Although Tintner raises interesting connections about art, she does not investigate Wharton's discussions of museums.

5. The Annual Report of the Trustees of the Metropolitan Museum of Art offers a clear picture of the trustees' attitude that one of the primary functions of the museum was to help refine public taste and that they believed by the end of the century that museums were certainly successfully accomplishing this goal. In the Third Annual Report for the Year Ending May 1, 1873, the trustees write that "the establishment of Museums of Arts is important for the purpose of educating and refining the people" (*The Metropolitan Museum of Art Annual Reports of the Trustees of the Association, 1871–1902,* 36). Already two years later, the trustees claim to see improvement: "the establishment of the Museum has already exerted a visible influence for good on the public mind" (ibid., 65).

6. *The Decoration of Houses* gave Wharton a reputation as an aesthete, perhaps somewhat unfairly, in part as a result of Walter Berry's review of it. Berry, who had also supervised Wharton's revision of the book, emphasized the text's virtue as an upholder of the traditions of "moderation, fitness, proportion." While he conceded that Wharton had used the terms in relation to her larger modern project, and that, for Wharton, "to advance may be to look backward," he also helped to cement an idea in the minds of readers that Wharton was an upholder of the better values of the past. The book, however, as my reading suggests, was equally—if not more—interested in the future. Berry's review is reprinted in Tuttleton, Lauer, and Murray, *Edith Wharton: The Contemporary Reviews,* 8–10 (orig. published in *Bookman* 7 [April 1898]: 161–63).

7. The question of what was the first museum in America is a source of some debate. Generally, a museum in Charleston, South Carolina, organized in 1773 by the Charles-Town Library Society is recognized as the first museum. See Ramsey, *Educational Work in Museums of the United States,* 1.

8. Two articles in *The Nation*—"A Museum of the Fine Arts for New York" (Jan. 6, 1870); and "A Museum of the Fine Arts for Boston" (Jan. 27, 1870)—suggest a lack of interest or knowledge about the founding of American museums by contemporaries. The article on Boston claims, "First, it appears to every one who looks into the matter that very few persons in the land know even what is meant by a Museum of Art" (32). The article on New York goes even further to say that "here, in New York,

everything is vague, undetermined, undefined. A few persons may know what they would have the Museum be . . . but these few persons have hardly compared notes, and as yet they hold no power over the premises" (63).

9. Wharton (with Ogden Codman Jr.), *The Decoration of Houses,* 186 (hereafter cited in the text as *DH*). Wharton's quotation recalls and reimagines Benjamin Franklin's antiaesthetic statement that " 'Nothing is good or beautiful but in the measure that it is useful' " (quoted in Rourke, *The Roots of American Culture and Other Essays,* 9).

10. During the period directly preceding World War I, museums were given larger government grants by retooling some of their collections for political purposes. See Coleman, *The Museum in America,* 1:143–53.

11. In the Annual Report of the Trustees of the Metropolitan Museum of Art for the Year Ending May 1, 1878, the trustees congratulate themselves for all that has been accomplished yet complain that "the reflection cannot be avoided that much more might have been accomplished had our fellow-citizens appreciated the value of such an institution and contributed liberally to its treasury" (*The Metropolitan Museum of Art Annual Reports of the Trustees of the Association, 1871–1902,* 144).

12. Wharton, *The Letters of Edith Wharton,* 77–78.

13. Wharton, *The Age of Innocence,* 185 (hereafter cited in the text as *AI*).

14. For Wharton's efforts at accuracy see Montgomery, *Displaying Women;* Waid, *Edith Wharton's Letters from the Underworld,* 90; and Ehrhardt, " 'To Read These Pages Is to Live Again.' "

15. See Tompkins, *Merchants and Masterpieces,* 58.

16. Jonah Siegel discusses the language and vocabulary of aesthetic ideas, particularly those of John Ruskin and William Hazlitt, in chapter 6 of his *Desire and Excess* (esp. 180–81).

17. See Bradley and Ousby, *Correspondence of John Ruskin and Charles Eliot Norton.* There are many passages in which Ruskin disparages the possibility of an artistic culture in the United States. Perhaps the clearest account is his explanation that America is an "*ugly* country" (32), in large part because those who consider themselves artistic are more interested in and drawn to what is ugly than what is beautiful. He uses as an example an American woman who was learning to draw from Ruskin and who, he believed, utterly lacked any aesthetic sense whatsoever, as though she were born into a country without one, too.

18. See Tylor, "The Study of Customs." George W. Stocking discusses Tylor's Darwinian claims that culture developed evolutionarily in his introduction to *Collected Works of Edward Burnett Tylor.* Nancy Bentley discusses Wharton's interest in anthropology in her *The Ethnography of Manners;* George Ramsden reports that Edith Wharton annotated her copies of Tylor's books in *Edith Wharton's Library.* Jane Marcus's generalizations on anthropology and modernism are helpful: "The 'modern' is as indebted to anthropology as the Victorian is to history. When Joyce wrote *Ulysses* he could expect that educated readers (with a little academic guidance) could at once read his book as a modern Odyssey, and readers of Eliot's *The Waste Land* hardly

needed his footnotes to recognize his sources in *The Golden Bough* and *From Ritual to Romance*" (Marcus, *Virginia Woolf and the Languages of Patriarchy*, 36–37).

19. Fry, *Vision and Design*, 37. Fry was also hired by the Metropolitan president John Pierpont Morgan to become the curator of paintings in 1906. His letters during this period express his admiration and horror at Morgan's personality and at Americans' cultural attitudes in general. See also Fry, *The Letters of Roger Fry*, 1:254–92.

20. Wharton met Berenson in 1903 at a dinner and famously made a very bad impression. They became good friends after a second dinner arranged in 1909. Both dinners and the subsequent friendship are discussed in Hermione Lee's and R. W. B. Lewis's biographies of Wharton, as well as in Ernest Samuels's *Bernard Berenson*, 388–89.

21. Berenson, *The Bernard Berenson Treasury*, 113.

22. Calo, *Bernard Berenson and the Twentieth Century*, 39–40.

23. Berenson, *The Bernard Berenson Treasury*, 157.

24. Calo, *Bernard Berenson and the Twentieth Century*, 91.

25. Berenson, *The Bernard Berenson Treasury*, 272.

26. Benjamin, "The Work of Art in the Age of Mechanical Reproduction," 221.

27. Wharton saw herself as a connoisseur, believing she could more correctly identify certain objects than some experts, as she described in *Italian Backgrounds*. In *Edith Wharton and the Politics of Race* Jennie Kassanoff connects Wharton's authentication of a work that had been misidentified to her disdain for the museums that house misappropriated objects: "Unlike her own dramatic discovery at San Vivaldo, where she had stumbled on 'the center of an unexplored continent,' the modern museum was a place of promiscuous contact, sham revelation and derivative knowledge" (157).

28. Originally, Cesnola's glass objects were held in the back of the second floor in Room F (of the Fourteenth Street site). See Howe, *A History of the Metropolitan Museum of Art*, 1:169.

29. *Sanctuary* is possibly the least discussed of Wharton's novels. Cynthia Griffin Wolff explains why: "Not to mince words, *Sanctuary* is a really bad little novel. . . . It will be mercifully forgotten here" (Wolff, *A Feast of Words*, 445). Although I would agree that *Sanctuary* is not Wharton's most engaging work, it is extremely interesting to consider as part of a series of what I call Wharton's "museum-novels," which include the better-known and frequently discussed novels such as *The House of Mirth*, *The Custom of the Country*, and *The Age of Innocence*. Brief discussions of *Sanctuary* do exist, but they tend to focus on the relationship between Kate Peyton and Clemence Verney. See, e.g., Goodman, *Edith Wharton's Women*, 9.

30. Wharton's uncle Frederick W. Rhinelander was the treasurer of the corporation (beginning in 1873) and also on two board-of-trustees subcommittees, for finance and for the creation of the new Central Park building site (both beginning in 1874). One of the frequent complaints in the early years of the *Annual Reports of the Trustees of the Metropolitan Museum of Art* is that European governments give massive amounts of money for the upkeep of national museums, whereas the United

States government and even the state governments are much less generous, limiting or significantly slowing down what the American museums are capable of accomplishing. See the Second Annual Report Ending May 1, 1872, in *The Metropolitan Museum of Art Annual Reports of the Trustees of the Association, 1871–1902*, 24.

31. Wharton, *Sanctuary*, 169 (hereafter cited in the text as *S*).

32. American Association of Museums, *Proceedings of the American Association of Museums* 1 (May 1906): 1–24.

33. Julia Noordegraaf explains Gilman's position: "Indeed, the aesthetic display of art was regarded [by Gilman] as the most accessible type of display for people without much training in looking at art works," and she argues that "Gilman's guidelines for the ideal museum were drawn up with the visitor and his or her comfort in mind. Typical of his approach is the fact that his definition of museum presentation includes visitor comprehension" (Noordegraaf, *Strategies of Display*, 93, 95).

34. Gilman, "The Triple Aim of Museums of Fine Art," 93–94. Gilman also wrote the important work *Museum Ideals of Purpose and Method* (1918), from which Marianne Moore took notes that I discuss in chapter 4. Gilman also became one of the main proponents of the idea of docents and the program of amateur guides leading visitors around a museum. Other curators resisted the program because they thought that proper education could not occur in this way. Gilman was also friends with Bernard Berenson and Isabella Stewart Gardner, so although there is no evidence that Wharton ever met him, she probably knew of his ideas.

35. Ward, "Labeling in Museums," 43.

36. Gilman, "An Open Reply," 48.

37. There were two committees organized to review Cesnola's collections: an Investigative Committee and an eight-member panel of Executive Committee members. Frederick W. Rhinelander was a member of the Executive Committee panel but not a member of the Investigative Committee. The Investigative Committee was a panel made up of both board members, including William Prime and J. Q. A. Ward, and external experts, including Frederick A. P. Barnard (Columbia University president), Charles P. Daly (American Geographical Seminary president), and Roswell D. Hitchcock (Union Theological Seminary president) (See Tompkins, *Merchants and Masterpieces*, 63). Cesnola also replied to the charges in an address to the Executive Committee. Both committees are mentioned briefly in *The Metropolitan Museum of Art Annual Reports of the Trustees of the Association, 1871–1902*, 262, as part of the Fourteenth Annual Report for the Year Ending Dec. 31, 1883. This brief mention, however, does not occur until 1883 (the first time *any* mention of the issue appears in the Trustee Reports); it occurs in brackets and states only that nothing problematic was found at all during the investigation. In Elizabeth McFadden's *The Glitter and the Gold* there is a brief reference to Cesnola's giving an account of his troubled excavations to eight members of the Executive Committee, including Rhinelander (200). Her source is the *New York Daily Tribune*, Dec. 12, 1883, as well as Cesnola's *Cyprus* (130). In Rhinelander's own file in the Metropolitan Archives, neither investigative panel is mentioned. Winifred Howe's *A History of the Metropolitan* names the mem-

bers of the Investigative Committee (1:222) but makes no reference to a separate internal committee made up of Executive Committee members. Calvin Tompkins's *Merchants and Masterpieces* (63–64) also names only the five members of the Investigative Committee. Tompkins also does not mention the Executive Committee's own investigation that McFadden references from 1883.

38. Edith Wharton's annotated copy of Henry James's *The American Scene* was sold in an auction, and the specific passages marked can no longer be identified (mentioned in Ramsden, *Edith Wharton's Library*, 63).

39. James, *The American Scene*, 189–93.

40. These scenes have been central to discussions of the *Age of Innocence*, but questions about why they take place in the Cesnola exhibit ignore the specific and controversial history of the antiquities. Two particularly useful readings can be found in Bentley, *The Ethnography of Manners*, 100–110; and Trumpener and Nyce, "The Recovered Fragments." Although I do not agree with Bentley's reading of the exhibit as providing "the field for securing the real" (108) for Archer and Olenska (since it assumes that the Cesnola objects are authentic objects from a more authentic past), her discussion of the museum's new authority in social culture is extensive and excellent. The most recent reading is offered in Kassanoff, *Edith Wharton and the Politics of Race*. In the book's "Coda: *The Age of Innocence* and the Cesnola Controversy," Kassanoff directly addresses the controversial history of the Cesnola antiquities, arguing that the inclusion of these objects underlines the novel's "preoccupation with such questions of authenticity" (161) and that these objects reaffirm both Wharton's efforts to find a "pure historical origin" of American identity and her repeated realizations of this impossibility since "to be American was to be denied the privilege of racial innocence" (162).

41. See Edbury, "Cyprus in the Nineteenth-Century."

42. Cesnola, *Cyprus*, 125–26.

43. Nancy Bentley explores Wharton's ambivalence about U.S. expansionist policies in "Wharton, Travel, and Modernity": "At a moment when most Americans greeted US expansions as an unequivocal force of progress, Wharton's view was far more wary and critically discriminating." Bentley goes on to argue that Wharton's view represents, in some ways, a double standard, believing that "Americanization destroys beauty, [but] European imperialism reveres and protects it. Art and beauty are her key to understanding global politics" (18). Although I do not think the distinction between American and European is quite as clear for Wharton as Bentley suggests, it is a helpful distinction to consider in this example since Wharton's analysis of the relationship between expansionist policies and what the Cesnola antiquities represent about the potential future of the Metropolitan Museum is so negative.

44. In the Third Annual Report for the Year Ending May 1, 1873, the trustees write: "The Trustees have become the depositories of a collection of antiquities so rare, so important, and so vastly interesting that they did not hesitate to make considerable sacrifices to display it to their fellow-citizens at the earliest possible moment. It is a curious fact that the most ancient specimens of art in the world should find their home

in the youthful of all museums." They continue: "For the possession of these treasures, the nation is indebted, in the first place, to the public spirit of General Cesnola, who preferred that they should be brought to his adopted country at the sacrifice of the larger sum for which he might have disposed of them abroad" (*The Metropolitan Museum of Art Annual Reports of the Trustees of the Association, 1871–1902*, 40, 42).

45. Duncan, "Art Museums and the Ritual of Citizenship," 92–93.

46. Wharton, *The House of Mirth*, 126 (hereafter cited in the text as *HM*).

47. There are many helpful readings of this famous scene, but none that I have found consider Carrie Fisher's understanding of museum culture as central to her plan for the evening. For an analysis of the social and economic implications of the scene in relation to Lily Bart's position see Dimock, "Debasing Exchange"; and Michaels, *The Gold Standard and the Logic of Naturalism*, 225–34. Another example of a house that is also a museum is Isabella Stewart Gardner's home. It is interesting that Wharton includes in a description of the Brys' house the detail that one "had to touch the marble columns to learn they were not of cardboard" (*HM*, 126), since one of the marble columns in Gardner's house was actually made of concrete, and she was reported to have told her architect that "no one would ever notice." I do not know if Edith Wharton ever heard the story, but she had met Gardner, attended a dinner at her home, and—though the two women did not like each other—they shared many close friends, most notably Bernard Berenson. See Tharp, *Mrs. Jack*, 238.

48. Throughout the first ten years of the museum's existence the Annual Reports of the Trustees include complaints about lack of commitment and interest of fellow citizens and the American government. One reason for the extent of the devotion to Cesnola made clear in these pages is his unwavering commitment to the museum. For example, in the Sixth Annual Report (for the Year Ending in 1876) the trustees write: "All the discoveries made by this laborious and indefatigable explorer should be added to the Collection" (*The Metropolitan Museum of Art Annual Reports of the Trustees of the Association, 1871–1902*, 80).

49. Clarence Cook gives the figure of $138,866 in *Art Amateur*, Aug. 1881, 47.

50. The story that Cesnola recounted of his excavations in *Cyprus: Its Ancient Cities, Tombs, and Temples* is officially discredited in McFadden, *The Glitter and the Gold.* Earlier charges against Cesnola can be found in Cook, *Transformations and Migrations of Certain Statues in the Cesnola Collection;* and Feuardent, *The Cesnola Collection and De Morgan Collection.*

51. Cesnola, *Cyprus*, vii–viii.

52. The magazine lasted for forty-nine issues, from 1879 to 1903.

53. In the Third Annual Report for the Year Ending May 1, 1873, the trustees include a quotation from an article in the *London Times* noting that " 'it is a European misfortune that they should cross the Atlantic' " (*The Metropolitan Museum of Art Annual Reports of the Trustees of the Association, 1871–1902*, 40). They were also insulted by the criticism from various European sources that, by sending the treasures to America, Cesnola was basically reburying the treasure. They responded to these attacks by arguing that "it is no less the duty of the Museum to see to it that the Cypriote antiquities should not even *seem* to be buried here" (ibid., 123).

54. McFadden, *The Glitter and the Gold,* 50.

55. A discussion of public grants and changes to museum administrative policies to meet government expectations can be found in Coleman, *The Museum in America,* 1:177–90.

56. Gaston L. Feuardent, "Letter to the Editor," *Art Amateur,* Sep. 1880, 68.

57. See Tompkins, *Merchants and Masterpieces,* 64.

58. *New York Times,* quoted in *Art Amateur,* March 1881, 68.

59. *Art Amateur,* March 1881, 68.

60. McFadden, *The Glitter and the Gold,* 33.

61. The trustees write: "[In this connection it is proper to make brief allusion to a subject which has recently commanded the attention of members as of the public. You are aware that from 1881, the first year of the complete arrangement and exhibition of the Cesnola Collection, it, and its discoverer, have been subjected to a continuous series of attacks in certain public prints, charging fraudulent manufacture and alterations of objects and deceptive restorations. It has not appeared to the Trustees that these statements required public notice from them]" (*The Metropolitan Museum of Art Annual Reports of the Trustees of the Association, 1871–1902,* 261). The accusations eventually culminated in a trial. The Board of Trustee member Joseph H. Choate defended Cesnola and won the case, though the accusations did not cease. See also note 37 above.

62. "Is Art Our Only Fashion?" *Art Amateur,* June 1881, 2.

63. In 1882 the Metropolitan hired Professor William Goodyear as its first curator. He served alone in that capacity for four years. In 1886 Cesnola reorganized the museum into departments using the British Museum's organizational plan: three departments, each with its own curator who reported to him. This organization remained in effect until Cesnola's death in 1904. See Howe, *The History of the Metropolitan Museum of Art,* 1:217–19. For other helpful and more general discussions on the professionalization of the museum see Wittlin, *The Museum,* 146–71; Rea, *The Museum and the Community;* Newsom and Silver, *The Art Museum as Educator,* 509–667; Conn, *Museums and American Intellectual Life, 1876–1926;* and Coleman, *The Museum in America,* 1:3–38. Also in Henry James's *The Golden Bowl* (1904), Maggie Verver's desire to be an expert or at least to be surrounded by experts is connected to her support of her father's plan to create the "museum of museums" in America. Henry James inscribed the book to Wharton personally, citing their mutual interest in the subject, although I think that Wharton differed from James on the subject of the expert. While James's female characters connect the gaining of knowledge to expertise Maggie Verver's enlightenment occurs in connection to her visit to the museum expert Mr. Crichton—Wharton's female characters are much more wary of the processes used to gain enlightenment.

64. Metropolitan Museum of Art, *Guide to the Cesnola Collections,* 13–23.

65. See the Annual Report for the Year Ending May 1, 1878, in *The Metropolitan Museum of Art Annual Reports of the Trustees of the Association, 1871–1902,* 121.

66. Cook, "Our Mismanaged Museum," *Art Amateur,* Aug. 1881, 46.

67. See Harris, "The Gilded Age Revisited." This is one of the first important es-

says on museums to challenge the idea that the developers of the earliest American museums were merely "ostentatious and grasping" figures, for whom "culture . . . meant possession and not creation, it meant acquisition" (546). Harris argues that this is not the true story of the development of the Boston Athenaeum and that early twentieth-century museum educators "incorrectly" (566) characterized the goals of the nineteenth-century founders of American museums in order to enhance the seeming importance of their own plans for improving museums' educational goals. Harris maintains that museums were founded with plans to implement some of the same educational goals that twentieth-century educators argued for a few decades later. Harris's argument helps explain the dynamic of the attacks on the Cesnola antiquities—and by relation—the founding trustees of the Metropolitan, who, despite blatant mistakes, certainly had some of the same educational goals in mind as those who challenged their leadership later.

68. See *The Metropolitan Museum of Art Annual Reports of the Trustees of the Association, 1871–1902*, esp. pages 24, 52, and 65.

69. In an early essay Wharton made arguments about the relationship between beauty and education that were very similar to those of the trustees, suggesting that surrounding oneself with beautiful objects was necessary to improving education. In "Schoolroom Decoration" (1897), an editorial published in the *Newport Daily News*, Wharton asks for "your help in completing the decoration of Newport schools . . . [and] in making the people feel that to put some beauty into the bare rooms of Newport is not only a good thing but a necessary thing . . . [because] beautiful pictures and statues may influence conduct as well as taste" (repr. in Wharton, *Edith Wharton*, 57–58).

70. Fisher, *Making and Effacing Art*, 10–12. Fisher defines the museum's act of preservation as the "resocialization of objects" and an effacing of an object's social history before it becomes a museum piece.

71. First published as Edith Wharton, "The Rembrandt," in the Aug. 1900 issue of *The Cosmopolitan*. This issue also includes an essay on Newport as the most obvious place in the United States to witness the remarkable growth in wealth and attitudes about luxury since the Civil War and an article on the new Paris Exposition.

72. Jennie Kassanoff reads this scene (and the label "use unknown") quite differently, as primarily about the erotic appeal of "inaccessibility": "As is the case in the museum, where the object is made precious by its mysterious inaccessibility, so Ellen retains the edge of reality by escaping the visible ravages of time. Her authenticity, like the Metropolitan's Cypriot antiquities, rests with her ability to transcend use. . . . For Archer, this impracticality is precisely the source of Ellen's erotic appeal: like the encased implements, her body remains for Archer unconsummated and her use unknown" (Kassanoff, *Edith Wharton and the Politics of Race*, 158).

73. "War-Time Service by Museums and by Museum Men," 34.

74. Dana, *A Plan for a New Museum*, 11–12. Dana published many other books about museums, including *Should Museums Be Useful?*

75. "Distance," *Museum Work* 1 (Feb. 1919): 130.

76. Cesnola, *Cyprus*, 2. Cesnola recounts the history of Cyprus as "a checquered character of war and conquest" in the introduction. This allows him to present his removal of the treasures as part of the "lively competition" over the island and its antiquities that had always taken place.

77. In *Edith Wharton and the Politics of Race* Jennie Kassanoff argues that for Wharton, an idea of democracy provided "a repressed but dynamic source of literary creativity" (162). In the scenes inside the Metropolitan Wharton seems to struggle between optimism about the good that the existence of any museum might accomplish by elevating the educational level and cultural knowledge of an indifferent public (an assumption with which she agrees) and a critical belief about the degree to which the early museum is already revealing some of the very ideas and attitudes that will keep it from providing this necessary enlightening function. She underlines her position in the introduction, explaining that "Wharton responded to the possibilities of racial and ethnic hybridity by forging a racial aesthetic and a theory of language and literature that encoded a deeply conservative, and indeed essentialist, model of American citizenship. If her native land generously welcomed the world's huddled masses, then the novel, under Wharton's neo-nativist laws of 'pure English' and her colonial determination to suppress 'pure anarchy in fiction,' formed an architectural, aesthetic and political bulwark against the menacing possibilities of democratic pluralism" (5).

78. Karageorghis, *Ancient Art from Cyprus*, 3–15.

79. Valéry, "The Problem of Museums." Wharton and Valéry were acquaintances in France. He personally inscribed his 1924 book of essays, *Varieté*, to her. The book does not include the 1923 essay although it does use similar arguments about the development of culture.

80. Adorno, "Valéry Proust Museum," 177.

81. Andre Malraux, like many of his fellow observers of museum culture, was concerned about losing the ability to contemplate works of art inside a museum and was anxious that the museum's volume of inventory meant that works of art were being put too closely together. "The practice of pitting works of art against each other, an intellectual activity, is at the opposite pole from the mood of relaxation which alone makes contemplation possible" (Malraux, *Museum without Walls*, 14). Katie Trumpener and James M. Nyce make a similar argument about Wharton's *The Age of Innocence* in "The Recovered Fragments." They contend that "the book's organizing principle is revealed in Edith Wharton's metaphor of society as a museum without walls. For Newland and the reader, Old New York becomes a study gallery where American society can be observed and understood" (168).

82. Although Wharton did not directly identify a source for this scene inaugurating "the new galleries" at the Metropolitan Museum, a similar event occurred on December 22, 1902, shortly after Frederick W. Rhinelander became president. In "Museum's Wing Opened," the *New York Times* (Dec. 23, 1902) reported on the celebration, which included a speech by the New York City mayor and a list of attendees, including Rhinelander, who sat onstage. In Winifred Howe's description, "the

ceremony of opening this, the most beautiful part of the Museum building, . . . was extremely simple. It was formally opened with prayer by the Right Reverend Bishop of Washington . . . presentation of the building to the Trustees by Hon. William R. Wilcox, President of the Department of Parks; the acceptance of it by Frederick W. Rhinelander, who upon the death of Henry G. Marquand had become President of the Museum; and an address by Hon. Seth Low, Mayor of the City" (Howe, *A History of the Metropolitan Museum of Art*, 1:277–78).

83. This moment in the Metropolitan's history, in fact, marked both the end of one era and the beginning of a new one. Because Cesnola was in his seventies, had struggled with health issues over the past few years, and had been in his position for almost twenty-five years, Frederick Rhinelander and the trustees began to search for his successor. As part of his extensive travels in Europe to secure new works of art and to study techniques of organization and preservation at museums and galleries, Rhinelander met with Bernard Berenson in Paris. He wrote to Cesnola in August about his interest in at least talking "with Berenson about his employment in future as Expert in his line—I am convinced that we must adopt this system in our purchases—I find he is generally acknowledged to be an authority—I am confident that he can be trusted in judging the authenticity and merit of the Italian Schools—and he is well acquainted with all other schools" (Letter to Louis di Cesnola, Aug. 6, 1904, Office of the Secretary of Records, Metropolitan Museum of Art Archives, Frederick W. Rhinelander file). Rhinelander's letters to Cesnola from Europe during two summers of travel suggest his indefatigable focus on learning from European museums and galleries both what to do and what not to do at the Metropolitan. He was appalled by the organization of the South Kensington Museum (later called the Victoria and Albert Museum) and very impressed by new methods of lighting and purifying air that he witnessed in several Paris galleries. He looked forward to his meeting with Berenson as part of this effort to improve the quality and authenticity of the collections themselves. (Edith Wharton had met Berenson for the first time a year before.) Ernest Samuels also adds that interest in making Berenson a buyer or giving him the directorship ended with Rhinelander's death and J. Pierpont Morgan's succession to the presidency. As Rhinelander was Berenson's advocate and neither Morgan nor his close adviser William Laffan, who became vice president, liked Berenson very much, the idea stalled. Samuels also notes that Berenson's wife, Mary, advised him not to take the post if he was offered it because she thought the museum on a recent visit was "a vast collection of horrors" (Samuels, *Bernard Berenson*, 421). Berenson, though, was interested in the job (420–22). Rhinelander's efforts to improve the museum and possibly secure its future through connecting with Berenson did not occur, as he died suddenly a little over a month later. Rhinelander's death marked the end of the early era of the building of the Metropolitan. At his funeral on September 27, 1904, the pallbearers—including Louis di Cesnola, Rutherford Stuyvesant, and J. Pierpont Morgan—indicated the depth of Rhinelander's connection to the museum. (See "F. W. Rhinelander's Work as President—Funeral Today," *New York Tribune*, Sep. 27, 1904.) In *No Gifts from Chance* Shari Benstock notes that

Wharton mourned his death, wearing black clothes and canceling social engagements (143). Not long after, Cesnola also died. By the end of 1904, eleven of the museum's original trustees had died within the previous eight years, and J. Pierpont Morgan, who finally agreed to take over the presidency following Rhinelander's death, began the next era of museum work. (See Howe, *A History of the Metropolitan Museum of Art,* 1:278–83.)

84. Benjamin, "The Work of Art in the Age of Mechanical Reproduction," 219.

85. In "A Little Girl's New York," Wharton's brief sequel to *A Backward Glance,* she critiques collecting and displaying practices at museums, accusing museums of draining life from the real objects by displaying them removed from what gives them purpose or meaning: "I know few sadder sights than the Museum collections of these Arachne-webs that were designed to borrow life and color from the nearness of young flesh and blood. Museums are cemeteries, as unavoidable, no doubt, as the other kind, but just as unrelated to the living beauty of what we have loved" (Wharton, *Edith Wharton,* 277).

86. See Wharton, *Edith Wharton,* 267.

87. Lynch, *The Image of the City,* 7, 109.

88. Dwight, *Edith Wharton,* 228.

89. On individual novels from the 1920s see Millicent Bell's description of the unsentimentality of a few of the late novels in *Edith Wharton and Henry James,* 298; Mary Schriber's begrudgingly positive account of *Twilight Sleep* as "artistically disappointing but . . . satiric" in *Gender and the Writer's Imagination,* 167–70; and Dale Bauer's argument that *Twilight Sleep* is "brilliant" in its depiction of a woman's place in culture in *Edith Wharton's Brave New Politics,* 105. For critiques of Wharton's late novels see Wegener, "Form, 'Selection,' and Ideology in Edith Wharton's Antimodernist Aesthetic"; and Hoeller, *Edith Wharton's Dialogue with Realism and Sentimental Fiction,* 20–23.

90. Coolidge, *Edith Wharton, 1862–1937,* 191.

91. Wolff, *A Feast of Words,* 362.

92. She was thinking about this collection when she wrote *The Age of Innocence* and originally considered *Old New York* as the title for the novel (Wolff, *A Feast of Words,* 339).

93. Wharton, *Twilight Sleep,* 21.

94. Wharton, *Hudson River Bracketed,* 415. Versions of the phrase are used at other points in the novel: " 'big New York novel' " (388) and "a big American novel" (398).

95. Wharton, *A Backward Glance,* 379.

96. Quite a bit has been made of Wharton's memory of hours spent happily in her father's private library: "But the library calls me back, and I pause on its threshold, averting my eyes from the monstrous oak mantel . . . and looking past them at the rows of handsome bindings and familiar names . . . I could at any moment visualize the books contained in those low oak bookcases" (Wharton, *A Backward Glance,* 64–65). Less, however, has been made of the fact that toward the end of her life, as Wharton became less enamored of the prospects for museums, she devoted

increasing attention to perfecting her own private libraries. Hermione Lee writes that "her last improvement was a smaller version of the I Tatti Library. . . . In 1928, she moved about two thousand of her books to Ste-Claire. . . . Once completed, the library with the elegant floor-to-ceiling wooden shelves, matting and dark wood side tables, had a cooler, more minimalist look than the living-rooms, which had a distinctly nineteenth-century air" (Lee, *Edith Wharton,* 547). Lee notes that Wharton had always been thinking about the library as both a physical and intellectual space: "Wharton was particularly eloquent about the need for a well-designed library . . . develop[ing] the 'gentleman's library' which Wharton was now beginning to make her own in *The Decoration of Houses,* in her own homes, and in her fiction" (133).

97. Fisher, *Making and Effacing Art,* 9.

Chapter 3

1. Larsen began as a volunteer at the 135th Street Library in the fall of 1921. *The Board of Trustees of the New York Public Library Minutes* makes the following statements about her progress: "Mrs. Nella L. Imes has had one year at Fiske [*sic*] University and two years at the University of Copenhagen. She passed the recent examination for entrance to Grade 1 and has been substituting for us since September 1921 with satisfactory reports" (Jan. 4, 1922, 7); "Mrs. Nella L. Imes, from Grade 1 to Grade 2, with an increase in salary from $82.66 to $109.75 per month, from November 1st" (Dec. 5, 1923, 389); "Mrs. Nella L. Imes, from Seward Park Branch to 135th Street Branch, October 1st, to take charge of Children's Room, in place of Miss Hope Green, transferred, with an increase in salary from $109.75 to $124 per month" (Nov. 5, 1924, 378). Larsen had worked for a few months at the Seward Park branch of the New York Public Library as part of her requirements for library school in 1923. The last entry in the *Board of Trustees Minutes* reads, "Mrs. Nella Imes to grade 2 from $124 to $150" (Jan. 1, 1926, 17). She resigned from the library in January of 1926, returning occasionally for short periods between 1926 and 1929 when she needed money or work, though her letters indicate that she did not want to do so. Thadious M. Davis gives a detailed report of her employment files at the end of her library career in *Nella Larsen, Novelist of the Harlem Renaissance,* 170–71. Larsen's most recent biographer, George Hutchinson, gives much more attention to Larsen's library career, noting the silence that has generally surrounded her extensive library work: "Larsen's [role at the 135th Street branch] has been almost entirely ignored" (Hutchinson, *In Search of Nella Larsen,* 176).

2. Wall, *Women of the Harlem Renaissance,* 13; and Davis, *Nella Larsen, Novelist of the Harlem Renaissance.* Another recent example of a reading challenging the Harlem Renaissance's aesthetic is Sharon Jones's *Rereading the Harlem Renaissance.* George Hutchinson's very positive critiques of Davis's and Charles Larson's biographies of Larsen in "Nella Larsen and the Veil of Race" is worth mentioning here, as is Yves Clemmen's positive comments on Wall's readings of *Quicksand* in "Nella Larsen's *Quicksand,*" 258–466. Hutchinson clarifies that while Davis's excellent reinter-

pretation of Larsen explains her talent and her important aesthetic position in the Harlem Renaissance, there is still room to debate certain arguments about her role in that process. My chapter takes issue only with the notion that Larsen's library work provides a means to read her work as "genteel," not with any of the other enormously helpful aspects of Davis's important biography or Wall's useful readings of *Quicksand* as a "great" novel.

3. In her scathing book about the feminization of the library profession, Garrison argues against the description of library work as an "extension of a woman's traditional role" because it required neither the woman nor the library to claim to have professionalized. Garrison concludes that the results of this attitude, which included practical consequences such as lower pay for female librarians, were ultimately devastating to all working women. See Garrison, *Apostles of Culture.*

4. Barbara Johnson explores the critical works that consider Larsen's implicit and explicit critiques of gentility. For example, Johnson writes, "The Harlem Renaissance was indeed the literary coming of age of the black middle class, but as Hazel Carby and others have pointed out, it was as much a critique of middle-class values as an espousal of them" (Johnson, "The Quicksands of the Self," 188). In Hazel Carby's seminal text, *Reconstructing Womanhood,* Carby argues much earlier that Larsen's dismissal as a "minor figure" ought to help illustrate the way she has been misread: "Nella Larsen in *Quicksand* refused the resolutions offered by this developing code of black middle-class morality at the same time as she launched a severe critique against the earlier but still influential ideology of racial uplift. The *Quicksand* of 1928 did not just explore the contradictory terrain of women and romance; its sexual politics tore apart the very fabric of the romance form" (Carby, *Reconstructing Womanhood,* 166, 168).

5. Tate, "Desire and Death in *Quicksand,* by Nella Larsen," 240. Throughout her essay Tate explores "Larsen's frequent protests against racial discrimination" (238) and the ways in which Helga is continuously "both escaping and embracing her identity as an African American" (245). I will explore Tate's concern with Helga's movements toward both escape and inclusion through Larsen's broader understanding of these terms as the almost inescapable intellectual categories within which Helga recognizes that people learn to think.

6. Rose, *The Public Library in American Life.*

7. She complained about the school's attitude toward black people in the "Author's Statement" for Alfred K. Knopf (Nov. 24, 1926, in the Alfred A. and Blanche Knopf Collection, Harry Ransom Humanities Research Center, University of Texas Libraries). Davis discusses this statement in *Nella Larsen, Novelist of the Harlem Renaissance* (147–51).

8. Scarupa, "The Energy-Charged Life of Dorothy Porter Wesley," 302–3.

9. Dewey, *Decimal Clasification,* 14.

10. Other students at the Library School voiced concerns about what they saw as the school's overemphasis on the Dewey decimal classification system. An undated special report was filed in the early 1930s based on student evaluations of the courses.

The evaluations were composed between 1928 and 1933, a few years after Larsen left and after the school had been absorbed by Columbia University, but most of the courses and faculty remained the same. In the comments about the "classification" course—"LS 211"—students complained about the overuse of the Dewey system and showed an understanding of some of the limits of the system. Examples include L. B. Pratt, 1928, who writes that there should be "more comparison and study of classification systems other than Dewey"; R. A. Miller, 1930, who writes that "in place of the sanctity of D.C. [Dewey Classification] should like to see substituted theory that modifications are necessary and that nothing is finally learned"; and B. M. Franz, 1933, who asks for "less emphasis on D.C." and "more on L.C." (*New York Public Library Library School Records,* Box 14, Columbia University Rare Book and Manuscripts Library).

11. Reece, *The Curriculum in Library Schools,* 3–6.

12. The five required textbooks are American Library Association, *Catalogue Rules;* American Library Association, *List of Subject Headings for Use in Dictionary Catalogues;* Cutter, *Rules for a Dictionary Catalogue;* Dewey, *Decimal Clasification;* and Kroeger, *Guide to the Study and Use of Reference Books.*

13. Reece, *The Curriculum in Library Schools,* 12–19.

14. Rose, "A Librarian in Harlem." The preface to the article states that Rose presented the essay at the most recent American Library Association (ALA) meeting.

15. Rose, *The Public Library in American Life,* 22.

16. Peterson, "The American Scholar: Emerson and Jefferson," 24.

17. Rose published essays about this branch throughout the 1920s in various journals. In an early article, "Serving New York's Black City," even the title of the essay suggests that Rose sees the 135th Street Library as functioning independently from the main branch, with its own goals for the future.

18. Rose, *The Public Library in American Life,* 36.

19. Christian, *Black Feminist Criticism,* 145.

20. "Since August first, an interesting exhibition of Negro art and of rare books and prints by and about the Negro has been held on the third floor of the 135th Street branch" (*New York Public Library Minutes* [Oct. 5, 1921], 295). There are several other references to similar exhibits over the next few years.

21. Anderson, "Black New York," boxes 10 and 11 of Scm 87-5, Schomburg Center Records, 1921–48, Schomburg Center for Research in Black Culture, Manuscripts and Archives (hereafter cited as Schomburg MSS).

22. See Wingfield, "A Jewel of Harlem," 33–36. Hughes writes: "On a bright September morning in 1921, I came up out of the subway at 135th and Lenox into the beginnings of the Negro Renaissance. I headed for the Harlem Y.M.C.A. down the block, where so many new, young, dark, male arrivals in Harlem have spent early days. The next place I headed to that afternoon was the Harlem Branch Library just up the street. There, a warm and wonderful librarian, Miss Ernestine Rose, white, made newcomers feel welcome, as did her assistant in charge of the Schomburg Col-

lection, Catherine Latimer, a luscious café au lait" (Hughes, "My Early Days in Harlem," 312).

23. Lewis, *When Harlem Was in Vogue,* 105.

24. Anderson, *This Was Harlem,* 186.

25. Rose, "A Librarian in Harlem," 207.

26. Ibid., 207.

27. Catherine Latimer became the first curator of the Division of Negro History, Arts, and Prints. See Sinette, *Arthur Alfonso Schomburg,* 141.

28. Rose, *The Public Library in American Life,* 21.

29. All references to Larsen's novels are to Larsen, *The Complete Fiction of Nella Larsen* (hereafter cited parenthetically in the text).

30. Recent criticism on the epigraph is rather divided as to how to read the poem in relation to Larsen's novel. In the 1970s and 1980s criticism stressed the importance of the image of the "tragic mulatto" in the novel. In the late 1980s and early 1990s there was a backlash against these readings. Articles in the last six or seven years treat the passage quite differently. In "Nella Larsen's *Quicksand*" Yves Clemmen argues that seeing the image (or the novel) as a tale of the "tragic mulatto" is too limiting. Barbara Johnson argues just as passionately that "Nella Larsen herself suggests that her novel should be read through the grid of the mulatto figure" (Johnson, "The Quicksands of the Self," 185). George Hutchinson's essay "Nella Larsen and the Veil of Race" returns to the subject of the mulatto but with the benefit of "the best recent criticism . . . particularly feminist themes" (329).

31. Several critics have given readings of Naxos as Tuskegee. See, e.g., Davis, *Nella Larsen, Novelist of the Harlem Renaissance,* 89–110; Rayson, "Foreign Exotic or Domestic Drudge?"; and Monda, "Self-Delusion and Self-Sacrifice in Nella Larsen's *Quicksand.*" Though the idea of linking Naxos to a specific school such as Tuskegee (where Larsen worked for a year as a nurse) is illuminating, it is only necessary for my purposes here to make clear that Booker T. Washington's ideas for Tuskegee originated in the Hampton model and in his training under Samuel Armstrong, who, according to James Anderson, "viewed industrial education primarily as an ideological force that would provide the type of instruction suitable for adjusting blacks to a subordinate social role in the emergent New South" (Anderson, "The Hampton Model of Normal School Industrial Education, 1868–1900," 62).

32. "Report of Cataloging for the Division of Negro Literature," signed by G. Franklin, Aug. 1940, Box 1, Folder 10/1, Schomburg Center Records, 1921–1948, Schomburg MSS.

33. "Report of Cataloging for the Schomburg Collection," Box 1, Folder 10/1, Dec. 12, 1946, Schomburg Center Records, 1921–1948, Schomburg MSS.

34. Ibid.

35. Woodson, *The Mis education of the Negro,* ix xii. Woodson's ideas recall Langston Hughes's essay "The Negro Artist and the Racial Mountain."

36. This is not the only reference to *Hamlet* in Larsen's novels. Toward the end of

Passing, Felise Freeland tells Irene Redfield (at the final party) that she looks like "the second gravedigger" (252).

37. Anderson, "The Hampton Model of Normal School Industrial Education, 1868–1900," 73.

38. Santayana, "The Genteel Tradition in American Philosophy," 40.

39. Brooks, *America's Coming-of-Age,* 3–35.

40. Cowley, "The Revolt against Gentility," 18.

41. Du Bois writes: "The history of the American Negro is the history of this strife,—this longing to attain self-conscious manhood, to merge his double self into a better and truer self. In this merging he wishes neither of the older selves to be lost. He would not Africanize America, for America has too much to teach the world and Africa. He would not bleach his Negro soul in a flood of white Americanism, for he knows that Negro blood has a message for the world. He simply wishes to make it possible for a man to be both a Negro and an American, without being cursed and spit upon by his fellows, without having the doors of Opportunity closed roughly in his face" (quoted in Franklin, *Three Negro Classics,* 215).

42. Ann E. Hostetler notices a similar point—that Helga's interests in difference are still in opposition to a spirit of dividedness: "Through her love of color Helga attempts to create a spectrum rather than an opposition, a palette that will unify her life rather than leave it divided" (Hostetler, "The Aesthetics of Race and Gender in Nella Larsen's *Quicksand,*" 35).

43. Criticism of the ending began with its first mostly positive review in *Opportunity:* "nothing has prepared us for the sudden shift in her. . . . She turns to revivalistic religion of a stupid sort, then more illogically, to a flabby dull minister who happens to take her home from the church meeting. . . . The end is, I suppose, a sordid death" (Walton, review of *Quicksand,* 212–13). Claudia Tate's "Desire and Death in *Quicksand,* by Nella Larsen" also takes issue with the "unsatisfying ending" (236).

44. Helga has resisted marriage and motherhood. When she sees James Vayle, her ex-fiancé and fellow teacher from Naxos, at a party in Harlem, his argument for wanting to marry makes her angry and makes her want to reject him all over again (which she does). He claims that "the race is sterile at the top. Few, very few Negroes of the better class have children, and each generation has to wrestle again with the obstacles of the preceding ones: lack of money, education, and background. I feel very strongly about this. We're the ones who must have children if the race is to get anywhere" (132). James misunderstands Du Bois's ideas about the "Talented Tenth" (which Du Bois explains in *The Negro Problem,* 31–75). James's restatement of Du Bois's ideas is self-serving. Du Bois does encourage those with money and access to elite opportunity to have children, but he does this as part of a larger plan to promote a vision for the possibilities of education and intellectual achievement. Helga's sympathy to some of Du Bois's ideas (which she expresses while working for Mrs. Hayes-Rore) makes her that much more angry at James for misstating them. The scene is particularly interesting because, although Helga's reaction to James's speech about marriage is quite

bitter, it is also the point at which the novel introduces the last of the social institutions that Helga will reject (and then join): marriage and motherhood.

45. Van Vechten's cataloging practices became increasingly serious throughout the 1920s and 1930s. His six-hundred-plus-page catalog of his Harlem Renaissance materials, including his collections of letters, documents, and books, was eventually given to the Beinecke Library and became the basis for the James Weldon Johnson collection. He thought seriously about the organization of this collection and wrote excitedly about his cataloging progress in letters to Langston Hughes in the 1930s and 1940s. Van Vechten's organization of this material has raised questions at the Beinecke about whether to keep collections' classification systems intact when they are transferred to a library. He created a system whereby he divided his collection into writings by African Americans and writings by everyone else. As a result, in order to know where to look for something in his collection, one must first know the race of the person with whom he corresponded.

46. An early critical recognition of this point is Labaree, review of *Passing*. Labaree writes that "in her new novel, Miss Larsen has forsaken the direct telling of *Quicksand* for an indirect telling, thereby losing the advantage of straight impact upon the sense and sensibility of her readers" (255).

47. Linda Dittmar, who explores Larsen's general thoughts on race, class, and gender, concludes that "Larsen's struggle is with an ideology designed to oppress her by caste as well as gender . . . the woman artist . . . thwarted by a 'social positionality' she feels powerless to change" (Dittmar, "When Privilege Is No Protection," 151).

48. Nella Larsen Imes to Carl Van Vechten, Sep. 29, 1926, Jan. 26, 1928, Beinecke Rare Book and Manuscript Library, Elmer Imes Manuscripts.

49. Box 2, Folder 3, Oct. 1924–June 1925, New York Public Library 135th Street Branch Collection, Schomburg Center Records 1921–1948, Schomburg MSS.

50. There are many examples of Larsen's comments about not knowing how to write; see, e.g., Nella Larsen Imes to Carl Van Vechten, Dec. 7, 1926, Beinecke Rare Book and Manuscript Library, Elmer Imes Manuscripts.

51. Larsen's letters are in Gertrude Stein's papers at the Beinecke Rare Book and Manuscript collection. Thadious M. Davis mentions the letters in her introduction to a recent edition of *Quicksand* (Davis, introduction to *Quicksand*). Debra B. Silverman argues that "even though Larsen praised Stein's text, she effectively rewrote Melanctha's narrative to deconstruct the very stereotypes which kept Stein from fully writing black women's experience in a way that was empowering" (Silverman, "Nella Larsen's *Quicksand*," 606).

52. Bettye J. Williams also writes that "Nella Larsen treats as complex and significant the struggle of her protagonists to form positive self-definitions in the face of multiple systems of oppression" (Williams, "Nella Larsen," 165). Williams thus suggests that Larsen's own novel functions for the author in the way that Helga Crane's repeated efforts at redefining herself through new systems of experience function within *Quicksand*. Larsen repeatedly returns to *Passing* to redefine its achievement

in the few years following its publication as she continued to use its success to apply for writing grants and new contracts.

53. Nella Larsen [Imes], "Three Scandinavian Games"; and Nella Larsen [Imes], "Danish Fun." Larsen's letter to the readers at *Forum* was a defense of "Sanctuary," a story she had published in the January 1930 issue and for which she was subsequently accused of plagiarizing. The story closely resembles Sheila Kaye-Smith's "Mrs. Adis," which was originally published in *Century* magazine in January 1922.

54. Larsen complains about the quality of her final novel, *Passing*, because she thought it was too easy to write (she completed the manuscript—originally titled *Nig*—in less than two months). Perhaps this complaint suggests an anxiety that she was already becoming too professionalized as a writer—the uncertainty about whether or not she could finish her first book and whether anyone would publish it was not part of the experience of writing her final novel. See Nella Larsen Imes to Carl Van Vechten, Oct. 15, 1928, Beinecke Rare Book and Manuscript Library, Elmer Imes Manuscripts.

55. The names she used at various points included Nellie Larson (given name), Nella Imes (married name), Allen Semi (married name backward), Nella Larsen, and Nella Larsen Imes.

Chapter 4

1. Bishop, *The Complete Poems*, 82–83.

2. Bishop writes about this meeting in the essay "Efforts of Affection." I do not know if Bishop knew this, but in 1932 Moore wrote to her brother that she had seen "bower-birds" during a visit to the Museum of Natural History. See Moore, *The Selected Letters of Marianne Moore*, 266.

3. Andrew Kappel explains Moore's philosophy of omission in terms of her famous statement that "omissions are not accidents," as she notes in the epigraph to her *Complete Poems*, and he discusses her practice of revisions in terms of this idea of "omission." Here I will extend Kappel's discussion in order to consider Moore's decision to omit certain poems from *Observations* in terms of not only "omission" but her developing interest in "accidents" as a term of equal weight and importance. See Kappel, "Complete with Omissions."

4. In a typescript of comments by Mary Warner Moore that Marianne Moore began in the 1930s, Moore quotes her mother as saying, "In St. Louis if a girl was ready to come out no one would think of having her go to college. Anything so mildly intellectual as going to Vassar was looked on askance, as for studying medicine!" (May 24, 1936). Mary Warner Moore's criticism of negative attitudes she witnessed toward women wanting to go to college offers one clear explanation for her view that Marianne Moore's college education entitled her to something better professionally (see Marianne Moore's reading notebook, ser. III, box 04, folder 08, Marianne Moore Collection, Rosenbach Museum and Library [hereafter cited as MMC]).

5. Moore's diaries list the concerts and museums she attended and usually a few

sentences about what she saw. Perhaps the most famous examples of her catalogs of visits are her "Sojourn in the Whale" letters detailing her first trip to New York and her recognition that the very first place she must see to begin her modern poetic education was Alfred Stieglitz's Gallery 291.

6. Most recently Cristanne Miller concluded that Moore's poems of the 1940s show a significant shift: "as others have suggested, Moore's World War II poems are indeed written in a register different from her poems of *Observations* (1924) and *Selected Poems* (1935)" (Miller, "Distrusting," 353). Laurence Stapleton argues in *Marianne Moore: The Poet's Advance* that "Marianne Moore's latest poems suggest a shift in emphasis" (225). And Margaret Holley's study *The Poetry of Marianne Moore* suggests that "the second significant turn in Moore's verses of the forties that will be amplified in her later work is their more frequent and explicit attention to issues of contemporary history" (114).

7. Paul, *Poetry in the Museums of Modernism.* In the chapter "Discovery, Not Salvage" (141–93) Paul focuses on Moore's use of the American Museum of Natural History to develop poems published in *Selected Poems* and *What Are Years* (1941).

8. Marianne Moore to Mary Warner Moore, July 10, 1910, MMC.

9. Ibid.

10. Moore continued the practice of copying letters onto the backs of original letters in her private correspondence and particularly when she became editor at *Dial* magazine. See Collins, "Marianne Moore, Melvil Dewey, and Lake Placid," 54. Examples from Moore's editorship are in the Dial/Scofield Thayer Papers, Beinecke Library. Other than brief descriptions of Moore's work with Dewey in biographical accounts of Moore's life, this is the only essay I have found that considers Moore's experiences in Lake Placid in relation to the development of her poetic principles.

11. See Cole, "Storehouses and Workshops," 374.

12. Marianne Moore to Mary Warner Moore, July 13, 1910, MMC.

13. Mary Warner Moore to Marianne Moore, July 22, 1910, MMC.

14. Some of Moore's earliest crafts projects suggest this interest: creating a family newspaper by rearranging existing newspaper headlines and columns, organizing postcard books, and developing what will become her system of reading (and other) notebooks (complete with self-made indexes).

15. Moore, "Autobiography," 42–44.

16. See Longstreth, *The Adirondacks*, 231–58. By the time Moore goes to work for Melvil Dewey in 1910, he is a rather controversial figure. Because of accusations of anti-Semitism, he had been forced out of the establishments that he had created—the professional library school at Columbia University and the American Library Association—and had formed a network in Lake Placid to promote his ideas. Longstreth also explains how Dewey divided guests into "classes" and excluded Jews at his Lake Placid Club.

17. Marianne Moore to Mary Warner Moore, July 24, 1920, MMC.

18. Quoted in Willis, *The Complete Prose of Marianne Moore*, 182.

19. Moore's conciliatory tone is one explanation for the way her essays tend to be

read as statements of her aesthetics of order rather than as critiques of this aesthetic. For example, Louise Collins discusses Moore's aesthetic as "precision of phrase, deliberateness, and a concern with categorizing" (Collins, "Marianne Moore, Melvil Dewey, and Lake Placid," 53). My analysis of Moore's experience working for Melvil Dewey suggests that Moore became less enamored of the job the longer she worked for him. By the time she writes *Observations,* she critiques his aesthetics of categorization and classification as exclusionary and not conducive to thinking creatively.

20. Robin Schulze's very detailed and thoughtful account of Moore's resistance to the publication of *Poems* and her eventual agreement to publish the book for the Dial Press appears in Schulze's introductory essay to *Becoming Marianne Moore,* where Schulze writes: "Moore, at the time, saw her poetic career, at least in part, in evolutionary terms. She pictures herself and her texts as organisms ill adapted to their present context, her poems creatures, like their author, doomed to extinction by their lack of proper defenses against the stresses of a much-changed and infinitely harsher environment. Poems capable of surviving in the relative shadow of little magazines might not survive the more intense public glare of a full volume, particularly when the poet had not been given the opportunity to alter them to suit their new social, cultural, and textual conditions" (Schulze, "Moore's Early Volumes," 25).

21. In the poem called "Children's Room 42nd Street Library" Moore writes:

As she was coming out
He turned himself about
And begged that she would look at him,
Him, him
In his heart so bold
In his scarlet coat of gold
And all his other clothes in trim
trim
trim (reading notebook, VI.01.02.118, MMC)

22. Paul, *Poetry in the Museums of Modernism,* 147.

23. Reading notebook, VI.01.02.120, MMC.

24. "Concerning the Marvelous," Feb. 25, 1937 (typescript), II.01.30, MMC.

25. Both drafts are in the MMC. The majority of both drafts have crossed out or bracketed lines, but since I am less interested in how she thought about revising these poems than in what she said before abandoning them, I include Moore's original version.

26. Willis, *The Complete Prose of Marianne Moore,* 503.

27. Moore reaches a similar conclusion in her unpublished novel "The Way We Live Now" (1939). A character discovers through observation that what museums do to the objects inside of them is not altogether positive: "Useless, strange and tiring, valuables wrested from their setting are likely to become; yet to the returning observer, the . . . habitat has itself become the setting and in the Ashmolean, before leav-

ing Oxford, it was with a kind of gratitude Hugh and Alex recognized objects once looked at more casually. Among these were King Alfred's Jewell; and the Cypriote octopus vase, immense and whole beneath its pattern of sucker-edged tentacles; the unluminous likeness of Ashmole himself; and in the picture-gallery, besides much that was unfamiliar, the striplings in pari-coloured hose, of the anonymous Stag Hunt at night" (Moore, "The Way We Live Now," 261 [typescript], MMC). In this scene the objects in the museum have been viewed before—"casually"—and are therefore familiar to the visitors. This "casual" experience is crucial to the visitors' enjoyment of these things when they see them again within the museum.

28. Moore, "Autobiography," 48–52 (III.04.19, MMC).

29. This is a point that Paul Valéry makes in reference to the new authoritarian museum culture. In the essay "The Problem of Museums" he begins by suggesting that the "no smoking" signs and the signs directing one to check one's coat and umbrella are signs of the museum's authority and ultimately affect the type of relationship one can have with it. See Valéry, "The Problem of Museums."

30. Although Moore generally gave the impression that the public library job was simply a part-time relatively unimportant experience for her, the *New York Public Library Minutes: Committee on Circulation* show that she took the exams for promotion on Jan. 5, 1921, passed the test, and was promoted to grade two. Nella Larsen took the same test, the same year, with the same result. During the period that Moore worked at the Hudson Park branch, that branch is mentioned three times in the *Library Minutes* for sewage issues, an employee's fall, and problems with the children's room floor (New York Public Library, Manuscripts and Archives, RG5).

31. Moore, "The Way We Live Now," 253.

32. Eliot, introduction to *Selected Poems*," 8–9, 11.

33. See Moore, *The Selected Letters of Marianne Moore*, 171 (Marianne Moore to T. S. Eliot, July 15, 1921). Repeatedly in letters both to Bryher and many others during this period of being surprised by Bryher's gift of a first book, Moore wavers between gratitude and annoyance. She is grateful for the "beautiful construction" of the book and annoyed that the book does not fully represent her long-standing thinking about exactly what her first book ought to look like.

34. Robin Schulze states that although Moore included notes for her poems as she wrote them, it was actually Scofield Thayer who suggested in the summer of 1924 that she include those in the upcoming book. Schulze writes: "In mid-September [Moore] sent [Thayer] a copy of 'Sea Unicorns and Land Unicorns,' accompanied by a lengthy letter in which she carefully outlined the sources of the poem's many quotations. Thayer found the explanatory notes as intriguing as the poem itself, particularly in the interplay they revealed between the content of the transplanted sources and the context of her poem. On his suggestion, Moore's notes, not only for 'Sea Unicorns and Land Unicorns' but for all of the poems she chose to print in *Observations*, became a part of the volume and an enduring part of her oeuvre" (in Moore, *Becoming Marianne Moore*, 327).

35. Robin Schulze writes that Moore agreed to publish her book with Dial Press

on September 2, 1924, and said the earliest she could turn in the manuscript was in November, but by October 8 the manuscript had already gone to the printer. Schulze writes: "Faced with the Dial Press deadline, Moore revised and arranged her poems, completed a full set of notes to her verses, and compiled a general index for the book, including both title and subject headings, in less than four weeks" (Moore, *Becoming Marianne Moore,* 34). Mary Warner Moore refers to this busy period in a letter to her friend Mrs. Ira Shoemaker, describing the "very urgent request" for the book of poems and the enormous "amount of work involved in 'doing it right.'" She also notes that Moore has had to stay home from her library job for four days with "a curious kind of cold," suggesting that the deadline is somewhat overwhelming (Mary Warner Moore to Mrs. Ira H. Shoemaker, Sep. 10, 1924, VI.27.09, MMC).

36. Peterson, "Notes on the Poem(s) 'Poetry': The Ingenuity of Moore's Poetic 'Place,'" in Willis, *Marianne Moore,* 226.

37. In "Concerning the Marvelous" (1937) Moore points out that the catalog and ancillary materials are just as important to the overall experience of the exhibition as the paintings themselves (II.01.30, MMC). Catherine Paul makes this point also in *Poetry in the Museums of Modernism* (145).

38. Andrew Kappel discusses the details of the publication of *Selected Poems,* and T. S. Eliot's role as an editor of Moore, in "Presenting Miss Moore, Modernist."

39. "Marriage," at first, did stand alone. It was published by itself without notes or any accompanying texts by Monroe Wheeler in *Manikin,* no. 3 (New York: Monroe Wheeler, 1923). This version is slightly shorter than the version Moore published in *Observations.*

40. In one of the few readings of "To a Prize Bird" David Bromwich argues that the bird's powerfulness is mediated by its awkwardness and that the image of the bird includes within it a vision of both authority and resistance. He says that although the bird is "staunch against defeat," it is "not . . . assured of conquest"; instead, "the bird is impressive only in being uncomfortable." I also see Moore undercutting the power of the bird, but for a more historical, less personal purpose in the context of *Observations.* See Bromwich, "'That Weapon, Self-Protectiveness,'" 71.

41. The original title in the *Egoist* was "To the Soul of 'Progress'" (see Moore, *Becoming Marianne Moore,* 188–89).

42. Moore, "Autobiography," 47–48, MMC.

43. Bonnie Costello explains: "After 1914, however, when the family read Kenneth Grahame's 1908 children's classic *The Wind in the Willows,* their family nicknames changed. Moore, by this time a serious poet, became the poem-writing 'Rat' ('the hero of the book,' as her mother wrote to Warner on 24 May 1914)" (Moore, *The Selected Letters of Marianne Moore,* 76).

44. "Art and Interpretation" (3), Jan. 9, 1937 (typescript), II.01.03, MMC.

45. Readings of "Marriage" generally are extremely helpful in working out the meanings of phrases and the contexts for quotations in the long, complicated, and difficult poem. For helpful, though generally personal rather than historical, readings of "Marriage," see Bergman, "Marianne Moore and the Problem of 'Marriage'";

Keller, "'For inferior who is free?'"; and White, "Morals, Manners, and 'Marriage.'" Margaret Holley notes in *The Poetry of Marianne Moore* (56–57) that "Marriage," "An Octopus," and "Sea Unicorns and Land Unicorns" were written simultaneously, with phrases from one draft of a poem entering a draft of a different poem.

46. See Moore, *The Selected Letters of Marianne Moore,* 120. Laurence Stapleton, however, argues that the impetus for the poem was a conversation, quoted in her notebook, that Moore had with Alfred Stieglitz about his marriage to his first wife, as he uses the word *institution* to describe marriage (Stapleton, *Marianne Moore,* 40–41).

47. Marianne Moore to Bryher, May 3, 1921 (Moore, *The Selected Letters of Marianne Moore,* 158).

48. Cristanne Miller notes that in this section of the poem, "far from idealizing either sex, here Moore criticizes both harshly for their failure to see beyond their own selfishness. . . . Nonetheless Moore is more sympathetic to her female character than to her male, and analyzes relationships between them that are notably feminist" (Miller, *Marianne Moore,* 118–20).

49. Delivered in the United States Senate, Jan. 26, 1830. The complete last sentence is as follows: "Let their last feeble and lingering glance, rather, behold the gorgeous ensign of the republic, now known and honored throughout the earth, still full high advanced, erased or polluted, not a single star obscured—bearing for its motto no such miserable interrogatory as, *What is all this worth?* nor those other words of delusion or folly, *Liberty first, and Union afterward;* but everywhere, spread all over in characters of living light, blazing on all its ample folds, as they float over the sea and over the land, and in every wind under the whole heavens, that other sentiment, dear to every true American heart—Liberty *and* Union, now and forever, one and inseparable!" (Beinecke Library College Pamphlets, 2056 1, 184).

50. Ibid., 127.

51. Marianne Moore to John Warner Moore, Feb. 20, 1921 (Moore, *The Selected Letters of Marianne Moore,* 155).

52. Holley, *The Poetry of Marianne Moore,* 64–65. Patricia Willis offers perhaps the most insightful recent reading of this poem by tracing the evolution of the images in the poem and the history of their omissions and revisions (see Willis, *Marianne Moore and the Pipes of Pan,* 19–60). For other readings see Grogan, "Tomlinson, Ruskin, and Moore"; and Stapleton, *Marianne Moore,* 42–50.

53. Runte, *National Parks,* 66–67. See also Cranz, *The Politics of Park Design,* 157. Cranz describes park histories during the "preinstitutionalized municipal park movement," and she explains that the educational issues that arose in the park movement were also concerns in the institutionalization of the museum and the library: "Policymakers perceived a public need for cultural institutions that could be made sufficiently entertaining to create an enjoyable atmosphere: 'If we can give people information in a playful way in the park, it will be a good thing to do.' This early judgment justified the museums, botanical gardens, zoological gardens, aquariums, arboretums, meteorology observatories, and music halls we see in parks today. Even

small, informally organized collections of animals or plants, like the buffalo herds in [Golden Gate Park in] San Francisco were thought to serve the double purpose of instruction and pleasure" (14).

54. Bonnie Costello argues that Moore had a very specific idea of the great American poem in mind that she wished to achieve: "The great American poem, for Moore, would be one in which a rich variety of experience would be imagined into a classic unity, a neatness of finish that would leave no stray particular" (Costello, *Marianne Moore,* 252). Although my analysis comes to a very different conclusion about the poem, Costello's work on this poem has been very important to the development of my thinking about the ending.

55. Willis, *The Complete Prose of Marianne Moore,* 316–17.

56. In her reading notebook, on p. 46, June 28, 1924, Moore attributed this quotation to W. P. Pycraft's *The Courtship of Animals,* 266–69. As the title suggests, this book discusses primarily the way animals mate. The exact sentence that Moore copies down into her reading book is not in Pycraft's book. The section on octopuses is specifically on their unique mating rituals. Pycraft describes how the "sucker-bearing arms" of the octopus are "completely transformed to subserve the ends of sexual congress," a version, it seems, of what Moore describes (though using quite different language) in her notebook.

57. Kappel, "Complete with Omissions," 152. He argues that a significant change appeared in her *Collected Poems,* a text in which she made her omissions *visible* to her general readers in ways the omissions really had not been before, through ellipses and abrupt pattern shifts. He argues that in this volume her revisions were no longer private acts of inclusion or exclusion, as they had been up until then, but public and "conspicuous" acts of excision meant to draw attention to themselves. In other words, in this volume she began to *want* her readers to know that she was radically altering her poems.

58. In her 1968 diary Moore lists "Rosenbach" under Oct. 20 and orders *ASW Rosenbach* (a biography) from *The Strand* on Oct. 22, 1968. She had previously listed the University of Texas at Austin on May 1, 1968, and Vassar College Library on Oct. 15, 1968. Considering that Moore had been quite ill the previous year and her handwriting extremely shaky, these were big trips to undertake and suggested their importance to her (VIII.04.12, MMC).

59. Robin Schulze shares Andrew Kappel's theories about these two late volumes. For Schulze, Moore's desire to advertise the revision process begins in 1951 and continues in 1967 as part of her "poetics of radical instability." Schulze argues that for Moore this poetics of "instability" was a good thing and allowed her to resist the kinds of authoritarian gestures of her fellow modernists. Schulze writes, "Restoring Moore and her poetics of radical instability to a place of primacy in the study of modernist poetry does much to undercut the concept, dear to many critics, of a closed, totalized, ahistorical, authoritarian modernist aesthetic" (Schulze, "'The Frigate Pelican''s Progress," 120).

60. Willis, *The Complete Prose of Marianne Moore,* 673.

61. Kappel, "Complete with Omissions," 133.

62. Long before this moment Moore had first mentioned her fascination with A. S. W. Rosenbach's collecting in a letter: "Mother is excited over Stowe's House being sold; and I am, over Dr. A. S. W. Rosenbach's purchase of *A Lytell Treatyse on the Beauty of Women* and [R. Turner's] *The Garland of Greene Witte*—mentioned in your Sphere of March 19th" (Moore to Bryher, May 9, 1921, in Moore, *The Selected Letters of Marianne Moore,* 159; also see note 58 above on her reading of Rosenbach's biography).

63. Marianne Moore, will dated 1967, MMC.

64. Sargeant, *Humility, Concentration, and Gusto,* 9–10.

65. These items were placed in series XIV, "Vertical Files," MMC.

66. Foucault, "Of Other Spaces," 26.

67. In her 1969 reading notebook Moore writes shakily: "prose is today's medium" (Feb. 19, 1969; reading notebook, VII.03.06, MMC).

Chapter 5

1. Mead, *An Anthropologist at Work,* 110.

2. Lois W. Banner discusses the degree to which Benedict disliked Parsons, beginning with their meeting in Parsons's course that Benedict was enrolled in—"Women and the Social Order"—at the New School in 1919 (Banner, *Intertwined Lives,* 146–52). Despite their personal feelings for one another, their intellectual lives were closely linked throughout the 1920s and 1930s. Since Parsons's course was the first Benedict took in anthropology, it is worth noting that her early introduction to anthropology and her early interests centered on the subject of the professional prospects of women. In biographical notes from Benedict's archive at Vassar, Parsons's course is given a different title—"Sex and Ethnology" (course 27)—and was offered in the fall of 1919 as the only course Parsons ever taught at the New School. See the Ruth Benedict Papers, Box 39, Folder 3, Vassar College Libraries Archives and Special Collections (hereafter cited as VCASC).

3. Parsons, *Social Freedom* (hereafter cited as *SF*); and Parsons, *Social Rule* (hereafter cited as *SR*).

4. Benedict, *Patterns of Culture,* 14 (hereafter cited as *PC*).

5. Briscoe, "Ruth Benedict, Anthropological Folklorist," 459.

6. Quoted in Mead, *An Anthropologist at Work,* 59, 66 (from Benedict's diary: Friday, Jan. 12, 1923; Thursday, Jan. 11, 1923; and Thursday, Feb. 22, 1923).

7. Mead writes about how Franz Boas would assign topics and then the students would complete them in the library. Alfred Kroeber mentions Boas's style of assigning research as well. Despite the historical underpinnings of this style of dissertation, the idea that Benedict was a library-anthropologist persisted even as she began to do more fieldwork. In *Intertwined Lives* Banner discusses the way Benedict championed fieldwork (300).

8. In "An Introduction to Zuni Mythology" (1935), repr. in Mead, *An Anthropologist at Work,* 228.

9. As I have noted, Emerson was a strong proponent of libraries, but he worried

about the effect that reading books as a singular method of research had on students (see chap. 1, esp. notes 7 and 8, above).

10. Hegeman, *Patterns for America,* 36.

11. Ibid., 45.

12. In 1928, during an exchange of letters with her department about an upcoming lecture at Columbia, she asked the department to list her only as "Dr. Ruth F. Benedict, Dept. of Anthropology," rather than their suggested title that included a stated relationship with the American Museum of Natural History.

13. In "Anthropology and the Humanities" she criticizes the old-style anthropologists who learned about tribes from museums rather than seeing museums as the repository for more direct, current knowledge: "professional anthropologists of this period did not engage in conversations such as those of Montaigne and his Tupinamba boy; they studied marriage or religion or magic in the British Museum without benefit of any informant. William James reports that when he asked Frazer about natives he had known, Frazer exclaimed, 'But heaven forbid!' " (4) (Ruth Benedict Papers, Box 49, Folder 1, VCASC).

14. Quoted in Mead, *An Anthropologist at Work,* 74 (from Benedict's diary: Wednesday, Jan. 13, 1923).

15. James Clifford discusses the impact of writing poetry on ethnographic analyses of culture: "Malinowski's authorial identifications (Conrad, Frazer) are well known. Margaret Mead, Edward Sapir, and Ruth Benedict saw themselves as both anthropologists and literary artists. In Paris surrealism and professional ethnography regularly exchanged both ideas and personnel. But until recently literary influences have been held at a distance from the 'rigorous' core of the discipline. Sapir and Benedict had, after all, to hide their poetry from the scientific gaze of Franz Boas" (Clifford and Marcus, *Writing Culture,* 3–4). Benedict describes her choice to keep her writing life private in an unpublished autobiographical fragment in which she explains that she learned early on to keep the things she cared about to herself: "my feeling about my verse, and my nom-de-plume, my relations to Stanley, all are unintelligible without the rule of life I discovered" (3–4) (Ruth Benedict Papers, Box 39, Folder 4, VCASC).

16. Benedict's mother joined library work during a period when library jobs were being advertised as extremely secure. Carolyn Lipscomb explains: "A library school recruitment brochure in 1911, titled *Librarianship: An Uncrowded Calling,* claimed that 'the total product of all the library schools does not nearly supply the normal demands arising from marriage, death, and resignations.' " After World War I "the shortage of available trained librarians accelerated with rapidity. The profession responded by expanding opportunities for library education." As a result, the profession quickly became crowded with " 'certain over-production' " (Lipscomb, "Librarian Supply and Demand," 8). Benedict reacted strongly against what she saw as false advertising for her mother's generation of librarians and against joining what seemed like an increasingly overcrowded field.

17. Quoted in Mead, *An Anthropologist at Work,* 65 (from Benedict's diary: Tuesday, Feb. 13, 1923).

18. On April 29, 1924, the National Research Council in Washington, DC, denied her application; and on May 23, 1924, in response to a request for more information, the council sent a letter to Elsie Clews Parsons explaining that "the Board has been quite inflexible with reference to the rule not to consider applications from candidates over thirty-five years of age, and the reason for this rule is found in the stated purpose of the fellowships, to develop investigations with the idea of assuming the succession to university appointments. . . . It has been our experience . . . that a person who has not already become established in university work at about the age designated, is not very promising material for development" (Ruth Benedict Papers, Box 1, Folder 1, VCASC). Benedict received—and kept—other rejection letters from the American Council of Learned Societies in 1923 and the Committee on Social Science Research Projects in 1926.

19. McCaughey, *Stand, Columbia,* 512.

20. Ruth Benedict Papers, Box 42, *Employment Contracts,* VCASC.

21. "During those years as well [the late 1930s], Ruth moved out of the academy. Horrified at contemporary events, she looked at American society, its character and the sources of that character" (Modell, *Ruth Benedict, Patterns of a Life,* 259).

22. "The professionalization of the discipline had a number of interesting consequences, not the least of which I have already mentioned: the opening up of its ranks from the gentlemen explorers and military men who comprised the ethnologists of the nineteenth century to a much more socially diverse group, including women and men whose origins were in the working class, or who came from immigrant families" (Boas quoted in Hegeman, *Patterns for America,* 44).

23. Hegeman, *Patterns for America,* 11.

24. Mead, *An Anthropologist at Work,* 87–88.

25. Ibid., 90.

26. Ibid., 165. Eda Lou Walton, a friend of Benedict, was also, coincidentally, the initial reviewer of Nella Larsen's *Quicksand* (1928) in *Opportunity* (see note 43 of chapter 3 above).

27. The publication of Mead's book coincided with the depositing of Benedict's papers in the Vassar rare book and manuscript archives in 1959. Vassar librarians organized a special exhibition of material from the volume, and they corresponded enthusiastically with Mead about what to include in the exhibit. The volume served to highlight Benedict's papers; Mead not only knew the papers from her long relationship with Ruth Benedict, but she had also spent eleven years since Benedict's death sifting through them to pick the best and most representative for the published volume. Mead's organization of the papers enabled the six-part volume to function as a kind of complete retelling (and primarily in Benedict's own words) of her life. This organization also remained intact for about sixteen years, until the papers were again reorganized at Vassar in 1975 to reflect the library's new archival practices. By that time, some of the restrictions on material were lifted (other correspondence would not be opened until 1999).

28. Mead's influence on readings continues, even in recent analyses of Benedict's writing. According to the biographer Judith Modell, Benedict's attraction to poetry

developed because it offered her more opportunity to hide: "screened by metaphor, by the 'beat,' and by a pseudonym, Ruth Benedict posed questions about human existence that, her phrases revealed, touched her own experience closely and intimately" (Modell, *Ruth Benedict, Patterns of a Life,* 10). Modell continuously returns to this idea that poetry is what Benedict turned to at moments when she most wanted to understand herself. Discussing Benedict's realization that she was unhappily married, Modell writes that "she also started writing poetry again, using verse as a vehicle for and discovery of her feelings" (ibid., 99). Margaret Caffrey also interprets Benedict as writing "poetry as an outlet for her energies," although she is more skeptical of Mead's poetic analysis (Caffrey, *Ruth Benedict,* 116). Even anthropologists such as Clifford Geertz, James Boon, and Richard Handler, who in the 1980s and early 1990s seemed to reject Mead's autobiographical reading and turned to Benedict as a vanguard—an anthropologist who, because she was also a poet, understood very early on that ethnography was always also a form of literature—did not actually need to read any of Benedict's poems to reach that verdict. Geertz reiterates Mead's view even while critiquing previous discussions of Benedict's literary efforts. In the chapter on Benedict in *Works and Lives* he seeks to expand the notion of (quoting Roland Barthes) "Benedictine anthropology" (19), by calling attention to the way Benedict writes. He briefly reflects on how she might have mastered this original style: "It had, of course, a kind of prehistory in her college writing, in some abortive fragments of feminist biography quickly abandoned when she turned to anthropology, and (though the nature of its relevance is normally misconceived) in her poetry" (109). Geertz takes special issue with the way Judith Modell's biography misinterprets Benedict's poems as autobiographical accounts of events and feelings. Certainly Modell's method of using "literary analysis to accomplish goals similar to psychoanalysis" (Modell, *Ruth Benedict, Patterns of a Life,* 8) is representative of this complaint. Despite Geertz's reinterpretation of Benedict's writing and his evident interest in correcting the "misconceptions" that have developed around her work, he also reiterates Mead's point that she "quickly abandoned" immature creative writing for mature anthropology. See Geertz, *Works and Lives;* Boon, *Other Tribes, Other Scribes;* and Handler, "Ruth Benedict and the Modernist Sensibility."

29. Mead, *An Anthropologist at Work,* 90.

30. Mead's view that Benedict's poetic life is so closely linked to Sapir's, however, ought to remain a more open question than she allows. Since Benedict's side of the correspondence has been lost, her poetic ideas have generally been read through Sapir's replies to her unsaved questions and as reflections of his interests and responses, a questionable practice given Sapir's strong opinions and the obvious differences in their voices and goals.

31. Edward Sapir to Ruth Benedict, Dec. 12, 1924 (quoted in Mead, *An Anthropologist at Work,* 165).

32. Edward Sapir to Ruth Benedict, Jan. 19, 1925 (quoted in Mead, *An Anthropologist at Work,* 169).

33. Sapir, "The Heuristic Value of Rhyme"; repr. in Sapir, *Selected Writings of*

Edward Sapir in Language, Culture, and Personality, 496. There is a very interesting analysis of Sapir's discussions of rhyme in Hegeman, *Patterns for America,* 86–88; Hegeman's focus is on how Sapir's analysis contributes to his efforts at a definition of culture.

34. Edward Sapir to Ruth Benedict, March 6, 1925 (quoted in Mead, *An Anthropologist at Work,* 175).

35. Edward Sapir to Ruth Benedict, May 14, 1925 (quoted in Mead, *An Anthropologist at Work,* 179).

36. Edward Sapir to Ruth Benedict, Sep. 27, 1927 (quoted in Mead, *An Anthropologist at Work,* 185–86).

37. Edward Sapir to Ruth Benedict, Feb. 7, 1925 (quoted in Mead, *An Anthropologist at Work,* 172).

38. Modell says that Benedict "readily, and occasionally eagerly, accepted [Edward Sapir's] comments on poems, remaining wary of his remarks on anthropological points." But Modell makes similar points, as does Mead, in attributing to Sapir the explanation of certain ways of thinking that the lack of Benedict's replies to him affords: "Sapir took up the point and reworded it for her in her prose, in letters, and in conversation. He shed the sharp light of analysis on matters she intentionally left obscure in the rhetoric of her verse" (Modell, *Ruth Benedict, Patterns of a Life,* 141). Yet there is evidence that contradicts this argument. For example, the poem "This Breath," from *November Burning,* was one of the poems Benedict sent Sapir for comments, and he responded by suggesting that Benedict take out the line "We have for blocks to build with," from its first stanza. The line certainly has a different rhythm than the others. While it makes sense that he would not like that line, as it interrupts the natural imagery of the poem, the line is important to Benedict's overarching argument in this poem. Repeatedly, Benedict makes aesthetic choices that seem to fit the scope of her thinking over choices of form. The line is a necessary part of the poem's concern with how a person can keep her most precious ideas safe but still be open to questioning and changing them—an idea central to her entire volume. Benedict never removed the line, even when she rewrote the poem for Mead in 1941.

39. One of the particularly noticeable facts in Benedict's papers at Vassar College is how many rejection letters she kept. There is obviously a lot of her own history that she chose not to keep in her files, which makes the large number of rejection letters still present that much more obvious. These rejections are by both poets and editors from magazines in the 1920s, from academic research councils, and other funding sources. In Susan Van Dyne's *Revising Life: Sylvia Plath's Ariel Poems,* Van Dyne describes how Plath "pilfered" stationery from Smith College the year she worked there and then composed her poems on the backs of those letterheads. Benedict, unlike Plath, appears to have written only on scrap paper or discarded drafts of grants for herself or students. Still, the sense of a poetic relationship being worked out in light of an academic one seems similar. See Susan Van Dyne, *Revising Life,* 8.

40. Ruth Benedict Papers, Lecture 25, Dec. 1938, Box 58, Folder 16, VCASC.

41. See Hegeman, *Patterns for America:* "I will suggest that the vision of 'culture'

that enabled this estranged perception of collective identity is a complexly modernist one, related to other estrangements of context and perception that so influenced the more experimental artistic movements of the period" (4).

42. The four primary analyses of Benedict's poetry are in Mead, *An Anthropologist At Work;* Modell, *Patterns of a Life;* Caffrey, *Ruth Benedict;* and Banner, *Intertwined Lives.* Despite the different way in which I go about understanding these poems contextually, by considering the ways that Benedict continued to regroup and rearrange them, I am indebted to the discussions of Benedict's original composition. Mead considers the way she sees her relationship with Benedict reflected in the poems. Modell (132–40) and Banner (207–11) consider the poems as quite personal and often related to the letters (often to Edward Sapir or Margaret Mead) in which Benedict first introduced them. Caffrey considers the poems in terms of their order of composition (178–79; 193–94; 375–77).

43. Some of the best examples of Benedict's methodology and passion for ethnographic research occur in her correspondence with students and colleagues working in the field. For example, during an exchange of letters with the anthropologist Ella DeLoria, Benedict responded to DeLoria's questions with a long letter of advice about the best way to approach important interviews with tribal members in order to get the clearest and truest picture of village life. See Ruth Benedict to Ella DeLoria, Aug. 25, 1932, Ruth Benedict Papers, Box 28, VCASC.

44. Mead, *An Anthropologist at Work,* 491–93. There are also multiple drafts of this essay in the Vassar archives. These different versions all highlight that sense of Wollstonecraft as a contemporary, particularly because of her thinking that "women are more than men's playthings, that they have lives and understandings of their own, and that anything short of a full development of their powers is a duty left undone" (2) (Ruth Benedict Papers, Box 56, Folder 7, VCASC).

45. The most complete version is in the Ruth Benedict Papers, Box 46, Folder 24, VCASC, with a pencil notation suggesting that parts might be missing that she sent to Clyde Kluckhohn. Benedict also was not sure which name to go by in publishing the volume, crossing out "Anne Singleton" on one cover and replacing it with "Ruth Benedict." I have checked in Louis Untermeyer's papers, in the Princeton University collection of Albert Harcourt's papers, and I have been unable to trace the manuscript that she sent to Harcourt Brace in 1928 or any other manuscripts. A working title was "The Winter of My Blood."

46. She thought about places to send these poems and in the manuscript folder is both a "Manuscript Market" for 1935 and also a list of magazines with addresses. These magazines and newspapers include the *Atlantic Monthly, Harper's, Dial,* the *Herald Tribune, Scribner's Magazine, Yale Review, Century, Bostonian, Poetry, Saturday Review,* and *Vanity Fair.* In the letters file, however, there is no specific evidence that she did more than plan to send any of the poems to the editors or magazines she highlights.

47. There are no dates on any of the versions of the volume in the Vassar library. My analysis is based on the most complete volume among her papers: Box 46, Folder 24, VCASC. In *An Anthropologist at Work* Mead claims that she reprints the

very last version of Benedict's 1941 hand-copied book (not called *November Burning*), given as a present to Mead, but that Mead adds "Resurrection of the Ghost" because it was a recent published poem that Benedict had not included in the 1941 version. The version I work off of from the copies at Vassar includes "Resurrection of the Ghost" as the last poem in the first section. Since the version I work with begins with "Dedication," it is at least almost concurrent with the shorter version she gave to Mead yet represents her continued thinking about the perfect organization for *November Burning*, the revised 1928 book manuscript that she clearly kept thinking about and trying to improve through the 1940s. See also note 56 below.

48. There are three copies in the papers at Vassar. One is titled "Dedication," another "To - with Verses," and the third is handwritten with no title. The text remains the same. This poem is included in the group of poems Benedict gave Mead in 1941. Judith Modell suggests that "Dedication" was written to Margaret Mead in 1940 (Modell, *Patterns of a Life*, 311). Mead also suggests this in *An Anthropologist at Work* (563). While the title "To - with Verses" does give that impression, the vaguer "Dedication" (without a name attached) at the opening of this volume suggests that the poem is serving a different function.

49. Section 1: "But the Son of Man" (*AAW*, 475); "Ways Not Winds' Ways" (*The Nation*, 1933); "This Breath" (*AAW*, 474); Countermand (*Poetry*, 1930); "Intruder" (*AAW*, 474); "As a Dream" (unpublished), "Moth Wing" (*AAW*, 488); "Toy Balloons" (*Poetry*, 1926; *AAW*, 488); "Words in Darkness" (*AAW*, 489); "Dark Soil" (unpublished rewrite of "Nutriment"); "Resurrection of the Ghost" (*Herald Tribune*, 1934; *AAW*, 490).

50. Section 2: "Sleet Storm" (*AAW*, 484); "I Shall Not Call" (*Poetry*, 1928); "Withdrawal" (*AAW*, 482); "The Worst Is Not Our Anger" (*The Measure*, 1926; *AAW*, 70); "Earth Born" (*Poetry*, 1928; *AAW*, 487); "Reprieve" (*AAW*, 480); "For the Hour after Love" (*Poetry*, 1928; *AAW*, 480); "For Faithfulness" (unpublished).

51. Section 3: "Annunciation" (*AAW*, 478); ("In Likeness of a Dove" is not listed in section 3, but the poem is inserted after "Annunciation" in the existing manuscript copy at Vassar); "Price of Paradise" (*AAW*, 478); "The Wife" (unpublished); "Unicorns at Sunrise" (*Poetry*, 1930; *AAW*, 481); "For Seed Bearing" (*AAW*, 71); "For My Mother" (*Poetry*, 1928); "Lost Leader" (unpublished); "Unshadowed Pool" (*Poetry*, 1930; *AAW*, 477); "Monk of Ariege" (unpublished).

52. Section 4: "November Burning" (*Poetry*, 1930; *AAW*, 484); "Preference" (unpublished); "Our Task Is Laughter" (*AAW*, 167); "Miser's Wisdom" (*AAW*, 488); "Counsel for Autumn" (*AAW*, 483); "In Praise of Uselessness" (*AAW*, 489); "In Parables" (unpublished); "Lovers' Wisdom" (unpublished); "Serpents Lengthening Themselves over the Rock" (unpublished); "Flight" (unpublished); "Spiritus Tyrannus" (*AAW*, 486); "Love That Is Water" (*Poetry*, 1930; *AAW*, 474).

53. Section 5: "Death Is the Citadel" (*The Nation*, 1929); "You Have Looked upon the Sun" (*AAW*, 486); "She Speaks to the Sea" (*AAW*, 479); "Eucharist" (*The Nation*, 1928; *AAW*, 479); "This Gabriel" (*AAW*, 486); "And His Eyes Were Opened" (*AAW*, 187); "Burial" (*AAW*, 483); "Dead Star" (*Poetry*, 1930); "Resurgam" (*New York Herald Tribune*, 1934; *AAW*, 194).

54. Durkheim and Mauss, *Primitive Classification*, vii.

55. She offers an example of museums throwing out "religious" art in certain tribes because these objects, following a different set of criteria (both religious and creative) than other tribal enterprises, seem less well made (*PC*, 38).

56. "The selection [of poems] is one she herself made in 1941, when she wrote these poems out by hand in a little hand-bound book as a present for me, and it expresses the most recent personal choice of which there is any record of what she liked best" (Mead, *An Anthropologist at Work*, 563).

57. Ibid., 201.

58. Ibid., 535–36.

59. She wrote in "The Concept of the Guardian Spirit in North America" (1923): "Among the Kwakiutl, their social life and organization, their caste system, their concept of wealth, would be equally impossible of comprehension without a knowledge of those groups of individuals sharing the same guardian spirit by supernatural revelation. It is in every case a matter of social patterning—of that which cultural recognition has singled out and standardized" (Benedict, "The Concept of the Guardian Spirit in North America," 84).

60. Briscoe, "Ruth Benedict, Anthropological Folklorist," 449.

61. Mead, *An Anthropologist at Work*, 236.

62. Paper delivered at the "Congress of Americanists" (1928) (Ruth Benedict Papers, Box 58, Folder 27, VCASC).

63. Mead writes: "Universal mechanisms . . . all left her cold because they seemed to her both limiting and partial. Each was, it is true, one way of looking at human behavior, but . . . any attempt to set up an exclusive and exhaustive set of categories repelled her. In this preference she belonged more to the humanities than to the sciences and was more interested in the rich complexity of the real, historically unique situation than in those types of scientific analysis which, by devising a formula which could be applied to all cultures, stripped the cultures of the very uniqueness which she valued" (Mead, *An Anthropologist at Work*, 547).

64. Charles Altieri's essay on the modernist long poem provides a helpful exploration of this issue within the work of other modernist poets. He argues that "Eliot, Pound, Stevens, Williams, and Crane . . . all defined their long poems as explorations of forms of relationship defined largely in opposition to the kinds of thinking valued by their society" (653) and believed in "the imagination as counterpressure to oppressive cultural realities and reductive models of the psyche" (655), an argument for writing that I see Benedict as also making, although she does this work within the lyric rather than the long poem. Altieri adds, though, that these poets struggled "between the impulse to lucidity and the impulse to lyricism . . . [and] both Pound and Eliot . . . [placed] their critical visions of society within lyrical patterns sustained by the long poem" (Altieri, "Motives in Metaphor," 656).

65. Hegeman, *Patterns for America*, 15–16.

66. Geertz, *Works and Lives*, 109.

67. Mead, *An Anthropologist at Work*, 87–88.

68. Handler, "Ruth Benedict and the Modernist Sensibility."

69. Benedict called the "myth of master races . . . the world's most tragic myth" because "during the past hundred years [this myth has] constantly incited its makers to discrimination and terroristic acts and has been used to justify every kind of oppression" ("Superior Races: The World's Most Tragic Myth" [1], Ruth Benedict Papers, Box 58, Folder 28, VCASC).

70. In Francesca Sawaya's chapter on Ruth Benedict and Zora Neale Hurston in *Modern Women, Modern Work,* Sawaya makes a related point: "While anthropology cannot necessarily provide us with a reliable understanding of others (in part because of our own historically shaped subjective proclivities), she [Benedict] makes clear . . . that it can provide us with the tools to begin to understand our own culture's integration and how it shapes us" (124–25).

71. Mead, *An Anthropologist at Work,* 237.

72. In "Anthropology and the Humanities" she writes, "To my mind the very nature of the problems posed and discussed in the humanities is closer, chapter by chapter, to those in anthropology than are the investigations carried on in most of the social sciences. . . . For if anthropology studies the mind of man, along with his institutions, our greatest resource, it seems to me, is the humanities" (2, 6). This essay is ultimately about the necessity of embracing anthropology's connections to both science and the humanities and the idea that "commitments to methods which exclude either approach is self-defeating" (13) (Ruth Benedict Papers, Box 49, Folder 1, VCASC).

73. Wallace Stevens makes a similar point about modernism in a 1951 lecture. Charles Altieri explains how Stevens recasts the distinction between modernist form and content to give modernist ideas greater possibility for discussion:

> Essays such as "The Effect of Analogy" and "The Relations between Poetry and Painting" clearly take their sense of the parameters of Modernity and limitations of classical models of mimesis from Cubist ideals. But rather than defining those ideals in terms of stylistic principles, Stevens makes a sharp distinction between work that is modern by virtue of form, and work that is modern "in respect to what it says" or to what it expresses (*Necessary Angel* 168). From this angle, the effective Modernity of a writer is likely to be less a matter of specific devices than of the ends he or she pursues and of the overall impact of the work directed by those ends. (Altieri, *Painterly Abstraction in Modernist American Poetry,* 248–49)

Stevens, in his late modernist lecture delivered at the Museum of Modern Art, suggests that the distinction between modernist and nonmodernist has to transcend the distinction of form and become more inclusive—since many modern ideas present themselves in distinctly unmodernist forms. Benedict's idea about form is related to Stevens's more inclusive approach to understanding how to recognize a work as modern by examining both what it says and how it says it.

74. Mead, *An Anthropologist at Work,* 207.

75. Louise Bogan to Morton Dauwen Zabel, May 31, 1948 (quoted in Limmer, *What the Woman Lived,* 261).

76. Ridgely Torrence to Anne Singleton, Jan. 10, 1928, Ruth Benedict Papers, Box 1, Folder 4, VCASC.

77. Cora Du Bois Papers, Box 67, Tozzer Library Special Collections, Harvard University.

78. "The Study of Learned Cultural Behavior in Civilized Nations" (4). Given at a conference on March 14, 1947 (Ruth Benedict Papers, Box 58, Folder 27, VCASC).

79. See Hegeman, *Patterns for America,* 66–113, for detailed discussions of Benedict's contribution to the anthropological project of defining culture. Also very helpful is Daniel Rosenblatt's discussion in "An Anthropology Made Safe for Culture."

80. Hegeman discusses the discomfort many of Benedict's colleagues (at least those who did not join with her) and later generations of Boasians have felt with her choice to work for the Office of War Information. Hegeman writes, "Of course, this participation in government-sponsored research and service was every bit as much an abandonment of the Boasian legacy" (*Patterns for America,* 165, 248).

81. Ruth Benedict Papers, Box 58, Folder 8, VCASC.

82. Ruth Benedict Papers, Box 43, VCASC.

83. Rourke, *The Roots of American Culture and Other Essays,* 275. The two women probably knew each other as undergraduates at Vassar College, were intellectually aware of each other's work in the 1920s, and met in the 1930s. Joan Shelley Rubin discusses how Benedict and Rourke crossed paths in "Constance Rourke in Context."

Conclusion

1. Jonathan Rosen, "So It Is Written: Books Are Memory," *New York Times,* Sep. 19, 2003, Arts sec.

2. See www.nypl.org/branch/local/man/hpinfo.html.

3. See www.columbia.edu/about_columbia/tour/12.html.

4. Multiple sources have made this claim, including, most recently, the front-page article by Louis Uchitelle and Amanda Cox, "Age of Riches: The Richest of the Rich, Proud of a New Gilded Age," *New York Times,* July 15, 2007.

5. Sarah N. Lynch and Eugene Mulero, "Dewey? At This Library with a Very Different Outlook, They Don't," *New York Times,* July 14, 2007.

6. Weinberger, *Everything Is Miscellaneous,* 23.

7. Most of the Cesnola collection was sold by the Metropolitan Museum of Art in 1928, and much of the remainder was allocated to the basement of the museum. There were originally thirty-five thousand objects, and the museum still has six thousand, five hundred of which are now on display. For a reader of Wharton, the renovation of the Cesnola antiquities rooms at the Metropolitan Museum of Art brings her earlier discussion of those spaces into sharp focus. The curatorial choice to celebrate Cesnola's finds and his connection to the museum's history on didactic panels throughout the four rooms would have surprised and upset her. Nowhere in the now-

permanent exhibition does the museum mention the controversy surrounding the original excavation and exhibition of Cesnola's collection. The only indication that the objects are not necessarily authentic is the words "attributed to" listed above several of the individual objects. The museum's explanation for this omission is a lack of space on the didactic panels, but were Wharton alive, she might use Marianne Moore's helpful epithet—"omissions are not accidents"—to contend that the omission reveals a great deal about the relationship between current museum practices and social thinking. The way the current Metropolitan Museum of Art celebrates the original Cesnola finds (and Cesnola's tenure as the museum's first director) eliminates an enormous amount of the exhibit's and the museum's stories—of the questions they raise about American imperialism, subjugation of races and classes (for example, the natives who knew where the treasures were and did all of the digging and carrying), and the uses of money to obviate moral questions, just to name a few aspects of their shared history. See McFadden, *The Glitter and the Gold;* and Karageorghis, *Ancient Art from Cyprus,* 3–15.

Bibliography

Abel, Elizabeth, Barbara Christian, and Helene Moglen, eds. *Female Subjects in Black and White: Race, Psychoanalysis, Feminism.* Berkeley: University of California Press, 1997.

Addams, Jane, ed. *Philanthropy and Social Progress.* Freeport: Books for Libraries, 1893.

Adorno, Theodor. "Valéry Proust Museum." In *Prisms,* trans. Samuel Weber and Sherry Weber, 173–86. Cambridge, MA: MIT Press, 1990.

Allport, Floyd. *Institutional Behavior: Essays toward a Re-interpreting of Contemporary Social Organization.* Chapel Hill: University of North Carolina Press, 1933.

Altieri, Charles. "Motives in Metaphor: John Ashbery and the Modernist Long Poem." *Genre* 11 (winter 1978): 653–87.

———. *Painterly Abstraction in Modernist American Poetry: The Contemporaneity of Modernism.* University Park: Pennsylvania State University Press, 1995.

American Association of Museums. *Museum Work: Proceedings of the American Association of Museums.* Providence, RI: The Association, 1918.

———. *Proceedings of the American Association of Museums.* Pittsburgh, PA: The Association, 1906–1917.

American Library Association. *Catalogue Rules (American edition).* New York: ALA, 1908.

———. *List of Subject Headings for Use in Dictionary Catalogues.* 3rd edn. New York: ALA, 1911.

Anderson, James D. "The Hampton Model of Normal School Industrial Education, 1868–1900." In *New Perspectives on Black Educational History,* ed. Vincent P. Franklin and James D. Anderson, 61–95. Boston: G. K. Hall, 1978.

Anderson, Jervis. *This Was Harlem: A Cultural Portrait, 1900–1950.* New York: Farrar Straus Giroux, 1982.

Art Amateur. New York: Montague Marks, 1879–1903.

Banner, Lois W. *Intertwined Lives: Margaret Mead, Ruth Benedict, and Their Circle.* New York: Vintage, 2003.

Battles, Matthew. *Library: An Unquiet History.* New York: Norton, 2003.

Bauer, Dale. *Edith Wharton's Brave New Politics.* Madison: University of Wisconsin Press, 1994.

Bell, Millicent. *Edith Wharton and Henry James: The Story of Their Friendship.* New York: George Braziller, 1965.

Benedict, Ruth. "The Concept of the Guardian Spirit in North America." Menasha, WI: American Anthropological Association, 1923.

———. Papers. Vassar College Libraries Archives and Special Collections. Poughkeepsie, NY.

———. *Patterns of Culture.* Boston: Houghton Mifflin, 1934.

Benjamin, Walter. "The Work of Art in the Age of Mechanical Reproduction." In *Illuminations: Essays and Reflections,* ed. Hannah Arendt, 217–52. New York: Schocken, 1968.

Benstock, Shari. *No Gifts from Chance: A Biography of Edith Wharton.* New York: Charles Scribner's Sons, 1994.

Bentley, Nancy. *The Ethnography of Manners: Hawthorne, James, Wharton.* Cambridge, UK: Cambridge University Press, 1995.

———. "Wharton, Travel and Modernity." In *The Cambridge History of American Literature,* ed. Sacvan Bercovitch. Vol. 3, *Prose Writing, 1860–1920,* 224–46. Cambridge, UK: Cambridge University Press, 2005.

Berenson, Bernard. *The Bernard Berenson Treasury.* Ed. Hanna Kiel. New York: Simon and Schuster, 1962.

Bergman, David. "Marianne Moore and the Problem of 'Marriage.'" *American Literature* 60 (May 1988): 241–54.

Berry, Walter. Review of *The Decoration of Houses.* In Tuttleton, Lauer, and Murray, *Edith Wharton: The Contemporary Reviews,* 8–10.

Bishop, Elizabeth. *The Complete Poems: 1927–1979.* New York: Farrar, Straus and Giroux, 2000.

———. "Efforts of Affection: A Memoir of Marianne Moore." In *The Collected Prose of Elizabeth Bishop,* ed. Robert Giroux, 121–58. New York: Noonday Press, 1984.

Bone, Robert. *The Negro Novel in America.* New Haven, CT: Yale University Press, 1958.

Bontemps, Arna, ed. *The Harlem Renaissance Remembered: Essays.* New York: Dodd, Mead, 1972.

Boon, James A. *Other Tribes, Other Scribes: Symbolic Anthropology in the Comparative Study of Cultures, Histories, Religions, and Texts.* Cambridge, UK: Cambridge University Press, 1982.

Bradley, John, and Ian Ousby, eds. *The Correspondence of John Ruskin and Charles Eliot Norton.* Cambridge, UK: Cambridge University Press, 1987.

Briscoe, Virginia Wolf. "Ruth Benedict, Anthropological Folklorist." *Journal of American Folklore* 92 (Oct.–Dec. 1979): 445–76.

Bromwich, David. "'That Weapon, Self-Protectiveness.'" In *Marianne Moore: The*

Art of a Modernist, ed. Joseph Parisi, 67–82. Ann Arbor: UMI Research Press, 1990.

Brooks, Van Wyck. *America's Coming-of-Age.* New York: B. W. Huebsch, 1915.

Caffrey, Margaret. *Ruth Benedict: Stranger in This Land.* Austin: University of Texas Press, 1989.

Calo, Mary Ann. *Bernard Berenson and the Twentieth Century.* Philadelphia: Temple University Press, 1994.

Campbell, Ballard C., ed. *The Human Tradition in the Gilded Age and Progressive Era.* Wilmington, DE: Scholarly Resources, 2000.

Carby, Hazel. *Reconstructing Womanhood: The Emergence of the African-American Novelist.* Oxford: Oxford University Press, 1987.

Carnegie, Andrew. *The Gospel of Wealth and Other Timely Essays.* Ed. Edward C. Kirkland. Cambridge, MA: Belknap Press, 1962.

Cather, Willa. *Alexander's Bridge.* Boston: Houghton Mifflin, 1912.

Cesnola, General Louis Palma di. *Cyprus: Its Ancient Cities, Tombs, and Temples.* New York: Harper, 1878.

Chandler, Alfred. *Structure and Strategy: Chapters in the History of the Industrial Enterprise.* Cambridge, MA: MIT Press, 1962.

Christian, Barbara. *Black Feminist Criticism: Perspectives on Black Women Writers.* New York: Pergamon, 1985.

Clark, Kenneth. Papers. *Kenneth Clark Correspondence as Director, 1934–1948.* National Gallery Archives. London.

Clemmen, Yves. "Nella Larsen's *Quicksand:* A Narrative of Difference." *CLA* 4 (June 1997): 458–66.

Clifford, James, and George Marcus, eds. *Writing Culture.* Berkeley: University of California Press, 1986.

Cole, John. "Storehouses and Workshops: American Libraries and the Uses of Knowledge." In Oleson and Vloss, *The Organization of Knowledge in Modern America,* 364–85.

Coleman, Laurence Vail. *The Museum in America: A Critical Study in Three Volumes.* Washington, DC: American Association of Museums, 1939.

Collins, Louise. "Marianne Moore, Melvil Dewey, and Lake Placid." In Willis, *Marianne Moore,* 53–60.

Conn, Steven. *Museums and American Intellectual Life, 1876–1926.* Chicago: University of Chicago Press, 1998.

Cook, Clarence. *Transformations and Migrations of Certain Statues in the Cesnola Collection.* New York: Gaston L. Feuardent, n.d.

Cooley, Charles Horton. *Social Organization: A Study of the Larger Mind.* New York: Scribner, 1909.

Coolidge, Olivia. *Edith Wharton, 1862–1937.* New York: Scribner, 1964.

Costello, Bonnie. *Marianne Moore: Imaginary Possessions.* Cambridge, MA: Harvard University Press, 1981.

Cowley, Malcolm. "The Revolt against Gentility." In *After the Genteel Tradition*, ed. Malcolm Cowley, 9–25. New York: Norton, 1936.

Cranz, Galen. *The Politics of Park Design: A History of Urban Parks in America.* Cambridge, MA: MIT Press, 1982.

Cutter, C. A. *Rules for a Dictionary Catalogue.* 4th edn. New York: ALA, 1904.

Dana, John Cotton. *A Plan for a New Museum: The Kind of Museum It Will Profit a City to Maintain.* Woodstock, VT: Elm Tree Press, 1920.

———. *Should Museums Be Useful?* Newark, NJ: Elm Tree Press, 1927.

Davis, Thadious M. Introduction to *Quicksand.* Ed. Thadious M. Davis. New York: Penguin, 2002.

———. *Nella Larsen, Novelist of the Harlem Renaissance: A Woman's Life Unveiled.* Baton Rouge: Louisiana State University Press, 1994.

Dearborn, Mary V. *Pocahontas's Daughters: Gender and Ethnicity in American Culture.* New York: Oxford University Press, 1986.

Dewey, Melvil. *Decimal Clasification.* 11th edn. Adirondaks: Lake Placid, 1922.

———. "The Profession." *American Library Journal* 1 (1876): 5–6.

Dickson, Katherine Murphy. *Sexism and Reentry: Job Realities for Women Librarians.* Lanham, MD: University Press of America, 1997.

Dimock, Wai Chee. "Debasing Exchange: Edith Wharton's *The House of Mirth.*" In *Edith Wharton: Modern Critical Views*, ed. Harold Bloom, 123–38. New York: Chelsea House, 1986.

Dittmar, Linda. "When Privilege Is No Protection: The Woman Artist in *Quicksand* and *The House of Mirth.*" In *Writing the Woman Artist: Essays on Poetics, Politics, and Portraiture*, ed. Suzanne W. Jones, 133–54. Philadelphia: University of Pennsylvania Press, 1991.

Ditzion, Sidney. *Arsenals of a Democratic Culture: A Social History of the American Public Library Movement in New England and the Middle States from 1850 to 1900.* Chicago: American Library Association, 1947.

Douglas, Ann. *The Feminization of American Culture.* New York: Knopf, 1977.

———. *Terrible Honesty: Mongrel Manhattan in the 1920s.* New York: Farrar, Straus, and Giroux, 1995.

Du Bois, Cora. Cora Du Bois Papers. Tozzer Library Special Collections, Harvard University.

Du Bois, W. E. B. "Talented Tenth." *The Negro Problem: A Series of Articles by Representative American Negroes.* New York: J. Pott, 1903.

Duncan, Carol. "Art Museums and the Ritual of Citizenship." In *Exhibiting Cultures: The Poetics and Politics of Museum Display*, ed. Ivan Karp and Steven D. Lavine, 88–103. Washington, DC: Smithsonian Institution Press, 1990.

Durkheim, Emile, and Marcel Mauss. *Primitive Classification.* Trans. Rodney Needham. Chicago: University of Chicago Press, 1963.

Dwight, Eleanor. *Edith Wharton: An Extraordinary Life.* New York: Abrams, 1994.

Edbury, Peter W. "Cyprus in the Nineteenth-Century: Perceptions and Politics." In

Cyprus in the Nineteenth Century AD, ed. Veronica Tatton-Brown, 13–20. Exeter: Short Run Press, 2001.

Ehrhardt, Julia. "'To Read These Pages Is to Live Again': The Historical Accuracy of *The Age of Innocence*." In Edith Wharton, *The Age of Innocence*, ed. Candace Waid, 401–12. New York: Norton, 2002.

Eliot, T. S. Introduction to Marianne Moore's *Selected Poems*. New York: Macmillan, 1935.

———. *The Waste Land*. New York: Boni and Liveright, 1922.

Emerson, Ralph Waldo. "The American Scholar." In *Nature: Addresses and Lectures*, 75–111. Boston: Phillips, Samson, 1850.

———. "Quotation and Originality." In *Letters and Social Aims*, 157–81. Boston: James Osgood, 1876.

Fauset, Jessie. *This Is Confusion*. Boston: Northeastern University Press, 1989.

Feuardent, Gaston. *The Cesnola Collection and De Morgan Collection*. New York: American Numismatic and Archeological Society, 1878.

Fisher, Philip. *Making and Effacing Art: Modern American Art in a Culture of Museums*. Cambridge, MA: Harvard University Press, 1991.

Foucault, Michel. "Of Other Spaces." *Diacritics* 16 (spring 1986): 22–27.

Fox, Daniel M. *Philanthropy and Art Museums*. Madison: University of Wisconsin Press, 1963.

Franklin, John Hope, ed. *Three Negro Classics: Up from Slavery*. New York: Avon, 1965.

Fry, Roger. *The Letters of Roger Fry*. Vol. 1. Ed. Denys Sutton. New York: Random House, 1972.

———. *Vision and Design*. New York: New American Library, 1920.

Garrison, Dee. *Apostles of Culture: The Public Librarian and American Society, 1876–1920*. New York: Free Press, 1979.

Geertz, Clifford. *Works and Lives: The Anthropologist as Author*. Stanford, CA: Stanford University Press, 1988.

Gilman, Benjamin Ives. *Museum Ideals of Purpose and Method*. Cambridge, MA: Riverside Press, 1918.

———. "An Open Reply." *Proceedings of the American Association of Museums* 1 (1907): 48–49.

———. "The Triple Aim of Museums of Fine Art." *Proceedings of the American Association of Museums* 1 (1907): 91–95.

Goldsmith, Meredith. "Edith Wharton's Gift to Nella Larsen: *The House of Mirth* and *Quicksand*." *Edith Wharton Review* 11 (fall 1994): 3–5, 15.

Goodman, Susan. *Edith Wharton's Inner Circle*. Austin: University of Texas Press, 1994.

———. *Edith Wharton's Women: Friends and Rivals*. Hanover, NH: University Press of New England, 1990.

Gould, Eric. *The University in a Corporate Culture*. New Haven, CT: Yale University Press, 2003.

Grogan, Ruth. "Tomlinson, Ruskin, and Moore: Facts and Fir Trees." *Twentieth Century Literature* 35 (summer 1989): 183–94.

Handler, Richard. "Ruth Benedict and the Modernist Sensibility." In *Modernist Anthropology: From Fieldwork to Text*, ed. Marc Manganaro, 163–80. Princeton, NJ: Princeton University Press, 1990.

Harris, Michael H., and Gerard Spiegler, "Everett, Ticknor and the Common Man: The Fear of Societal Instability as the Motivation for the Founding of the Boston Public Library." *Libri* 24 (1974): 249–76.

Harris, Neil. "The Gilded Age Revisited: Boston and the Museum Movement." *American Quarterly* 14 (1962): 545–66.

Haviland, Beverly. "Passing from Paranoia to Plagiarism: The Abject Authorship of Nella Larsen." *Modern Fiction Studies* 43 (summer 1997): 295–318.

Hegeman, Susan. *Patterns for America: Modernism and the Concept of Culture.* Princeton. NJ: Princeton University Press, 1999.

Hoeller, Hildegard. *Edith Wharton's Dialogue with Realism and Sentimental Fiction.* Gainesville: University Press of Florida, 2000.

Holley, Margaret. *The Poetry of Marianne Moore: A Study in Voice and Value.* Cambridge, UK: Cambridge University Press, 1987.

Hoogenboom, Ari, and Olive Hoogenboom, eds. *The Gilded Age.* Englewood Cliffs, NJ: Prentice-Hall, 1967.

Hostetler, Ann E. "The Aesthetics of Race and Gender in Nella Larsen's *Quicksand.*" *PMLA* 105 (winter 1990): 35–46.

Howe, Winifred E. *A History of the Metropolitan Museum of Art.* 2 vols. New York: Metropolitan Museum of Art, 1913.

Hughes, Langston. "My Early Days in Harlem." *Freedomways* 3 (summer 1963): 312–14.

———. "The Negro Artist and the Racial Mountain." In *The Harlem Renaissance Reader*, ed. David Levering Lewis, 91–95. New York: Viking, 1994.

———. Papers. The James Weldon Johnson Collection. Yale Collection of American Literature. Beinecke Rare Book and Manuscript Library. New Haven, CT.

Hutchinson, George. *In Search of Nella Larsen: A Biography of the Color Line.* Cambridge, MA: Harvard University Press, 2006.

———. "Nella Larsen and the Veil of Race." *American Literary History* 9 (summer 1997): 329–49.

James, Henry. *The American.* Boston: James R. Osgood, 1877.

———. 1907. *The American Scene.* Bloomington: Indiana University Press, 1968.

———. *The Golden Bowl.* New York: Scribner, 1904.

Johnson, Barbara. "The Quicksands of the Self: Nella Larsen and Heinz Kohut." In *Telling Facts: History and Narration in Psychoanalysis*, ed. Joseph H. Smith, 184–99. Baltimore: Johns Hopkins University Press, 1992.

Joint Committee on the Library. *Condition of the Library of Congress.* March 3, 1897. Washington, DC: Government Printing Office, 1897.

Jones, Sharon. *Rereading the Harlem Renaissance: Race, Class, and Gender in the Fic-*

tion of Jessie Fauset, Zora Neale Hurston, and Dorothy West. London: Greenwood Press, 2002.

Josey, E. J., ed. *The Black Librarian in America Revisited.* Metuchen, NJ: Scarecrow Press, 1994.

Joyce, James. *Ulysses.* London: Egoist Press, 1922.

Kappel, Andrew. "Complete with Omissions: The Text of Marianne Moore's Complete Poems." In *Representing Modernist Texts: Editing as Interpretation,* ed. George Bornstein, 125–56. Ann Arbor: University of Michigan Press, 1991.

———. "Presenting Miss Moore, Modernist: T. S. Eliot's Edition of Marianne Moore's *Selected Poems.*" *Journal of Modern Literature* 19 (summer 1994): 129–50.

Karageorghis, Vassos. *Ancient Art from Cyprus: The Cesnola Collection in the Metropolitan Museum of Art.* New York: Harry Abrams, 2000.

Karp, Ivan, and Steven D. Lavine, eds. *Exhibiting Cultures: The Poetics and the Politics of Museum Display.* Washington, DC: Smithsonian Institution Press, 1991.

Kassanoff, Jennie A. *Edith Wharton and the Politics of Race.* Cambridge, UK: Cambridge University Press, 2004.

Keen, Andrew. *The Cult of the Amateur: How Today's Internet Is Killing Our Culture.* New York: Doubleday, 2007.

Keller, Lynn. "'For inferior who is free?': Liberating the Woman Writer in Marianne Moore's 'Marriage.'" In *Influence and Intertextuality in Literary History,* ed. Jay Clayton and Eric Rothstein, 219–44. Madison: University of Wisconsin Press, 1991.

Killoran, Helen. *Edith Wharton: Art and Allusion.* Tuscaloosa: University of Alabama Press, 1996.

Koch, Theodore Wesley. *A Book of Carnegie Libraries.* New York: H. W. Wilson, 1917.

Kroeger, A. B. *Guide to the Study and Use of Reference Books.* Chicago: ALA, 1917.

Labaree, Mary Fleming. Review of *Passing. Opportunity* 7 (Aug. 1929): 255.

Larsen, Nella. *The Complete Fiction of Nella Larsen.* Ed. Charles Larson. New York: Anchor Books, 2001.

———. "Correspondence." *Opportunity* 4 (1926): 295.

———. "Danish Fun." *Brownies' Book,* July 1920, 219.

———. "Letter 5: The Author's Explanation." *Forum* (April 1930): xli.

———. "Sanctuary." *Forum,* Jan. 1930, 15–18.

———. "Three Scandinavian Games." *Brownies' Book,* June 1920, 191–92.

Larson, Charles. *Invisible Darkness: Jean Toomer and Nella Larsen.* Iowa City: University of Iowa Press, 1993.

Larson, Magali. *The Rise of Professionalism: A Sociological Analysis.* Berkeley: University of California Press, 1977.

Lee, Hermione. *Edith Wharton.* New York: Knopf, 2007.

Lentricchia, Frank. *Modernist Quartet.* Cambridge, UK: Cambridge University Press, 1994.

Lewis, David Levering. *When Harlem Was in Vogue.* Oxford: Oxford University Press, 1989.

Lewis, R. W. B. *Edith Wharton: A Biography.* New York: Harper and Row, 1975.

———. "A Writer of Short Stories." In *Edith Wharton: Modern Critical Views,* ed. Harold Bloom, 9–28. New York: Chelsea House, 1986.

Lewis, Sinclair. *Babbitt.* New York: Harcourt Brace, 1922.

———. *Main Street.* New York: Harcourt Brace, 1920.

Library School Bulletin. New York: New York Library, 1920.

Limmer, Ruth, ed. *What the Woman Lived: Selected Letters of Louise Bogan, 1920–1970.* New York: Harcourt Brace, 1973.

Lipscomb, Carolyn. "Librarian Supply and Demand." *Journal of the Medical Library Association* (Jan. 2003): 7–10.

Longstreth, Morris. *The Adirondacks.* New York: Century, 1920.

Lynch, Kevin. *The Image of the City.* Cambridge, MA: MIT Press, 1960.

Machlup, Fritz. *The Production and Distribution of Knowledge in the United States.* Princeton, NJ: Princeton University Press, 1962.

Malraux, Andre. *Museum without Walls.* Trans. Stuart Gilbert and Alistair Macdonald. New York: Random House, 1938.

Marcus, Jane. *Virginia Woolf and the Languages of Patriarchy.* Bloomington: Indiana University Press, 1987.

McAlmon, Robert. *Post-Adolescence.* Paris: Contact, 1923.

McCaughey, Robert A. *Stand, Columbia: A History of Columbia University in the City of New York, 1754–2004.* New York: Columbia University Press, 2003.

McDonald, Gail. *Learning to Be Modern: Pound, Eliot, and the American University.* Oxford: Oxford University Press, 1993.

McFadden, Elizabeth. *The Glitter and the Gold.* New York: Dial, 1971.

McMullen, Haynes. "Ralph Waldo Emerson and Libraries." *Library Quarterly* 25 (Jan. 1955): 152–62.

Mead, Margaret. *An Anthropologist at Work: Writings of Ruth Benedict.* Boston: Houghton Mifflin, 1959.

———. *Blackberry Winter: My Earlier Years.* New York: Washington Square Press, 1972.

The Metropolitan Museum of Art Annual Reports of the Trustees of the Association, 1871–1902. New York: Metropolitan Museum of Art, 2006 (reprint).

Metropolitan Museum of Art. *Guide to the Cesnola Collections.* New York: Francis and Loutrei, 1877.

Michaels, Walter Benn. *The Gold Standard and the Logic of Naturalism: American Literature at the Turn of the Century.* Berkeley: University of California Press, 1987.

Miller, Cristanne. "Distrusting: Marianne Moore on Feeling and War in the 1940s." *American Literature* 80 (June 2008): 353–79.

———. *Marianne Moore: Questions of Authority.* Cambridge, MA: Harvard University Press, 1995.

Modell, Judith. *Ruth Benedict, Patterns of a Life.* Philadelphia: University of Pennsylvania Press, 1983.

Molesworth, Charles. *Marianne Moore: A Literary Life.* New York: Atheneum, 1990.

Monda, Kimberly. "Self-Delusion and Self-Sacrifice in Nella Larsen's *Quicksand.*" *African American Review* 31 (1997): 23–39.

Montgomery, Maureen. *Displaying Women: Spectacles of Leisure in Edith Wharton's New York.* New York: Routledge, 1998.

Moore, Marianne. "Autobiography: Coming About." Unpublished. In Papers and Collections. Rosenbach Museum and Library. Philadelphia.

———. *Becoming Marianne Moore: The Early Poems, 1907–1924.* Ed. Robin Schulze. Berkeley: University of California Press, 2002.

———. *Collected Poems.* New York: Macmillan, 1951.

———. *Complete Poems.* New York: Macmillan, 1967.

———. *Observations.* New York: Dial, 1924–25.

———. Papers. The Dial/Scofield Thayer Papers. Yale Collection of American Literature. Beinecke Rare Book and Manuscript Library. New Haven, CT.

———. Papers and Collections. Rosenbach Museum and Library. Philadelphia.

———. *Poems.* London: Egoist Press, 1921.

———. *The Poems of Marianne Moore.* Ed. Grace Schulman. New York: Viking, 2003.

———. *The Selected Letters of Marianne Moore.* Ed. Bonnie Costello. New York: Knopf, 1997.

———. *Selected Poems.* Ed. T. S. Eliot. New York: Macmillan, 1935.

"A Museum of the Fine Arts for Boston." *The Nation,* Jan. 27, 1870, 32.

"A Museum of the Fine Arts for New York." *The Nation,* Jan. 6, 1870, 63.

Newfield, Christopher. *Ivy and Industry: Business and the Making of the American University, 1880–1980.* Durham, NC: Duke University Press, 2004.

Newsom, Barbara, and Adele Silver, eds. *The Art Museum as Educator: A Collection of Studies as Guides to Practice and Policy.* Berkeley: University of California Press, 1978.

New York Public Library Library School Records. Papers and Collections. Rare Book and Manuscript Library. Columbia University, New York.

New York Public Library Minutes: Committee on Circulation, 1921. Papers and Collections. New York Public Library Manuscripts and Archives Division. New York.

Noordegraaf, Julia. *Strategies of Display: Museum Presentation in Nineteenth- and Twentieth-Century Visual Culture.* Rotterdam: NAi, 2004.

Oleson, Alexandra, and John Voss, eds. *The Organization of Knowledge in Modern America, 1860–1920.* Baltimore: Johns Hopkins University Press, 1979.

135th Street Library Records. Schomburg Center Records, 1921–1948. Schomburg Center for Research in Black Culture. Manuscripts and Archives. New York.

Page, Walter Hines, and Arthur Wilson Page. *The World's Work.* Garden City, NY: Doubleday, 1913.

Parsons, Elsie Clews. *Social Freedom: A Study of the Conflicts between Social Classification and Personality.* New York: Knickerbocker Press, 1915.

———. *Social Rule: A Study of the Will to Power.* New York: Putnam, 1916.

Paul, Catherine. *Poetry in the Museums of Modernism: Yeats, Pound, Moore, Stein.* Ann Arbor: University of Michigan Press, 2002.

Peterson, Merrill D. "The American Scholar: Emerson and Jefferson." In *Thomas Jefferson and the World of Books: A Symposium Held at the Library of Congress, September 21, 1976.* Washington, DC: Library of Congress, 1977.

Pycraft, W. P. *The Courtship of Animals.* New York: Henry Holt, 1914.

Ramsden, George, ed. *Edith Wharton's Library: A Catalogue.* York: Stone Trough, 1999.

Ramsey, Grace Fisher. *Educational Work in Museums of the United States: Development, Methods and Trends.* New York: H. W. Wilson, 1938.

Rayson, Ann. "Foreign Exotic or Domestic Drudge? The African-American Woman in *Quicksand* and *Tar Baby.*" In *Literary Studies East and West,* ed. Cristina Bacchilega and Cornelia Moore, 182–93. Hawaii: University of Hawaii Press, 1996.

Rea, Paul Marshall. *The Museum and the Community.* Lancaster, PA: Science Press, 1932.

Reece, Ernest. *The Curriculum in Library Schools.* New York: Columbia University Press, 1936.

Rhinelander, John B. *One Branch of the Rhinelanders in the USA—From 18th Century German Rotgerbers to 19th Century Old New Yorkers to 20th Century Dispersed Americans.* New York: New York Historical Society, 2000.

Rivers, W. H. R. *Social Organization.* Ed. W. J. Perry. New York: Knopf, 1924.

Rose, Ernestine. "A Librarian in Harlem." *Opportunity* 1 (July 1923): 206–7, 220.

———. *The Public Library in American Life.* New York: Columbia University Press, 1954.

———. "Serving New York's Black City." *Library Journal* 46 (1921): 255–58.

Rosenblatt, Daniel. "An Anthropology Made Safe for Culture: Patterns of Practice and the Politics of Difference in Ruth Benedict." *American Anthropologist* (2004): 459–72.

Rourke, Constance. *The Roots of American Culture and Other Essays.* New York: Harcourt Brace, 1942.

Rubin, Joan Shelley. "Constance Rourke in Context: The Uses of Myth." *American Quarterly* 28 (winter 1976): 575–88.

Runte, Alfred. *National Parks: The American Experience.* Lincoln: University of Nebraska Press, 1987.

Samuels, Ernest. *Bernard Berenson: The Making of a Connoisseur.* Cambridge, MA: Harvard University Press, 1979.

Santayana, George. "The Genteel Tradition in American Philosophy." In *The Genteel Tradition: Nine Essays,* ed. Douglas L. Wilson, 37–64. Cambridge, MA: Harvard University Press, 1967.

Sapir, Edward. "The Heuristic Value of Rhyme." *Queen's Quarterly* 27 (1920): 309–12.

———. *Selected Writings of Edward Sapir in Language, Culture, and Personality.* Ed.

David G. Mandelbaum. 1949. Repr. Berkeley: University of California Press, 1985.

Sargeant, Winthrop. *Humility, Concentration, and Gusto: A Profile of Marianne Moore.* Brooklyn, NY: Pratt Adlib Press, 1957.

Sawaya, Francesca. *Modern Women, Modern Work: Domesticity, Professionalism, and American Writing, 1890–1950.* Philadelphia: University of Pennsylvania Press, 2004.

Scarupa, Harriet Jackson. "The Energy-Charged Life of Dorothy Porter Wesley." In *The Black Librarian in America Revisited,* ed. E. J. Josey, 298–315. Metuchen, NJ: Scarecrow Press, 1994.

Schriber, Mary. *Gender and the Writer's Imagination: From Cooper to Wharton.* Lexington: University Press of Kentucky, 1987.

Schulman, Grace. *Marianne Moore: The Poetry of Engagement.* Chicago: University of Illinois Press, 1986.

Schulze, Robin. "'The Frigate Pelican''s Progress: Marianne Moore's Multiple Versions and Modernist Practice." In *Gendered Modernisms: American Women Poets and Their Readers,* ed. Margaret Dickie and Thomas Travisano, 117–39. Philadelphia: University of Pennsylvania Press, 1996.

———. "Moore's Early Volumes: From *Poems* (1921) to *Observations* (1924)." In Moore, *Becoming Marianne Moore,* 18–38.

Scott, Geoffrey. *The Architecture of Humanism: A Study in the History of Taste.* London: Constable, 1914.

Siegel, Jonah. *Desire and Excess: The Nineteenth-Century Culture of Art.* Princeton, NJ: Princeton University Press, 2000.

Silverman, Debra B. "Nella Larsen's *Quicksand:* Untangling the Webs of Exoticism." *African American Review* 27 (1993): 599–614.

Sinette, Elinor Des Verney. *Arthur Alfonso Schomburg: Black Bibliophile and Collector.* New York: New York Public Library, 1989.

Small, Herbert. *Handbook of the New Library of Congress.* Boston: Curtis and Cameron, 1897.

Snyder, Thomas D., ed. *120 Years of American Education: A Statistical Portrait.* Washington, DC: U.S. Department of Education, 1993.

Stapleton, Laurence. *Marianne Moore: The Poet's Advance.* Princeton, NJ: Princeton University Press, 1978.

Stielow, Frederick. "Reconsidering Arsenals of a Democratic Culture." In *Libraries and Democracy: The Cornerstones of Liberty,* ed. Nancy Kranich, 3–14. Chicago: American Library Association, 2001.

Sutton, Tiffany. *The Classification of Visual Art: A Philosophical Myth and Its History.* Cambridge, UK: Cambridge University Press, 2000.

Tarbell, Ida M. *The History of the Standard Oil Company.* 2 vols. New York: McClure, Phillips, 1904.

Tate, Claudia. "Desire and Death in *Quicksand,* by Nella Larsen." *American Literary History* 7 (1995): 234–60.

Taylor, Francis Henry. *Babel's Tower: The Dilemma of the Modern Museum.* New York: Columbia University Press, 1945.

Tharp, Louise Hall. *Mrs. Jack: A Biography of Isabella Stewart Gardner.* Boston: Little, Brown, 1965.

Thomas, M. Carey. *Education of Women.* Ed. Nicholas Murray Butler. Albany: Lyon, 1900.

Tintner, Adeline R. *Edith Wharton in Context: Essays on Intertextuality.* Tuscaloosa: University of Alabama Press, 1999.

Tompkins, Calvin. *Merchants and Masterpieces: The Story of the Metropolitan Museum of Art.* New York: Henry Holt, 1970.

Toomer, Jean. *Cane.* New York: Liveright, 1923.

Trachtenberg, Alan, ed. *Democratic Vistas, 1860–1880.* New York: Braziller, 1970.

———. *The Incorporation of America: Culture and Society in the Gilded Age.* New York: Hill and Wang, 1982.

Trumpener, Katie, and James M. Nyce. "The Recovered Fragments: Archeological and Anthropological Perspectives in Edith Wharton's *The Age of Innocence.*" In *Literary Anthropology: A New Interdisciplinary Approach to People, Signs, and Literature,* ed. Fernando Poyatos, 161–69. Amsterdam: John Benjamins, 1988.

Tuttleton, James, Kristin O. Lauer, and Margaret P. Murray, eds. *Edith Wharton: The Contemporary Reviews.* New York: Cambridge University Press, 1992.

Tylor, Edward. *Collected Works of Edward Burnett Tylor.* London: Routledge, 1994.

———. "The Study of Customs." *MacMillan's Magazine* 46 (1882): 50–51.

Valéry, Paul. "The Problem of Museums." 1923. Repr. in *Arts* 34 (March 1960): 40–41.

Van Dyne, Susan. *Revising Life: Sylvia Plath's Ariel Poems.* Chapel Hill: University of North Carolina Press, 1993.

Van Slyck, Abigail. *Free to All: Carnegie Libraries and American Culture, 1890–1920.* Chicago: University of Chicago Press, 1998.

Van Vechten, Carl. *Nigger Heaven.* New York: Knopf, 1926.

———. Papers. James Weldon Johnson Collection. Yale Collection of American Literature. Beinecke Rare Book and Manuscript Library. New Haven, CT.

Varg, Paul A. *Edward Everett: The Intellectual in the Turmoil of Politics.* London: Associated University Press, 1992.

Wadlin, Horace G. *The Public Library of the City of Boston: A History.* Boston: Trustees, 1911.

Waid, Candace. *Edith Wharton's Letters from the Underworld: Fictions of Women and Writing.* Chapel Hill: University of North Carolina Press, 1991.

Wall, Cheryl A. *Women of the Harlem Renaissance.* Bloomington: Indiana University Press, 1995.

Walton, Eda Lou. Review of *Quicksand. Opportunity* 6 (July 1928): 212–13.

Ward, Henry. "Labeling in Museums." *Proceedings of the American Association of Museums* 1 (1907): 42–44.

"War-Time Service by Museums and by Museum Men." *Museum Work: Including the Proceedings of the American Association of Museums* 1 (Nov. 1918): 34.

Watson, Steven. *Prepare for Saints: Gertrude Stein, Virgil Thomson, and the Mainstreaming of American Modernism.* Berkeley: University of California Press, 1995.

Wegener, Frederick. "Form, 'Selection,' and Ideology in Edith Wharton's Antimodernist Aesthetic." In *A Forward Glance: New Essays on Edith Wharton,* ed. Clare Colquitt, Susan Goodman, and Candace Waid, 116–38. Newark: University of Delaware Press, 1999.

Weinberger, David. *Everything Is Miscellaneous: The Power of the New Digital Disorder.* New York: Henry Holt, 2007.

Wharton, Edith. *The Age of Innocence.* Ed. Candace Waid. New York: Norton, 2002.

———. *A Backward Glance.* New York: Appleton, 1937.

———. *The Custom of the Country.* New York: Scribner, 1913.

———. *The Decoration of Houses* (with Ogden Codman Jr.). New York: Scribner's, 1897.

———. *Edith Wharton: The Uncollected Critical Writings.* Ed. Frederick Wegener. Princeton, NJ: Princeton University Press, 1996.

———. *The Gods Arrive.* New York: Appleton, 1932.

———. *The House of Mirth.* 1905. Repr. New York: Bantam, 1984.

———. *Hudson River Bracketed.* New York: Appleton, 1929.

———. *The Letters of Edith Wharton.* Ed. R. W. B. Lewis and Nancy Lewis. New York: Scribner, 1988.

———. *The Mother's Recompense.* New York: Appleton, 1925.

———. Papers. Yale Collection of American Literature. Beinecke Rare Book and Manuscript Library. New Haven, CT.

———. *The Reef.* New York: Appleton, 1912.

———. "The Rembrandt." *The Cosmopolitan: A Monthly Illustrated Magazine,* Aug. 1900, 429–37.

———. *Sanctuary.* 1903. Repr. Philadelphia: Pine Street Books, 2001.

———. *Summer.* New York: Appleton, 1917.

———. *Twilight Sleep.* New York: Appleton, 1927.

———. Wharton Mss. Collection. Lilly Library. Indiana University, Bloomington.

———. *The Writing of Fiction.* 1924. Repr. New York: Touchstone, 1997.

White, Heather Cass. "Morals, Manners, and 'Marriage': Marianne Moore's Art of Conversation." *Twentieth Century Literature* 45 (Winter 1999): 488–510.

Wiebe, Robert. *The Search for Order, 1877–1920.* New York: Hill and Wang, 1967.

Williams, Bettye J. "Nella Larsen: Early Twentieth Century Novelist of Afrocentric Feminist Thought." *CLA* 39 (Dec. 1995): 165–78.

Willis, Patricia, ed. *The Complete Prose of Marianne Moore.* New York: Viking, 1986.

———. *Marianne Moore and the Pipes of Pan: Mt. Rainier and Mt. Olympus.* Athens: Attica Tradition Educational Foundation, 2001.

——, ed. *Marianne Moore: Woman and Poet.* Orono, ME: National Poetry Foundation, 1990.

Wingfield, Valerie. "A Jewel of Harlem: The Countee Cullen Regional Branch from 1905–1951." Master's thesis, Columbia University, 1994.

Wire, G. E. "The Library Assistants of the United States." *The Library Assistant: The Official Organ of the Library Assistants' Association* 18 (1899): 214–17.

Wittlin, Alma. *The Museum: Its History and Its Tasks in Education.* London: Routledge, 1949.

Wolff, Cynthia Griffin. *A Feast of Words: The Triumph of Edith Wharton.* New York: Oxford University Press, 1977.

Woodson, Carter G. *The Mis-education of the Negro.* Washington, DC: Association Publishers, 1933.

Woolf, Virginia. *A Room of One's Own.* 1929. Repr. San Diego: Harvest, 1957.

——. *A Writer's Diary.* Ed. Leonard Woolf. San Diego: Harcourt, 1954.

Zakaria, Fareed. *From Wealth to Power: The Unusual Origins of America's World Role.* Princeton, NJ: Princeton University Press, 1998.

Index